The Official ACT!™
QuickStudy Guide

|ACT!

The Official ACT! QuickStudy Guide

Developers: Cornerstone Solutions, Inc. (www.cornerstonesolutions.com)

Printed in the United States of America
Version 6.0
April 15, 2003 [Update]

The Official ACT! QuickStudy Guide

Get It In Writing   153

Using E-mail   179

Database Design & Layouts   297

Running and Designing Reports   347

Introduction

Thank you for investing in **The Official ACT! QuickStudy Guide**. We hope you'll gain a better understanding of ACT!...and that a greater understanding benefits your business.

This guide is not intended to replace the ACT! User's Guide, but to complement it with real-life product walk-throughs and hands-on exercises. It includes information that will help a first-time ACT! user get up and running immediately, while giving long-time ACT! users loads of advanced techniques that they may not even know existed. In short, we'll help you...regardless of your skill level...take full advantage of ACT!.

In addition to giving you step-by-step instructions for specific features, this guide gives you real-world business examples...and how you can use them to give your business a competitive advantage.

We hope you'll find this book to be an easy, yet enlightening way for you to maximize ACT!. Go through the guide chapter by chapter, or jump around to those topics you specifically want to know more about. Even though you may already know a lot about ACT!, you'll be even more amazed by what you don't know!

We welcome your feedback about **The Official ACT! QuickStudy Guide**. Tell us what was valuable...and areas where we could improve...by sending an e-mail to acttraining@act.com.

Thanks again...and now it's time to begin mastering ACT!.

The Basics

To become acquainted with the basics of working in ACT!, you will:

☑ Discuss the concept of contact management software.

☑ Start ACT!.

☑ Identify basic Windows screen elements.

☑ Review how to communicate with your computer using a mouse and/or a keyboard.

☑ Familiarize yourself with the ACT! program window.

☑ Add new contact records to the ACT! database.

|ACT!

Using This Study Guide...Hey Don't Skip This

This Self-paced Study Guide has a very simple and straightforward flow. A **description** of each topic is displayed first. Following each "Description" is a step-by-step "**How to...**" (We would never bury this important information in a paragraph!) This way you can also use this guide as a reference tool.

...understand the Study Guide

1. This column displays the commands, like...

   Choose **File, Open...**
   or
   click the Open toolbar icon.

   This column is used for comments or more complete descriptions. All of our procedures are clearly displayed in a numbered format with comments for clarification.

2. Click on the file displayed in the **Filename:** list.

   Any command references will be displayed in **Bold** with the appropriate character underlined for quick recognition.

3. **OK**

   We never miss a step.

After you have reviewed the basic procedure outlined in the "**How to...**" section, you can "**Try it...**" in the practice section. We have made an effort to ensure that no practice session is dependent upon the completion of a previous session. That way you can stop and start where you like or even skip around.

Practice: *Topic to try*

Step	What to do	How to do it/Comments
1.	The "What to do" column of each Practice gives the instructions on what is to be accomplished.	If you need help, this column provides step-by-step keystroke instructions. However, you can cover up this column to see if you can perform the practice on your own.

 These "helping hand" notations indicate that a valuable tip is being offered. Pay particular attention to these.

This icon indicates a keystroke alternative to the option, such as [Ctrl+O] for open. Notice that keystrokes are in bold and underlined and placed inside of square brackets. If the keys are to be pressed simultaneously, a plus sign (+) is placed between the keys.

This icon indicates how you can accomplish the same task using a right-mouse click.

Oh . . . by the way . . . our Study Guide also contains a bit of tongue-in-cheek humor every now and then. We hope you'll forgive us and not groan too loudly.

What's Contact Management Software?

Your computer can do a lot for you if you let it. All you need is the right software and you can create professional looking printed documents, perform complex calculations quickly and accurately, keep track of accounting information, and keep track of inventories and employees. For these purposes most people use word processors, spreadsheets, and databases. All three of these applications are popular, flexible, and easy to use, at least up to a point....

Word processors write documents, database and spreadsheet programs keep track of, and perform calculations on, large amounts of data, but these programs were not designed to provide all the tools you need to perform effective "contact management".

The purpose of contact management software is to help you keep track of the people (contacts) and companies you do business with…or would like to do business with. ACT! is the number one selling Contact Management Software in the world. Not only does it keep track of names, addresses, and phone numbers, but it also performs a few other important tasks:

✔ Provides easy ways to lookup contacts by not only their name and address information, but also by other details about them.

✔ Creates correspondence (sending personalized letters or e-mails to individuals or groups of people should be quick and easy) and remembers when it was sent, who sent it, and what was said.

✔ Provides one-click access for scheduling and keeping track of meetings, phone calls, and important tasks *with the contact* (not just with yourself like you would find in Outlook or a Palm device.) Displays or prints appointment calendars so you can keep a perspective on your schedule.

✔ Allows easy input of extensive notes, as well as quick display of all notes and histories associated with a contact. ("When did I last have lunch with Clark and what did we talk about?")

✔ Keeps a record of each "touch" you make with your contacts all in one easy to view place, on the contact's record. You can see the last time you or anyone in your company called them, the last time you met with them, what you talked about, and so on.

✔ Tracks sales opportunities that you hope to close, those that did close, and (gulp!) the ones that got away.

✔ Effortlessly shares this data with other users in your office or on the other side of the world.

✔ Synchronizes this data with a Palm device so you don't have to take your PC with you everywhere.

✔ Generates reports on the information you keep about your contacts. You can print out summaries of your meetings, notes you may have taken, changes in your relationships, or maybe something as simple as a phone number list. You can print a report displaying the number of calls you made, letters or emails or faxes you sent, meetings you attended, etc.

To be successful in most any business, you need to know the people with whom you do business. In addition to their names and address information, you want to know when you talked to them last, what you said, what *they* said, what their spouse's name is (do they *have* a spouse?), what their interests are, what their dislikes are, when you are supposed to call them again, and so on, and so forth, ad infinitum.

ACT! understands that the more you know about your customers, the more effective you can be in doing business with them. Keeping track of all these details could be a daunting task, especially if you deal with hundreds or even thousands of people. However, that is one of the reasons why ACT! has become so popular. With everything linked to the contact, these details are only a mouse-click away. ACT! is a powerful, flexible, and above all, **EASY TO USE** software program that has one goal in mind:

To turn your contacts into relationships,
and your relationships into results.

Starting ACT!

Now that we've talked a bit about how this Study Guide is set up and about contact management software, let's start up ACT! and see what all the fuss is about.

When normal installation is performed, ACT! creates the program icon in a program group called **ACT! 6**

ACT! may also create a desktop icon you can click on to run the program.

...start ACT! from the Start menu

1. Click the **Start** button, point to **All Programs**.

   Click the **Start** button (it is most likely on the lower left corner of your screen) and point to **All Programs**. A menu opens to the right.

2. Point to **ACT! 6**

   Point to the program group that contains ACT!. Your group might have a slightly different name.

3. Click the **ACT!** icon. ACT!

   ACT! will start.

...start ACT! from a desktop icon

1. Double-click the icon.

   ACT!

☞ *If you use Windows 98 or above, the ACT! icon appears on the Quick Launch Toolbar to the right of the Start button. You can also single-click this icon to start ACT!.*

ACT! Icon

The QuickStart Wizard

When you start ACT! for the first time, it runs a utility called the QuickStart Wizard. This program guides you through the basic configuration of ACT! and the creation of a new database. This is a great way to get started with a new ACT! installation. If you cancel the **QuickStart Wizard** you can run it at any time by choosing **Help, QuickStart Wizard** from the main menu.

 *This guide assumes you have already set up ACT!, therefore, should the **QuickStart Wizard** show its face, click the **Cancel** button. You can return to it anytime you wish.*

Login

It is possible you may be asked to login to your ACT! database when you start up. If this happens to you, don't worry about it. ACT! is just asking who you are so it knows what information to display (it may also be asking you to input your password, if you have one).

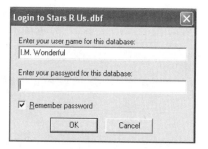

Practice: **Start Your Engines**

Step	What to do	How to do it/Comments
1.	Start ACT!.	**Start, All Programs, ACT! 6, ACT!**
2.	If a **QuickStart Wizard** dialog box is displayed click **Cancel**. Observe the screen.	

 At the completion, you either see a relatively blank screen, or a database is open and visible in the ACT! window. It does not matter at this point which is displayed.

Using the Menu and Function Keys

There are four ways to issue an ACT! command: using the menu, pressing special key combinations, clicking toolbar buttons, or right-clicking certain areas of the screen. In this Study Guide, we'll show you all of the ways. You don't have to remember them all, just pick one that seems easy for you.

Menu

Menu commands are usually chosen with the mouse by pointing and clicking on the desired option. Menu options will change depending upon what you're doing in ACT!. If they display as dimmed (this is often called "grayed out") that means the option is not appropriate or active at this time. For example, **Edit, Undo** is dimmed if you haven't done anything.

In this Guide, all menu options will be displayed in Bold and appear just as they do on the screen. If you are to click a submenu option, the commands will be separated by a comma...like this:
Edit, Sort...

The Keyboard

If you prefer, you can invoke ACT! menu commands using the keyboard. You may have noticed that every menu command has an underlined letter. It's not because the programmers liked to underline things.

...use the keyboard to choose a menu option

1.	Press **[Alt]**.	This activates the menu bar to the keyboard.
2.	Type the underlined letter.	Notice that the **Edit** menu command has un underlined **E**
3.	Press the underlined letter for the submenu option.	When the **Edit** menu displays, you will notice that the submenus also have underlined options. Press the letter of the option you wish to perform. (e.g. **S** would allow you to **Sort** the contacts in your database.)

ACT!™

You can also use keystroke combinations to make ACT! perform some commands. For example, instead of pressing **[Alt+F]** and then **X** to execute the **File, Exit** command in ACT!, you could also press and hold the **[Alt]** key while you tap the **[F4]** key to exit.

 *As you go through this Guide, keyboard alternatives like **[Alt+F4]** (which is used to exit ACT!) will be displayed with the icon shown at the left. Notice that keystrokes are in bold and underlined and placed inside of square brackets. If the keys are to be pressed simultaneously, a plus sign (+) is placed between the keys.*

Toolbars

Toolbar icons make your life easier as you work on your PC. If you can do it by clicking on an icon, we'll display it to the right of the command like this.

Right-Click

Finally, if you right-click certain areas of the screen, ACT! will display a small menu (called a shortcut menu) with options for whatever you are right-clicking. After the menu displays, you left click on the menu item you want to perform.

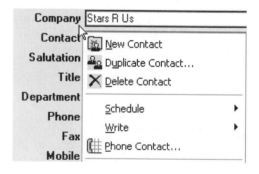

 *If **right**-click options are available, they will be displayed with this icon.*

Opening a Database

There is more to contact management than names, addresses, and phone numbers. An **ACT! database** will also provide you with a calendar, a task list, access to e-mail, and other tools with which to make you the most efficient person in your company (maybe even the world!).

So let's open a practice database and see what ACT! is all about. We have prepared a sample database to use for this self-paced study guide.

Setting Up For Your Self-Study

In the back of this guide, a CD has been provided that contains a database that we will use while we work through this Self-Study Guide (don't say we never gave you anything).

If ACT! already opened a database for you, humor us and use ours. First we need to restore the database to your system.

...install the files used in this Quick Study Guide

1. Insert the CD found in the back of this guide into your CD-Rom drive.

2. In ACT!, click **File**, **Restore**

   The **Restore** dialog box appears.

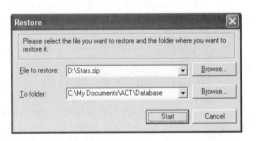

3. In the **File to restore:** text area, type:

   d:\stars.zip

4. Click **Start**.

Your PC may have assigned a different drive letter to your CD-ROM or DVD-ROM drive. If so, you can click **Browse...** , then locate the drive and select the file.

You should not have to change the **To folder:** location (even if it doesn't match the example above). The location is set by a combination of what version of Windows you use and whether or not you have upgraded from a previous version of ACT!.

5. If prompted to close your database, click **Yes.**

If you already have a database open, you will be asked if it is OK to close the current database and open the restored one.

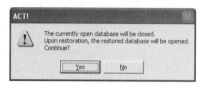

👉 *In the unlikely event that you should already have a database named "Stars R Us" on your PC, you will be warned before it overwrites your work.*

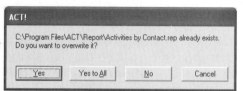

6. If prompted to rollover your activities in our practice database, click **Cancel**.

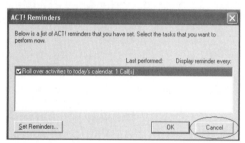

Returning to Real Life

If you are already using a database for your business, you will want to know how to easily move back and forth from the practice database we just opened and the one you need to use everyday.

Remember, in this Study Guide, you should review the "**How to…**" section to understand the procedure involved and then proceed to the practice to "**Try it…**".

...open a database

1. Choose **File, Open...**
   or
   click the Open toolbar icon.

Regardless of which method you use, the **Open** dialog box appears.

Normally, the **Open** dialog box displays a list of the databases in a folder called **Database** that was created for you. It is possible your database may be stored in another drive or folder.

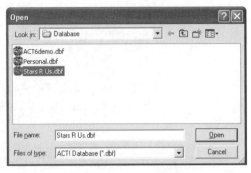

2.   If necessary, change to the drive and folder where your database is stored. Select the database you want to open.

Once you have located the database, click the name in the list, or type it yourself in the **File name:** box.

3.   Click **Open.**

The database opens in ACT!.

    *ACT! can only have one database open at a time. If you have a database open and choose to open another, ACT! closes the first one for you before it opens the second. **This does no harm to either**.*

If you are constantly moving between 2 or more databases, you can usually do it quickly by selecting from the "Recent Files" list at the bottom of the **File** menu. The number 1 option will always be the name of the current database. Usually the number 2 option will display the database that you just left.

    *Some menu options display keystroke shortcuts to the right of the menu command. [**Ctrl+O**], for example, can be use to open a database file instead of choosing **File, Open...**.*

If you have not yet started using a working database for your business, you can skip this practice (moving back and forth between the practice database and your real one) and go straight to the "Windows Screen Elements" on the next page.

 After we have reviewed the basics of ACT!, you will find a section later in this guide (page 298) on creating a working database for you to use.

Practice: *Open Another Database*

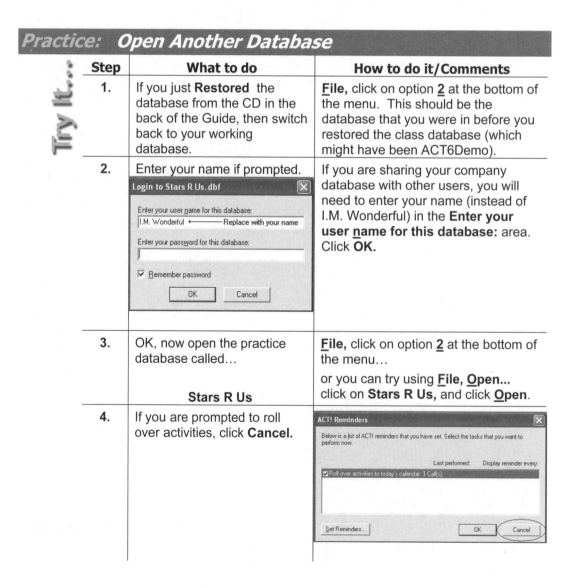

Step	What to do	How to do it/Comments
1.	If you just **Restored** the database from the CD in the back of the Guide, then switch back to your working database.	**File,** click on option **2** at the bottom of the menu. This should be the database that you were in before you restored the class database (which might have been ACT6Demo).
2.	Enter your name if prompted.	If you are sharing your company database with other users, you will need to enter your name (instead of I.M. Wonderful) in the **Enter your user name for this database:** area. Click **OK.**
3.	OK, now open the practice database called… **Stars R Us**	**File,** click on option **2** at the bottom of the menu… or you can try using **File, Open...** click on **Stars R Us,** and click **Open.**
4.	If you are prompted to roll over activities, click **Cancel.**	

Windows Screen Elements

Over the next few pages, we will briefly review some basic Microsoft Windows®
and PC terms and functions. These tips will be especially helpful if you have
never taken a basic Windows class before. If you are a Windows expert you
can skip ahead to page 16, but then again you might learn something. Hey it's
only 3 pages.

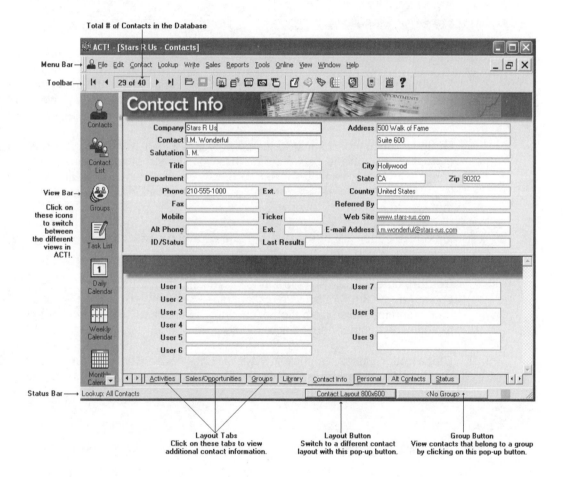

Total # of Contacts in the Database

Menu Bar →

Toolbar →

View Bar →
Click on
these icons
to switch
between
the different
views in
ACT!.

Status Bar → Lookup: All Contacts

Layout Tabs
Click on these tabs to view
additional contact information.

Layout Button
Switch to a different contact
layout with this pop-up button.

Group Button
View contacts that belong to a group
by clicking on this pop-up button.

ACT! runs in a Windows environment. As such, it has a similar look and feel to
other Windows applications. There are certain screen elements that are
common to all Windows programs. This adds a great deal of consistency to
"Windows programs" and makes them easier to learn. ACT! is *not* an exception
to this. (Life is good!)

ACT!

Title bar displays the name of the program, ACT!, and the current database name (if a database is open and its window is maximized).

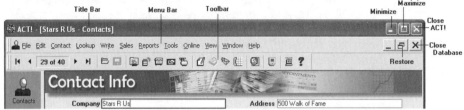

Menu bar displays the commands that are available for the active window.

Toolbar holds icons that, when clicked, will perform some of the most commonly used features. Icons that display on the toolbar will change as you work in the different screens in ACT!.

Minimize button allows you to temporarily leave your work and place the current window in the background while you do something else on your computer. When minimized, the current window is reduced to an icon in the lower part of the screen. It does not exit the application or close the file. Click that icon to reopen the window.

Maximize button fills the screen with the current window. The maximized window may hide other open windows.

Restore button displays if the window is maximized. Clicking the Restore button returns the window size to its original "medium" size. The Restore button and the Maximize button occupy the same place on the Title bar and replace one another depending on the current window size.

Close button closes the current window. Clicking the Close button on the ACT! title bar exits ACT!. Clicking the Close button below it closes the current database window.

The Mouse

The mouse is a pointing device. Although all operations can be accomplished with the keyboard, sometimes it's easier (and more fun) to use the mouse.

The mouse has six main functions (okay, seven if you count throwing the little rodent across the room):

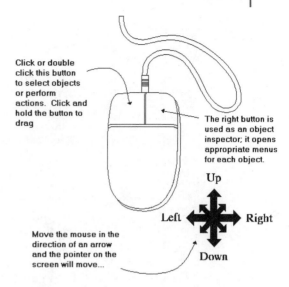

Click or double click this button to select objects or perform actions. Click and hold the button to drag

The right button is used as an object inspector; it opens appropriate menus for each object.

Up

Left   Right

Move the mouse in the direction of an arrow and the pointer on the screen will move...

Down

Action	Reaction
Point	Place the mouse pointer on an object, icon, or menu item to point to it (perhaps a helpful tool tip will display).
Click	With the mouse pointer on an object, icon, or menu selection, *press and release the LEFT mouse button. Do not hold the button down.*
Double-Click	Position the mouse pointer and ***without moving the mouse,*** *click the LEFT mouse button twice, **quickly**.* The trick here is not to move the mouse between the clicks.
Drag	Place the mouse pointer on the desired object, *press and hold the LEFT mouse button.* Move the mouse pointer to a new location and release the mouse button. Dragging is used to move objects or select specific text.
Right-click	Position the mouse pointer on an object, icon, or menu selection, *press and release the RIGHT mouse button* to display object specific menus.
Right-drag	Position the mouse pointer on an object, icon, or menu selection, *press and hold the RIGHT mouse button* while moving the object to a new location. When the button is released, a shortcut menu will appear.

Changing the View Bar

While we are viewing the basic screen, you may notice that the View Bar may not appear down the left side of the ACT! screen. (The View Bar contains great big icons with pictures that say **Contacts, Contact List, Groups**, and so on). If you don't see it there, the View Bar may be displayed on the lower-right side of the screen as a Mini View Bar. You can determine where you would like the View Bar to display.

Large View Bar

Mini View Bar

...change the position of the View Bar

How To...

1.	Point anywhere on the View Bar (or the Mini View Bar) and right-click.	A shortcut menu appears with choices related to the View Bar.

2.	Click **Mini View Bar** or **Large View Bar**	The bar moves to the opposite location in the ACT! window and the buttons resize themselves accordingly.

*If your screen size is small, you may not be able to see all of the View Bar icons on the left side of your window (can you see the **Monthly Calendar, E-mail,** or **Internet Services** icons?) You can have ACT! display smaller icons and text so that they all display at the left. Point anywhere on the View Bar and right-click. Click **Small Icons.***

Practice: *Admiring the View Bar*

Step	What to do	How to do it/Comments
1.	Practice switching between the Large View Bar and the Mini View Bar.	It's probably down the left side of your screen, but it also may be displayed in the bottom right corner. Right-click the current View Bar and select the opposite option.

Toolbar Buttons

ACT! usually displays one toolbar at the top of the screen. Many of the most common commands in ACT! can be invoked with a single click of the mouse on the appropriate toolbar button. The function of each button is represented by a small picture (or icon) on the button.

Some of the button icons are as clear as crystal in their meaning. The Open File icon, for example, makes sense (a picture of a file folder "opening"). Others are

as clear as chocolate milk. When the meaning of a toolbar button is unclear, just *point* to the icon (don't click it). After a moment, a label called a **tool tip** displays, and identifies the button for you. (We know it's not polite to point, but the buttons won't take offense if you do.) A more complete description of the toolbar button also displays on the ACT! Status bar on the lower-left side of the screen.

Step	What to do	How to do it/Comments
1.	What's the name of this icon?	Point to the icon, but *don't* click it. The tool tip appears telling you that it's the **New Contact** icon. The Status Bar displays "Insert a new contact".
2.	Find out the names of several other icons on the toolbars.	

Try It...

There are many useful icons on the ACT! toolbar. Much of your work can be accomplished without menus, if you take the time to learn the meaning of these tools.

 As you work in ACT! and find that you have questions about a screen or a dialog box, press the [F1] key to display a context sensitive Help screen.

Layouts

There is more information associated with a contact record than you could shake a stick at (we want to go on record as being against shaking sticks at your computer--but there *is* a lot of information there!).

There are times when you may find it advantageous to see less (or more) information or to see it ordered in a different way. You may be on a laptop which allows you to display lots of information on the screen, but your co-workers may be using older PCs that are not capable of displaying as much information.

ACT! comes with several pre-defined Contact layouts. Layouts allow you to display the information stored in your Contact database in many different ways (the same data, just arranged differently). The Layout button is used to switch between available layouts.

...change to a different layout

1. Click the Layout button.

The Layout button is displayed at the bottom of the Contact window (to the left of the <No Group> button). The name of the current layout is displayed on the button. When you click the Layout button, a list of choices appears.

3rd Contact

3rd Title

Contact Layout 2000/5.0
Contact Layout 640x480
Contact Layout (16 Colors)
Contact Layout 1024x768
Essentials 1024x768
Essentials 800x600
Contact Layout 800x600

Contact Layout 800x600

☞ *If your list is different from the one shown here, don't worry about it. Different PCs often have different layout choices. Trust us...you already have the ones that count!*

2. Click the desired layout.

The screen display changes to the new layout.

The *[F6]* key toggles between the two most recently chosen layouts. (To switch layouts, press *[F6]* to return to the original, and *[F6]* again to switch back.)

Try It...

Step	What to do	How to do it/Comments
1.	Switch to the **Contact Layout 640x480** layout and notice the changes in how the data is displayed. Web Site, Ticker, and some phone numbers have moved from the top half of the screen.	Click the Layout button at the bottom of the window and choose **Contact Layout 640x480** from the subsequent pop-up menu.
2.	Switch to the previous layout without using the mouse.	Press **[F6]**.
3.	Switch to the **Essentials 800x600** layout and notice the different color scheme.	Click the Layout button and choose **Essentials 800x600**.
4.	Switch to some of the other layouts and note the differences.	Some of them are pretty similar, aren't they?
5.	Switch back to the **Contact Layout 800x600**, layout, if necessary.	This may not be the optimal size for your PC, but we will be using this layout as we go through the Study Guide.

 The numbers to the right of the layout name (640x480 or 1024x768) indicate that the layout is optimized for that screen size. If you don't know your PC's screen resolution, just find a layout that seems to fill up your screen without the need for using scroll bars to see the information.

Layout Tabs

At the very bottom of the Contact View, ACT! displays the Layout Tabs. You are going to want to keep track of lots of information about your contacts (far more information than can comfortably fit on your screen at one time). Each notebook style tab provides you with an extra "page" on which you can record additional data about your contacts. Click a tab to display the information stored on its page. The names on the tabs describe the type of information stored on them.

| Notes/History | Activities | Sales/Opportunities | Groups | Library | Contact Info | Personal |

*You can also use the keyboard to display a Layout tab. Note that each layout tab name has an underlined letter. Press and **hold** the **[Alt]** key, while you tap that underlined letter on your keyboard and the associated layout tab displays.*

Practice: *View Layout Tabs*

Step	What to do	How to do it/Comments
1.	What layout tab is being displayed right now?	If you look carefully, one of the tabs appears to be in front of the others. The contents of its "page" are displayed in the bottom part of the window.
2.	Display the **Alt Contacts** tab using the mouse.	Click the **Alt Contacts** tab to see if there are any additional contacts listed for the current record.
3.	Use the keyboard to display the **Notes/History** tab.	Press **[Alt+N]** to display the Notes/History entries for the current contact (the meaning of these will be explained soon).
4.	Click on some additional tabs to view their contents. What kind of information do you think you will find there?	
5.	When you are finished browsing, click the **Notes/History** tab.	Let's all be on the same page, shall we?

Try It...

Sizing the Contact Window

There are two parts to the contact screen, the **top** part and the **bottom** (we have just got to stop using those *obscure* technical terms!). The top contains the Company Name, Contact name, Address, and Phone number information. The bottom half displays the information contained in the layout tabs.

✔ A horizontal bar divides the two parts.

✔ This dividing bar can be used to change the relative size of the top and bottom portion of the layout.

...resize the parts of the contact window

1. Place the mouse pointer on the bar that divides the top and bottom of the layout.

The mouse pointer turns in to a double-headed arrow when it is positioned properly.

2. Click and hold the left mouse button and drag the bar up or down to resize the two window parts relative to each other.

The two parts of the screen stay the size that you make them, until you change them back.

Practice: *Size the Parts*

Step	What to do	How to do it/Comments
1.	Change the size of the bottom portion of the Contact screen. Adjust the size so you can see the maximum information on both the top and bottom of the window.	Place your mouse pointer on the bar that divides the top and bottom of the screen. Look for the double-headed arrow that indicates you are positioned properly, click and hold the left mouse button, and drag up or down to resize the bottom half of the window.

 If you have a computer with a large Screen Area setting, you will want to adjust the bar tightly to the top half of the screen (so that you can just see all of the fields in the top half) with all of the extra room in the bottom half. That way, as you continue to enter notes and histories, you can see more of them without scrolling.

Contact Record Basics

Now that you have a feel for the ACT! screen, we need to look around. The ACT! database consists of a number of contact records. First, let's find out just what a "contact record" is.

The Anatomy of a Record

All of the related information about each contact in your database is called a **contact record** (or simply a **record**). Records hold a great deal of information. That information is displayed on your screen when you are in an ACT! database.

✔ The Contact screen displays information about the current contact record.

✔ Each bit of information is displayed in its own text box. These boxes are called **fields**.

✔ To the left of each text box is a label that describes the data stored in that box. These labels are called **field labels**.

✔ There are many more fields than can be displayed easily on your computer monitor so they are divided among the tabs in your layout.

The "My Record" Contact Record

When you first opened the Stars R Us database, you landed on the record for I.M. Wonderful. This was not a random occurrence. In fact, any time you open this database, the same record displays since ACT! thinks that is who you are. In your own business database, this record should contain *your* name and personal information.

Now you may wonder why your name and related information needs to be in a list of contacts. After all, you know who you are and where you live, and whether or not you need to talk to yourself. This record is called the **"My Record"**, (yes, that is its official designation) and there is a very good reason for its existence. It provides ACT! with information for letters, faxes, etc. about the current user...you. For example, when you write a letter, you may want your name and title to be included at the bottom under the space for your signature. It is from the "My Record" record that this information is obtained. However you input your title (Supreme Commander?), your Fax number, your e-mail address, etc., that is how it will display in your correspondence.

"I Feel So Us(er)ed"

An ACT! database can be opened at the same time by more than one person if your PCs are networked. Each person who can have access to the database should have a logon user name. When they do, each user who can login to the database has their own "My Record."

✔ When a database has more than one user, it prompts for the user name when the database is opened with a login screen. This way, you can identify yourself to the database. When the file opens, the corresponding "My Record" displays which should contain all the information that you might want to use in your correspondence.

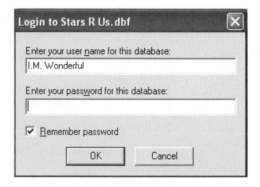

✔ ACT! also uses the logon name to keep track of and separate all of the activities each user is planning. In other words, each logon user can have a separate calendar. In addition, a note entered on any contact will be marked with the name of the logon user who entered it

✔ While you may be the only user of your database now, it's good to know that ACT! can grow with you.

☞ *For the purposes of this study guide, you are based in Hollywood and your name is I.M. Wonderful. (The meaning of the initials is a secret, so secret, even we don't know.) You are the president of Stars R Us.*

Fields

The purpose of most of the fields is fairly evident, but let's go through each of the tabs and review what information we are capturing on this contact. In the top half of the layout, you will find what we call "business card" information (data found on almost everyone's business card). However there are a couple of fields that are worth discussing in each area of the screen.

Salutation: The Salutation field is automatically filled in when you enter the Contact field. You can always change it (from Robert to Bob or to Dr. Smith). This field will display in your correspondence: Dear Bob

Alt Phone: Alt phone is just another phone number you can use if you can't reach anyone on the regular Phone: field. Sometimes we use this field to enter the Main Phone number for a company so we can get to a live operator if we seem stuck in voice mail with the normal Phone: number.

ID/Status: ID/Status field can be used to segment your database into Customers, Prospects, Vendors, Friends, etc. Don't ignore this field. It is a quick way to group your database for mail outs or other quick lookups (**ID/Status** is one of the options on the **Lookup** menu.) This field is also what is known as a "history" field. Anytime you type something in this field, it automatically gets posted to the **Notes/History** tab with the current date and time, along with who changed the information.

Ticker Symbol: If your contact is with a publicly traded company, you can input their Stock Exchange Ticker Symbol here so that you can lookup their current stock price before making that next phone call (sometimes it is a good talking point, other times it is a sore point).

Referred by: Keeping track of how new leads reach you can help you decide how to spend your marketing dollars next year. It can also help remind you to thank your friend for the lead that turned into a client. ACT! has a built-in report (**Reports, Source of Referrals**) that will sort and count the number of contacts by referral source.

Web Site: If you enter the contact's web site information, you can click on the field ACT!'s Internet Services window will open with the client's web site displayed. Handy to refresh your memory about what services or products the company provides.

Last Results: This field is also a "history" field and posts all changes to the **Notes/History** tab with the current date and time, along with who entered the information (handy if you are sharing this database with other users). So, Last Results could display…well…the last results of your contact with this person. If the field displays "Planning to sign the contract next month", you can look in the **Notes/History** tab to see what year that information was entered.

Contact Info

User 1 - User 9: ACT! provides you with some "blank" fields where you can begin to enter other information about your contacts. Perhaps you would like to keep an "Industry" field so that you can focus your marketing efforts on specific groups. Maybe you would like to make one of the fields "Account Exec" or "Directions" (How to get to this contact). We'll learn how to change the field names later in this Study Guide. If you don't change the field names, just be sure you use the same field each time you enter the information (User 1=Industry, User 2=Account Exec, etc.)

Personal

Birth Date: Birth date allows you to keep track of your clients' birth dates. While it is a date field (which records month, day AND year), you don't have to be that precise here (unless you are in the insurance business)...just the month and day will do. This field is also designated as an Annual Event field, meaning that you can lookup all contacts that have a birth date in the current week, month or other specified time period.

Spouse: All things being equal, people do business with people they like. You don't have to ask the contact what their spouse's name is, just record it sometime when they mention the name in conversation. How impressive is it if you remember their name and ask about them? Very!

Alt Contacts

Assistant: If you find yourself going through assistants to get to your contacts, you will find this field invaluable in building a relationship with the contact. Remembering the Assistant's name the next time you call makes a great impression and might help get you past this gatekeeper.

2nd and 3rd Contacts: It is recommended that you use these fields for non-decision makers. If someone has any impact on whether the company will buy from you, they deserve their own record. However, there may be times when you just want to record someone's name for later use (e.g. an accounts payable contact and phone number).

Status

Public/Private: No this isn't asking whether it is a publicly or privately held company. All contacts by default are marked as Public. If you are sharing the database with other users in your company, you can opt to change this field to Private for certain records. After a contact is marked as Private, only the listed "Record Manager" can see it (not even the administrator can see it unless they log in to the database as that Record Manager.) This will also affect the total number of contacts displayed in the record counter.

Private records will be included in your count, but not in anyone else's count.

Last Reach	7/15/2002	Create Date	12/6/1995
Last Meeting	8/16/2002	Edit Date	8/16/2002
Last Attempt		Merge Date	11/20/2001
Public/Private	Public	Letter Date	
Record Creator	I.M. Wonderful		
Record Manager	I.M. Wonderful		

System fields: The fields on this tab that are grayed out are system fields that cannot be changed by the user. As you work in ACT!, the dates are automatically recorded here. In this example, we entered the contact into our database on 12/6/1995. The last time we called the contact was 7/15/2002. The last meeting we attended together was 8/16/2002. The Edit Date will always display the last date that a field was changed, or the completion date of an activity, whichever is the most recent date.

User 10 - User 15: ACT! provides a few more fields for you to use.

Inserting a New Contact Record

The list of people you know and do business with is in a constant state of change. As you make new contacts, you will need to add them to the list. When a company goes out of business, you need to delete that data.

...add a contact to a database

1. Choose **Contact, New Contact...**

   or

   press the **[Insert]** key on your keyboard.

   A blank Contact window appears.

2. Enter the information for the new contact.

   Press **[Tab]** to move from field to field. **[Shift+Tab]** takes you back to the previous field.

*You can also right-click anywhere on the background of the Contact layout screen and choose **New Contact** from the shortcut menu.*

☞ *The information entered into ACT ! is saved as you go.*

Drop-down Fields

Certain fields in your contact database can display drop-down lists. These lists often contain common entries for their particular field. Making use of these drop-down fields can help speed your data entry, but if you need to enter something not in the list, you may do so. **Title**, **ID/Status**, **City**, and **State** are some examples of drop-down fields.

...use a drop-down field

1. Click in the desired field.

   When the field is active, a drop-down list button appears to the right of the field box.

2. Click the drop-down list button to display the list.

   A list "drops down" from the field box.

3. Click the desired entry.

   The list closes and your selection appears in the field.

To select multiple items, press [F2] and click first item, then [Ctrl+click] each additional item.

There are several ways to enter data from a drop-down list. You can display the list using the mouse (as described above) or you can type the entry. If the item you are typing is in the list, ACT! displays it as you type the first few letters. Once you see the appropriate entry, even if you haven't finished typing, you can move on to the next field and the displayed item is entered. If the item you are entering is not in the list, just finish typing it and move on.

City Boston

We typed "bo"

Practice: *Adding a Contact*

Try It...

Step	What to do	How to do it/Comments
1.	Add a new record to the database. **Casablanca Films** Ingrid Bergman	**Contact, New Contact...** or press **[Insert]**. Use **[Tab]** to move from the **Company** field to the **Contact** field. Notice the Salutation field automatically filled in after you entered Ingrid's name.
2.	Her **Title** is **President.** Select it from the drop-down list. Phone **310-555-8860** Fax **310-555-8869**	Click in the field and then click the down arrow. Click **President.** Notice that ACT! inserts the hyphens for you in the phone numbers
3.	Use **[F2]** to choose an **ID/Status** of **Prospect.**	**[Tab]** to the **ID/Status** field and press **[F2]**. Click **Prospect, OK.**
4.	Her company address is: **1250 Palm Drive Los Angeles, CA 91010**	Notice how ACT! helps you fill in **Los Angeles** and **CA.**
5.	Enter a **Last Results** of: **Met her at Selznick's party.**	
6.	Spouse = **Dr. Peter Lindstrom**	

Duplicating Contacts

ACT! isn't just about the companies you do business with, it is about the people who work for those companies. It is very possible you will have more than one contact for any given company.

Example: You leave a meeting clutching three business cards. All three are important people, and all three work for the same company. Therefore, the **Company**, **Address**, and some of the phone information are the same on all the cards. This could mean a lot of repetitive data entry.

ACT! can duplicate data from certain fields in the currently displayed record and place them in a new record. All you have to do is fill out the name of the contact, and those items that are different.

...enter a duplicate (almost) contact

1. Display the first contact.

   This is the contact that has the company information you want to duplicate.

2. **Contact, Duplicate Contact...**

   *You can also right-click anywhere in background of the Contact screen and choose **Duplicate Contact**... from the shortcut menu.*

3. Click the **Duplicate data from primary fields** or the **Duplicate data from all fields** option, click **OK**.

   Duplicate data from primary fields duplicates only those fields that are likely to be the same. The default primary fields are **Company, Address 1, Address 2, Address 3, City, State, Zip, Country, Phone,** and **Fax**. All other fields are left blank.

   Duplicate data from all fields duplicates everything (including fields like Spouse) from the current record... *except* the Contact name.

4. Make necessary entries or changes.

   Change whatever fields need to be changed.

Try It...

Practice: *Duping Ingrid*

Step	What to do	How to do it/Comments
1.	You should still be on Ingrid Bergman's record.	
2.	Let's enter another employee for the same company. After you duplicate the record (and before entering the contact information below), notice which fields were duplicated.	Choose **Contact, Duplicate Contact...**, or right-click anywhere on the layout background and choose **Duplicate Contact... OK** Company name and address fields were duplicated, but not ID/Status, Last Results, or Spouse.
3.	Enter the following information: Contact: **Isabella Rosellini** Title: **Vice President** Phone: **310-555-8862**	Check it out! All you had to enter was the information that was different from Ingrid's record.
4.	Change the Salutation to **Izzy**.	

Deleting Contacts

You would think deleting a contact would be easy wouldn't you? Then again, do you really want it to be easy? After all the trouble you go through to record your data, it would be a shame if you could delete it too easily.

ACT! takes pains to make sure you won't lose data accidentally. You can delete individual contacts or an entire lookup, but it requires more than one confirmation step. That's a good thing.

...delete a contact record or lookup

1. Display the record you want to delete, or perform a lookup that displays all of the records you wish to delete.

   If you are going to delete a lookup, make sure to review the records to make sure you really want to delete all of them.

2. Choose **Contact, Delete Contact** from the menu

   or

    *Press [**Ctrl**+**Delete**]*

   or

    *Right-click anywhere on the background of the Contact layout and you can choose **Delete Contact** from the shortcut menu.*

A warning dialog box appears. *Read the warning carefully!*

ACT!

Deleting contacts cannot be undone. Would you like to delete the current contact or the entire contact lookup?

Delete Contact | Delete Lookup | Cancel

3. Click **Delete Contact** to delete the current contact *only*, click **Delete Lookup** to delete *the entire lookup*.

The default button is **Delete Contact**, so unless you deliberately click **Delete Lookup**, only the current contact will be deleted. The type of the current lookup is displayed at the lower-left corner or your screen. Regardless of which choice you make, another warning is displayed. *Read this one carefully also.*

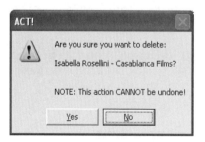

ACT!

Are you sure you want to delete:

Isabella Rosellini - Casablanca Films?

NOTE: This action CANNOT be undone!

Yes | No

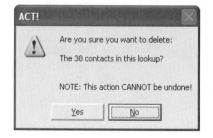

ACT!

Are you sure you want to delete:

The 38 contacts in this lookup?

NOTE: This action CANNOT be undone!

Yes | No

4. If the described action is really what you want to do, click **Yes**.

Now really, to delete something by accident, you would almost have to be asleep wouldn't you?

Practice: *So Long, Sweetheart*

Try It...

Step	What to do	How to do it/Comments
1.	You should still be on **Isabella Rosellini's** record.	
2.	Never mind. She is the contact with Casablanca Films that is already in the database, so let's delete this record that you just entered.	Choose **Contact, Delete Contact**, click **Delete Contact**, and click **Yes**. Because Isabella was the only record in the lookup, ACT! displays the "Are you sure…" message. **Yes** All contacts (well, all the contacts that are left) are displayed.
3.	You should now be viewing **Ingrid** again.	
4.	By the way, click on the **Notes/History** tab of Ingrid's record and notice that both your ID/Status and Last Results entries were recorded when you entered her record a few minutes ago.	Both ID/Status and Last Results are history fields. Anything typed in either of these fields will be recorded in the **Notes/History** tab as a History type of "Field Changed". It will also display the date and time of the entry and the name of the person who changed the field.

|ACT!

Changing a Few Preferences

As we go through this Study Guide, we want to point out a few areas where you might want to change your ACT! setup. You can change how ACT! responds on your PC without affecting anyone else who may be using ACT! in your company. However, rather than go through every option now, we will return to this area several times throughout the Guide to make changes relating to the topics at hand.

 We will only cover a few options, but remember, if you would like to know more about an option in a dialog box, press [F1] to display a context-sensitive help screen for the feature you are using.

...edit some of the ACT! preferences on your PC

1. **Edit, Preferences...**   The Preferences dialog box displays.

2. Click on the **General** tab, if necessary. As you are entering the Company name for a new contact record would you rather press **[Tab]** or **[Enter]** to move to the Contact field to enter the name?

    It makes no difference which you choose...whichever feels more comfortable to you. Best of all, you can change it back any time.

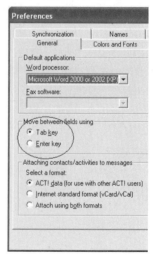

3. Next click on the **Names** tab

When you enter a Contact's name, by default, ACT! fills the Salutation with the contact's first name. If you work with a more formal clientele, you can change the default to **Use contact's last na_me_.** Then when you enter the contact's name as:

Dr. John Smith

the Salutation will be filled in as…

Dr. Smith

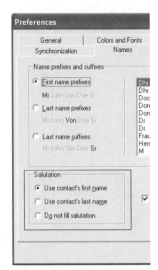

 If you fill in the contact name as John Smith, the Salutation will simply read "Smith". If you select the last name option, you must enter a title in the Contact field (Ms. Jane Doe, Professor Pat Smith, etc.)

Review: The Basics

Try It…

1.	What record do you see every time you open a database in ACT!?
2.	Display the **Activities** information for the current record.
3.	Display the **Personal** information for the current record.
4.	Change your Preferences to use **[Enter]** as the key to move from field to field. While you are there, change the default Salutation to the last name.
5.	Add yourself as a contact record. Don't forget to add the title prefix to your name (Mr., Ms., Dr., etc.)
6.	Change the Salutation to something a little less formal.
7.	Add all of your address information, including your e-mail address.
8.	Duplicate the primary fields in your record and add a co-worker.
9.	Never mind…delete your co-worker.
10.	Change the Preferences to your …well…your preferences. Select whichever key you like best to move between fields. Select the Salutation default that you would like to use (first name or last name).
11.	Leave the database open on your screen.

Working With Your Contacts

To get a feel for how ACT! can be put to work for you every day,
you will:

☑ Learn to locate contacts with Browse icons and the
Lookup menu.

☑ Work with your contacts in the Contact List view.

☑ Create a Note for a contact.

Locating Contacts

Let's continue by using some ACT! features that you'll use every day. One thing you'll do over and over is locate people and companies in your database. The better you are at finding names, the more valuable ACT! becomes.

Browsing Records

Most of what we have seen up to now involves the My Record contact record and the one we added to the database. There are other contacts in the database and you need to know how to view them. Located at the upper-left side of the toolbar, there are 4 buttons that help you to move from record to record using the mouse.

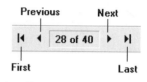

✔ Click the inside buttons to go to the next or previous record; click the outside buttons to go to the first or last record.

✔ The record counter in the middle of the browse buttons indicates the current position in the database. You see a phrase such as **28 of 40**, which means you are looking at contact number 28 of 40 available records.

To Move:	Keyboard	Mouse
To the previous record	**[Ctrl+PageUp]**	◄
To the next record	**[Ctrl+PageDn]**	►
To the first record	**[Ctrl+Home]**	I◄
To the last record	**[Ctrl+End]**	►I

Practice: Movin' On Up

Step	What to do	How to do it/Comments
1.	What is the number of the current record? How many records are available to view?	The Record counter displays this information. I◄ ◄ 29 of 41 ► ►I
2.	View the next 4 or 5 records.	Press **[Ctrl+PageDn]** or click the Next button. ►
3.	Display the 1st record.	Press **[Ctrl+Home]** or click the First icon. I◄

Try It...

Step	What to do	How to do it/Comments
4.	View the last record.	Press **[Ctrl+End]** or click the Last icon. ▶❙
5.	View the previous 4 or 5 records.	Press **[Ctrl+PageUp]** or click the Previous icon several times. ◀

The Lookup Menu

Looking up contact records is what the **Lookup** menu does. Used properly, the Lookup menu can help you locate not just specific people, but groups of people based on more than one criterion.

Example: You want to see a list of all contacts in Los Angeles who are movie directors.

Provided you keep track of things like professions somewhere in your database, the Lookup menu can accomplish this easily. Many common lookup fields are already set up for you to use in the Lookup menu itself.

...lookup a record

1. Choose **Lookup** from the menu. A number of common fields are displayed, like **Company...**, **First Name...**, **Last Name...**, etc. Click the appropriate item.

    Note: the **Lookup** dialog box reminds you of the Lookup menu item you chose (**Last Name** in this case).

    A **Lookup** dialog box appears for the item you chose.

2. Type part or all of the name or number you wish to lookup. The lookup dialog box for some fields contains lists from which you may choose (**City** is an example of this).

    You must type the *beginning* of the data for which you want to search. The more you type, the more specific the lookup.

3. **OK**

    ACT! scans all available records and displays only those records that fit the lookup.

☞ *Extra points for you if you noticed the __Empty field__ and __No__n-empty field
options. Click one of these options to lookup all records where the
chosen field is empty (so that you can fill in the blanks) or all non-empty
fields where there is something typed (like all contacts with fax numbers).*

Lookups are easy if you remember just a few things:

✔ Lookups are not case sensitive - all you have to do is spell it right!

✔ The more you type, the more specific the lookup is. The less you type,
the less specific it is.

> **Example:**   You are looking up a Last Name. Type the letter **g** to
> lookup all contacts that begin with the letter **G.** Type **gab**
> to locate all contacts with last names that begin with **Gab.**
> Type **gable** to look up only the last name of **Gable** (now
> how many of *those* could there be? Well there could be a
> Gables…nah!).

> **Example:**   You want to lookup only those people in a certain area
> code. Do a lookup on **Phone** and type the area code
> only. The result is all those contacts whose phone
> numbers begin with that code.

✔ With a simple lookup, you cannot lookup data in the middle of a field, only
at the beginning.

> **Example:**   You want to lookup all contacts that live in both
> **Cleveland Heights** and **East Cleveland**. Both cities
> contain the name **Cleveland**, but not in the same place
> within the City field. A lookup on **Cleveland** displays only
> **Cleveland Heights**.

The Effects of a Lookup

When you do a lookup, the records that match are displayed in the Contact window. The record counter reflects the number of records that fit the lookup and which of those contact records you are currently viewing. You may use normal navigation keys or the mouse to browse these contacts.

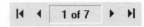

Seven contacts matched the lookup example

When you have performed a lookup, the Status Bar reflects this by showing the current **Lookup** at the bottom left corner of the ACT! window. If this indicator says **All Contacts**, then all records are accessible.

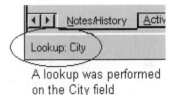

A lookup was performed on the City field

☞ *To return to viewing all contact records, choose **Lookup**, **All Contacts**.*

☞ *Every time you perform a Lookup, ACT! scans **all** records, not just those currently displayed (unless you change the options.) It is **not** necessary to lookup all contacts before performing a new Lookup.*

Practice: *Simple Lookups*

Step	What to do	How to do it/Comments
1.	Lookup the record for **Marilyn Monroe** by searching for her last name.	Choose **Lookup, Last Name...**, type **mon**, and click **OK**.
2.	How many records did ACT! find to match your entry?	The indicator at the top of the window says **1 of 1**. Notice also that the status bar says **Lookup: Last Name**. This is the current lookup.
3.	Try to move to another record.	Click the Previous button or press **[PageUp]**. It doesn't do much good, does it?
4.	Display all of the records in the database.	Choose **Lookup, All Contacts**.
5.	What record is displayed? What number is it?	Hello, Marilyn! Her contact record is still displayed, but now the record number is **19 of 41**.
6.	Now try to move to another record.	Now you can move to other records because the lookup is **All Contacts**.
7.	Lookup Roy Rogers' record by searching for his last name. How many records does ACT! find? Why?	Choose **Lookup, Last Name...**, type **rog**, click **OK**. Two records are displayed. It seems Roy is not the only Rogers in your database. Ginger is there, too!
8.	Lookup all records from the city of **Hollywood**. How many records are displayed? Are they all from the same state?	Choose **Lookup, City...** type **hollywood**, click **OK**. Browse the records. Some are from Hollywood, California, and two are from Hollywood, Texas (hey, it could happen!).

Try It...

Wait, We Didn't Tell ACT! the Last Name

We just finished searching for several contacts by their last name. Do you see a First Name or Last Name field in ACT!? How does ACT! do that?! We're glad you asked. ACT! looks at the first word you entered in the Contact field and designates it as the First Name. It looks at the last word you entered and assigns it to the Last Name. That works great for Marilyn Monroe, but what about Dr. William Smith III? We certainly don't want Dr. to be labeled as the first name and "III" as the last name.

That's OK. ACT! knows how to handle more complicated names as well. Let's go back to the Preferences dialog box.

...edit name preferences

How To...

1. **Edit, Preferences...,** click on the **Names** tab.

   The Preferences dialog box displays.

2. **First name prefixes** are a list of words that ACT! ignores if they are the first word typed (e.g. Doctor, Dr., Mrs. Ms., Mr., etc.) So if you type Mrs. Jane Doe, ACT! ignores the first word (Mrs.) and uses the second word that you type as the first name...pretty smart!

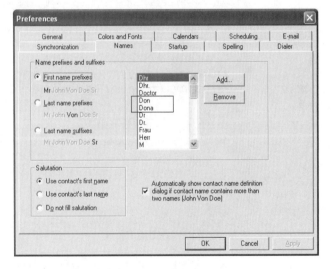

There is a potential problem here though. The prefixes of Don and Dona will be ignored (as in Don Juan Alejandro). However, many North Americans use the first name of Don. If you enter a name of Don Jones, you will not be able to **Lookup, First Name**, Don. Unless you do a lot of business with a Spanish-speaking country, you might want to click on Don and click **Remove**. While you are there, you might as well remove Dona as well in case you have any contacts that spell Donna with only one "n".

3. **Last name prefixes** are words that if found immediately to the left of the last name should be included *with* the last name (e.g. Jolly Old St. Nicholas…his last name would be St. Nicholas, not just Nicholas).

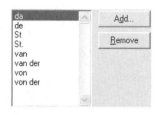

4. **Last name suffixes** are a list of words that ACT! ignores if they are the last word typed in the Contact field (Jr., Sr. PhD, CPA, etc.) If you work with contacts that have a common certification after their name, you should verify that their certification is listed here so that ACT! will ignore the title and use the next to last word for the Last Name.

5. **OK**

If you have worked with a database for a while, you may have some names where ACT! could not correctly identify the first and last names. As you find these problematic names, they are easy to fix.

…fix a problem name

1. Click in the Contact field

2. Click on the button to the right of the name.

3. Use the drop-down arrows to correct the name.

4. Click the **Automatically show this dialog if contact name contains more than two names** to avoid this problem in the future.

5. **OK**

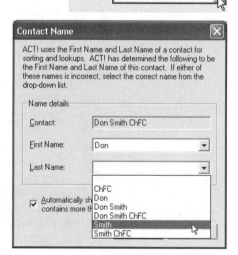

Practice: *Fixing Names*

Step	What to do	How to do it/Comments
1.	Find Van Johnson by looking up his first name.	**Lookup, First Name**, Van, **OK**. Sorry, can't find him. **OK Cancel**
2.	Look him up using his last name and then fix his name.	**Lookup, Last Name**, johnson, **OK** There he is! Click on the button beside his name and select Van from the drop-down list for his first name. Since "Van" is a Last name prefix, ACT! thought his last name was Van Johnson (as in Rip Van Winkle).

OK, we digress…back to more Lookups.

Lookup Variations

The simple lookups, like those we have just performed, will serve most of your lookup needs...or not! Face it, there will be times when you need to lookup more than one city, or more than one last name. There are also times when a simple lookup displays too many matching contacts and you want to "whittle it down" to a more manageable size. There are several ways you can refine your lookups. You can:

✔ Add to the current lookup.

✔ Narrow the current lookup.

✔ Perform a Keyword lookup.

"Why do I care?" we hear you say. Well, let's get back to an average day. Let's say you want to send out an introductory letter about yourself to a bunch of people in your database. This is how you find them!

Adding to Lookups

It's pretty easy to lookup all contacts from a given city. But what if you want to see all contacts from two cities, or three? Easy! All you need to know is how to add to an existing lookup.

...add to a lookup

How To...

1.	Perform a first lookup.	You can't add to something you don't have yet.
2.	To add to the first lookup, choose **Lookup** once again and another option.	Display the **Lookup** menu and choose the desired lookup option. You do not have to choose the same lookup option as the previous lookup.
3.	With the **Lookup** dialog box displayed, choose the **Add to lookup** option, type your lookup criteria in the text box.	Don't forget to choose **Add to lookup** or this lookup will replace the previous lookup instead of adding to it. 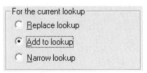
4.	Click **OK**.	All contact records that fit your new criteria will be added to your previous lookup of contacts.
5.	Repeat steps 2 through 4 as desired.	You may add multiple lookups together.

*When you are adding several lookups to the current lookup, it's pretty easy to forget to choose **Add to lookup** before you click **OK**. When this happens, you lose everything you have done to that point. Don't panic, just choose **Lookup, Previous** from the menu, and the previous lookup is restored so you can try again.*

Practice: *Lookup, Then Lookup More*

Step	What to do	How to do it/Comments
1.	Lookup all Contacts from the city of **Beverly Hills**.	Choose **Lookup, City...** type **bev**, and click **OK**. 6 contacts work in Beverly Hills.
2.	Look up all contacts from the city of **Hollywood**. Are any of the **Beverly Hills** contacts still displayed?	Choose **Lookup, City...** type **holly**, and click **OK**. 8 contacts work in Hollywood. When you performed the second lookup, it replaced the previous.
3.	Display the previous lookup.	Choose **Lookup, Previous**. Beverly Hills is back (dahhhhling!!!).
4.	Add **Hollywood** to the **Beverly Hills** lookup. Are both cities displayed?	Choose **Lookup, City...** type **holly** (if necessary), select **Add to lookup**, and click **OK**.
5.	Can you add **Brentwood** to the current lookup?	You're on your own on this one. You should end up with 15 contacts.

Try It...

Narrowing Lookups

With **Add to lookup**, you can add records to create a complex lookup one step at a time. This is great if your first lookup does not yield all of the contacts you wanted. But what do you do if your first lookup displays too many records? Simple! Narrow the lookup.

...narrow a lookup

1.	Perform a lookup.	This first lookup should display more records than you can easily use.
2.	Determine a different field to use to narrow the lookup and display the **Lookup** dialog box for that field.	Choose **Lookup** from the menu and choose the field you wish to narrow the lookup by.
3.	Type the desired lookup criteria and choose **Narrow lookup**.	Don't forget to choose **Narrow lookup**. Otherwise this lookup replaces the previous lookup instead of narrowing it.
4.	Click **OK**.	The current lookup is narrowed to display only those records that fit the new criteria *and* the original criteria.
5.	Repeat steps 2 through 4 as desired.	You can continue to narrow the lookup until you have only the contacts you want displayed.

How To...

For the current lookup

- ○ Replace lookup
- ○ Add to lookup
- ● Narrow lookup

Practice: *Lookup, Then Lookup Less*

Try It...

Step	What to do	How to do it/Comments
1.	Lookup the **City** of **Hollywood**. As before, we get 8 contacts from both Texas and California.	Choose **Lookup, City...**, type **holly** and click **OK**.
2.	We only wanted records from **Hollywood, CA**. Can you narrow the lookup to only those records?	Choose **Lookup, State...**, type **ca**, select **Narrow lookup**, click **OK**.
3.	Can you add records in Los Angeles to the current lookup?	Yes! You can combine **Narrow** and **Add** to create very complex lookups.

Lookup Other Fields

The standard Lookup menu options offer the most commonly used fields for quick lookups, but not all the fields are listed. What if you want to lookup a fax number or find out how many contacts have been referred to you by Kittie Carlisle? These lookup fields are not on the menu. For these kinds of searches we can use the **Other Fields...** option.

...lookup information in other fields

How To...

1. **Lookup, Other Fields...**   The same dialog box displays.

2. Click on the **Lookup** drop-down arrow and select the field in the database that you want to query.

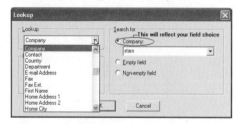

3. Enter your **Search for** criteria

4. **OK**

☞ *In addition to clicking the drop-down arrow, you can also type the name of the field to move quickly to it.*

Practice: Looking up other stuff

Try It...

Step	What to do	How to do it/Comments
1.	How many contacts in our database have fax numbers.	Choose **Lookup, Other Fields...**, select **Fax**, click on **Non-empty field** and click **OK**. Should be about 35 (if you entered Ingrid).
2.	How many people has Kitty Carlisle referred to us?	Choose **Lookup, Other Fields...**, select **Referred by**, notice that you have to change the options in the **Search for** section before we can type in Kitty's name. Should be 3.

|ACT!

Keyword Searches

The pre-set fields in the Lookup menu work well as long as you know how the data in the field begins. If, however, you want to look for a word, number, or phrase that is "inside" the text in a field, the pre-set fields don't help you any. So ACT! provided an option called **keyword** search.

Example: You want to locate all companies with the word **Film** in their name. Unless **Film** is at the beginning of the company name, using the **Lookup, Company** option does not work.

...perform a keyword search

1. **Lookup, Keyword Search...**

   The **Keyword Search** dialog box appears.

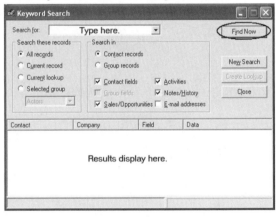

2. Type the keyword or phrase in the **Search for:** box.

   Be as specific or as general as you need. Keyword lookups are not case sensitive (all you have to do is spell it right).

3. Click the appropriate check box(es) to specify which part(s) of the database ACT! is to search.

   ACT! searches database **Contact fields, Sales/Opportunities, Activities, Notes/History** by default. You can also add **E-mail addresses**, among other things.

4. **Find Now**

   ACT! searches the specified area(s) of the database for your word or phrase and displays a lookup of the records containing those criteria.

5. **Create Lookup**

If you're only interested in one of the records found in the keyword search, double-click the record you wish to view. The Keyword Search dialog box minimizes, and ACT! displays the selected record with the keyword(s) highlighted.

Keyword lookups have two limitations:

✔   They cannot be combined with other lookups using the **Add** or **Narrow** options.

✔   They can be time consuming because they search all fields (not just the contact name), instead of specific fields (as with other lookups).

 The **Keyword Search** dialog box stays open until you close it. When you click **Create Loo<u>k</u>up** or double-click a record found in the dialog box, the box minimizes down to a bar at the lower left corner of the ACT! window.

You can close it (like any minimized program or document) by clicking its Close button.

 If you need to do a lot of keyword searches, feel free to leave the dialog box in its minimized state until you are ready for it again. At that point, just click the Restore button on the minimized bar and type your keyword.

Practice: *Performing a Keyword Lookup*

Try It...

Step	What to do	How to do it/Comments
1.	Lookup all records that contain the word **film**.	**Lookup**, **Keyword Search...**, type **film**, **Find Now**, and let the search run. When it's finished, click **Create Lookup**.
2.	How many items are found that contain the keyword?	There are 17 items found (if you entered Ingrid).
3.	Create a lookup of the companies that were found. How many companies are there?	Click **Create Lookup**. There were 15 with the word film somewhere in the **Company** name field …some at the end of the field and some in the middle. You could *not* perform this lookup using **Lookup**, **Company....**
4.	What was the reason for the discrepancy of 17 items and only 15 companies?	Click on the Restore icon of the Keyword Search dialog and view the items. There is also one record with the word "films" in the **Note** field and one record that had recorded a History using the word "film."
5.	View the note.	Double-click the record to see how the record opens in ACT! and highlights the word "film" in the Note field. Handy if you have entered lots of notes.
6.	Close the **Keyword Search** dialog box.	Click the **Close** button on the minimized Keyword Search dialog bar at the lower left corner of the ACT! window.

Lookup Annual Events

Missing a contract renewal (or a birthday for that matter) is serious stuff. You probably have an activity scheduled to take care of this, but sometimes you just need to get a list of all contracts that come up for renewal next month or next quarter.

If a date field in your database is classified as an Annual Event, ACT! makes that field available for lookups based on the month and day only (ignoring the designated year). From the lookup, you can then use ACT!'s Mail Merge feature to generate birthday announcements, contract renewal letters, etc.

☞ *To classify a date field in your database as an Annual Event, click in the field and select **Edit, Define Fields....** Place a check in the **Annual Event** option. Click **OK**. If you have an existing character-based field in ACT! (where you can type in December 5 or 12/5 without the year) and you want to take advantage of the Annual Event feature, see the section later in this book (starting on page 300) about creating fields.*

When you create a *new* database in ACT!, one pre-defined annual event field is included; Birth Date, however, you can add as many annual event fields as you like.

...lookup annual events

1. **Lookup, Annual Events...**

   or

    [Ctrl+Shift+A]

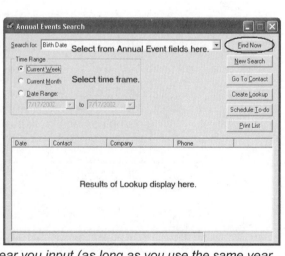

2. Select an event using the drop-down arrow in the **Search for:** list.

3. Select a time frame.

   ☞ *If you select **Date Range:** It makes no difference what year you input (as long as you use the same year for both fields). Only the month and day will be considered..*

4. **Find Now**

5. **N̲ew Search** clears the list so that you can start another search without exiting the window.

Go To C̲ontact displays the record of the selected contact and minimizes the **Annual Events Search** dialog box for later use.

Create L̲ookup creates a lookup of the contacts that matched your search criteria. This option would be great to use for mail merges or printing address labels!

Schedule T̲o-do starts the scheduling of a To-do for the selected contact only. The Regarding field is populated with the field name.

P̲rint List prints the results of the lookup with the same four columns.

6. Click **Close**.

Practice: *Generating a Birthday call list*

Step	What to do	How to do it/Comments
1.	Lookup all birthdays for the current month.	**L̲ookup, Annual Events...,** click **Current M̲onth,** click **F̲ind Now**
2.	Lookup the birthdays for July (I.M.'s favorite month)	**L̲ookup, Annual Events...,** click **D̲ate Range,** and select 7/1 for the starting date and 7/21 for the ending date. Click **F̲ind Now.**
3.	Create a lookup for the July birthdays.	Click **Create L̲ookup.** Notice that the **Annual Events Search** dialog box is minimized and its title bar appears at the lower-left corner of your screen.
4.	Restore the Annual Events dialog box and lookup Louis Mayer's record.	Click on the Restore button and then double-click Louis B. Mayer or select his name and click **Go To C̲ontact.**
5.	Close Annual Events.	Click the **Close** button

Try It...

Lookup Internet Directory

This feature requires that you have access to an LDAP (Lightweight Directory Access Protocol) server. These servers are similar to e-mail phone books and are usually used by universities or large companies to maintain their centralized up-to-date phone books. These servers are usually password protected in order to keep the data private.

There are public Internet Directory services, however you must subscribe to them to use them. If you have access to an LDAP server, you can add it to ACT!'s directory services list and after it is properly configured, use it to look for your ACT! contacts on one of these web based databases.

The Contact List

When you view contacts in the Contact screen, you get to see a lot of information about *one contact at a time.* There are times when you would like to see information about more than one contact, even if it means seeing less information.

When you display the Contact List window, the current lookup is displayed in list form. Field names are displayed at the top of the columns, and the list is sorted by Company name (usually).

...display the Contact List

1. Choose **View, Contact List**
    or

     press [F8],
    or
    click the Contact List button on the View Bar.

    Contact List

    The Contact List window displays. The current record is usually displayed at the top of the list.

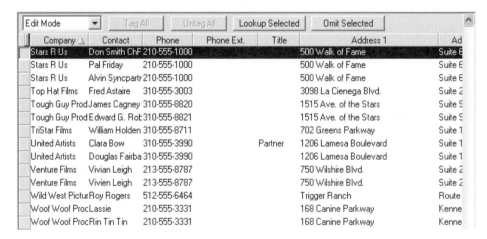

Edit Mode ▼	Tag All	Untag All	Lookup Selected	Omit Selected	
Company △	Contact	Phone	Phone Ext.	Title	Address 1	Ad
Stars R Us	Don Smith ChF	210-555-1000			500 Walk of Fame	Suite 6
Stars R Us	Pal Friday	210-555-1000			500 Walk of Fame	Suite 6
Stars R Us	Alvin Syncpartr	210-555-1000			500 Walk of Fame	Suite 6
Top Hat Films	Fred Astaire	310-555-3003			3098 La Cienega Blvd.	Suite 2
Tough Guy Prod	James Cagney	310-555-8820			1515 Ave. of the Stars	Suite 9
Tough Guy Prod	Edward G. Rot	310-555-8821			1515 Ave. of the Stars	Suite 9
TriStar Films	William Holden	310-555-8711			702 Greens Parkway	Suite 1
United Artists	Clara Bow	310-555-3990		Partner	1206 Lamesa Boulevard	Suite 1
United Artists	Douglas Fairba	310-555-3990			1206 Lamesa Boulevard	Suite 1
Venture Films	Vivian Leigh	213-555-8787			750 Wilshire Blvd.	Suite 2
Venture Films	Vivien Leigh	213-555-8787			750 Wilshire Blvd.	Suite 2
Wild West Pictur	Roy Rogers	512-555-6464			Trigger Ranch	Route
Woof Woof Proc	Lassie	210-555-3331			168 Canine Parkway	Kenne
Woof Woof Proc	Rin Tin Tin	210-555-3331			168 Canine Parkway	Kenne

✔ If you have performed a lookup prior to displaying this list, only the records in the lookup display in the list.

✔ You can use the Lookup menu to perform lookups when the list is displayed, just as you normally would.

✔ When you first display the list, the current contact displays at the top of the list. Be aware that this may not be the first record in the list. There may be many more contact records above the current record in the list.

Address 2

Not the top →Suite 100
of the list

✔ Watch the scroll bar at the right side of the window. If the scroll box is not at the top of the bar, you are not viewing the first item in the list.

✔ You can use the scroll bar to browse the list. You can also use the Up and Down arrow keys and the **[PageUp]** and **[PageDn]** keys on your keyboard if you wish.

Practice: *Display the Contact List*

Try It...

Step	What to do	How to do it/Comments
1.	Lookup all contacts, if necessary.	If all 40 records are not displayed, choose **Lookup, All Contacts**.
2.	Display the Contact List.	Press **[F8]** or click the Contact List button on the View Bar. Contact List
3.	Observe the list.	Whatever record you were on when you displayed the list is at the top of the list. This is not necessarily the top record in the list.
4.	Try moving up and down in the list.	Try the scroll bar. Try the arrow keys on your keyboard, try **[PageUp]** and **[PageDn]**.

Sorting the Contact List

When the Contact List is displayed, it is a bit easier to see how the database is sorted. Normally it is sorted by the Company field, which just happens to be the first column in the list (unless someone has changed it). When you are browsing the list, looking for someone by name, it would be better if you could sort the list by that column, don't you think?

...sort using the Contact List

How To...

1. Observe the column headings in the list. One heading contains a triangle. The triangle points either up or down.

    Ascending

Company △
Acme Matador Pictures
Americana Productions

    Descending

Company ▽
Woof Woof Productions
Woof Woof Productions

    This triangle is the sort indicator. When it appears in a column heading, the list is sorted by that column. When it points up, the sort is ascending (0-9, A-Z). When it points down, the sort is descending (Z-A, 9-0).

2. Click once on any column heading by which you want to sort.

Company △
Acme International Pictures
Acme Matador Pictures

    The list sorts in Ascending order by that column.

3. Click again on the same column to sort in descending order.

Company ▽
Woof Woof Productions
Woof Woof Productions

☞ *When you sort the **Contact** column, ACT! assumes you wish to sort by **Last Name**.*

☞ *You cannot view notes, histories or activities while displaying the Contact List View. Once you have found the desired record, you can display the regular Contact screen for that contact by double-clicking the row heading for that record.*

Double-click here to display the contact record ⟶

RKO Pictures
Ruby Pictures
Santiago Productions
Sherwood Forrest Films

Practice: *Sorting the List*

Try It...

Step	What to do	How to do it/Comments
1.	Sort the Contact List by the **Contact** column.	Click the **Contact** column heading once to sort the list in ascending order.
2.	Sort the list by **State** in descending order.	You may have to scroll right to display the **State** column. Click the **State** column heading two times to sort in descending order.
3.	Sort by **Contact** again.	Click the **Contact** column heading.
4.	Double-click the row header for Fred Astaire to view his record.	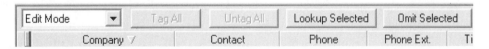
5.	Return to the Contact List View.	Press **[F8]** or click the Contact List button on the View Bar.
6.	Leave the list displayed.	

Tag Mode vs. Edit Mode

You may have noticed the specialized controls at the top of the Contact List.

The drop-down list at the left of these controls allows you to switch from **Edit Mode** to **Tag Mode**. In Edit Mode, you can edit any of the fields in the contact's record by just clicking the field you wish to change and typing the changes.

In Tag Mode, you can **tag** records. No, it's not a kid's game! Tagging a record means marking a record so you can perform an action on it. When you tag multiple records, any action you take is performed on all of the tagged records.

Example: If you tag 10 contacts and then press **[Ctrl+Delete]**, you will (after a confirmation step) delete all 10 records.

How To...

...tag records in the Contact List

1. Choose **Tag Mode** from the drop-down list at the top of the Contact List view.

   ☞ *If any records are tagged, you can click **Untag All** to remove the tags.*

   Tagged records display a **+** to their left.

   ☞ *You cannot edit the contents of a field when you are in Tag Mode.*

Click the drop-down button, then click **Tag Mode**. When you are in **Tag Mode**, the row headings disappear and a blank space appears to the left of each record.

2. Click on the record anywhere to tag or untag it. You can also use the arrow keys to move to different records, pressing the **[Spacebar]** to tag or untag.

A **+** appears when the record is tagged.

☞ *When you are in Tag Mode, the buttons that normally say **Lookup Selected** and **Omit Selected** will say **Lookup Tagged** and **Omit Tagged**.*

Practice: *Tagging Stuff*

Try It...

Step	What to do	How to do it/Comments
1.	While still in Contact List view, lookup the "My Record" and change the title to **Grand Poobah**.	You can do lookups in Contact List view. **Lookup, My Record,** click in the title field and enter the new title.
2.	Display the list in **Tag Mode**. Try to change the title again to something else.	Change from Edit Mode to Tag Mode using the drop-down list. You will not be able to make any edits to a contact record.

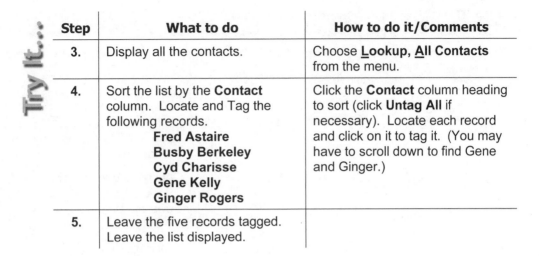

Step	What to do	How to do it/Comments
3.	Display all the contacts.	Choose **Lookup, All Contacts** from the menu.
4.	Sort the list by the **Contact** column. Locate and Tag the following records. **Fred Astaire** **Busby Berkeley** **Cyd Charisse** **Gene Kelly** **Ginger Rogers**	Click the **Contact** column heading to sort (click **Untag All** if necessary). Locate each record and click on it to tag it. (You may have to scroll down to find Gene and Ginger.)
5.	Leave the five records tagged. Leave the list displayed.	

Lookup and Omit Tagged Records

Once you have contacts tagged, you can create a lookup from the tagged records. There are two variations of this process.

✔ Create a lookup consisting only of those contact records you have tagged. This is a "**Lookup Tagged**" action.

✔ Create a lookup consisting of those contact records that are not tagged. This is an "**Omit Tagged**" action.

Note that there are buttons for each of these actions at the top of the Contact List.

...lookup or omit tagged Contacts

1. Tag the records you wish to Lookup/Omit.

2. Click **Lookup Tagged** to display only the tagged records.   `Lookup Tagged`   This performs a real lookup. If you return to the Contacts window, only the remaining records are available.

Click **Omit Tagged** to display only those contacts that are not tagged.   `Omit Tagged`

Practice: *Lookup and Omit*

Step	What to do	How to do it/Comments
1.	Lookup the currently tagged contacts.	You should still have the 5 contacts tagged from the previous exercise. Click the **Lookup Tagged** button at the top of the Contact List.
2.	Observe the list. Display the Contacts view.	Only the tagged records are displayed. Click the **Contacts** button on the View Bar.
3.	How many records are displayed?	There should be 5 records available in the Contacts window as well.
4.	Return to the Contact List. Are the records still tagged?	Click the **Contact List** button on the View Bar. The +'s still appear to the left of all 5 records.
5.	Untag all records but **Busby Berkeley**.	Click on each + to untag the other 4 records, or click Untag All and tag Busby again.
6.	Omit Busby from the lookup.	Click **Omit Tagged**. Only the dancers are left.
7.	Lookup all Contacts. Return to **Edit Mode**. Leave the Contact List displayed.	Choose **Lookup**, **All Contacts**. Choose **Edit Mode** from the drop-down list at the top of the Contact List.

Try It...

Adding and Removing Columns

The Contact List displays a selection of fields that will probably suit most users. However, you may find you would like to see a piece of information that is not currently displayed in the list. You can add columns to the Contact List view (and remove them) quite easily.

...add a column to the Contact List

How To...

1. Point to any column heading in the Contact List and **right-click**.

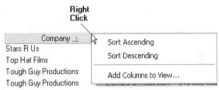

2. Choose **Add Columns to View...** from the shortcut menu.

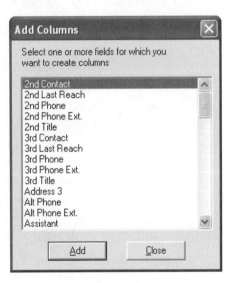

All of the fields in your database are displayed here in alphabetical order.

3. Select the first field you wish to add and click **Add**.

   ☞ *You can also drag a field from this dialog box to the screen. A heavy vertical line indicates where the field will be placed.*

4. Repeat step 3 until all the fields you want are added, then click **Close**.

The field will be added to the right side of the list. The **Add Columns** dialog box will remain displayed.

Practice: *Adding Last Reach*

Try It...

Step	What to do	How to do it/Comments
1.	Add the field named **Last Reach** to your Contact List.	Right-click one of the column headings and choose **Add Columns to View...**, locate and select **Last Reach**, click **Add**, click **Close**.
2.	Display the last column in the Contact List. Is it **Last Reach**?	Scroll to the right. Added columns are always added to the right of the list.
3.	Sort the list on the **Last Reach** column to see whom you haven't called in a while.	Click on the Last Reach column header. By default, blanks are displayed first and then the oldest dates to the newest dates. You could click the column again to display the column in descending order to see whom you have talked to most recently.
4.	Leave the list displayed.	

...move or remove a column from the Contact List

How To...

1.	Scroll to the column heading you wish to move or remove.	You are going to change the list using your mouse.
2.	Place the mouse pointer on the column header and drag it to its new location and drop it.	When you start to drag, the mouse pointer appears as a grabbing hand. The field will move with the mouse until your drop it at its new location. 
3.	If you continue to drag the column heading up toward the top of the screen, the mouse pointer turns into a trashcan. Release the mouse button at this point to remove the column.	Until the trashcan pointer is displayed, you are only moving, not removing the field. Remaining fields move to the left. 

☞ *Columns are only removed from the Contact List view. They are not removed from the database. You can always add them back to the view.*

☞ *As you scroll to the right, you can no longer see the contact name and phone number. If you need to work with more columns that you can see on one screen, you can "freeze" the columns at the left so that they always remain in place as you scroll to the right. Just drag the fat separator bar at the upper left corner of the screen and drop it after the last column to the right that you want to freeze in its place. Then you can scroll to the right and still see the contact's name. This setting will not be saved upon closing the window.*

Grab bar...   ...and drag to desired location.

Company	Contact	Phone		Title	Address 1
Stars R Us	Pal Friday	210-555-1000			500 Walk of Fame
Stars R Us	Alvin Syncpartner	210-555-1000			500 Walk of Fame

ACT!

Practice: *Removing Last Reach*

Step	What to do	How to do it/Comments
1.	We can't see the **Last Reach** column and the **Contact** name at the same time. Freeze the column display after Phone and then scroll to the right to see how this feature works.	As your mouse points to the separator bar in the upper right corner of the Contac List view screen, it changes to a double-headed arrow. Drag the bar to the right of Phone and release the mouse button. Use the scroll bar at the bottom of the screen to test this option.
2.	Close and reopen the Contact List view window. Notice that the separator bar returns to the home position.	Click on the lower Close button to close the Contact List view window without closing the program. Click on the Contact List view icon to open the window again. Contact List
3.	Let's remove some of the columns. Remove **Phone Ext., Title, Address1, Address 2, Zip**, and **E-mail Address**.	Position the mouse pointer on each column heading. Click and hold the left mouse button, and drag the fields up until the mouse pointer becomes a trashcan. Release the mouse button.
4.	Drag the **Last Reach** column to the right of the **Phone** number.	Drag the Last Reach column header to the left (the mouse pointer looks like it has grabbed the field label) and release the mouse button when the field is positioned between the **Phone** and the **City** field. Phone Last Reach City 210-555-1000 Hollywood
5.	Return to the Contacts window.	Click the Contacts button. Contacts

Taking Notes

Okay, back to using ACT! on a typical day. You cannot successfully sustain a good relationship without some memory for details. (Forget your spouse's birthday and see what it gets you!) The same is true in business. If you can display a clear memory of what was discussed the last time you talked, you show your contacts that you care about the details. If they know you care enough to remember the details, they are more likely to remember *you*. If they *remember* you, they are more likely to *think* of you when the time comes to do business.

While the contact layout provides a large number of fields to record various bits of information, there will invariably be something you want to record for which there is no field or that is too long to fit in any of the existing fields. You might want to record details about how a contact likes to do business, for example.

...add a Note to a contact record

1. Display the Contact for whom you want to make a Note.

    Use lookup or browse to display the Contact record.

2. Display the **Notes/History** tab.

    The **Notes/History** list displays.

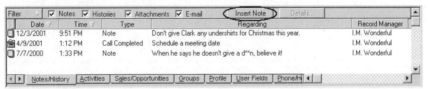

3. Click the **Insert Note** button at the top of the list.

    A new (empty) Note is inserted in the list. The date, time, type, and record manager information are entered for you.

4. Type the Note. Notes can be as long as you like. You can even cut and paste info into a note.

    Both Notes and History items are displayed in this list. The Note icon to the left of the date identifies notes.

☞ *Clicking the **Insert Note** toolbar button at the top of the ACT! window both displays the **Notes/History** tab and inserts a Note for the current contact.*

KB *Pressing the **[F9]** function key also displays the **Notes/History** tab and creates a Note for the current contact.*

Try It...

Practice: *Making a Note*

Step	What to do	How to do it/Comments
1.	Lookup the record for **Bing Crosby**.	**Lookup**, **L**ast **Name...**, type **cros**, **OK**.
2.	Create the following Note: **Bing plays golf every Wednesday and Saturday.**	Click the **Notes** icon or press **[F9]**. Type the Note.
3.	Lookup the record for **Rin Tin Tin**.	**Lookup**, **F**irst **Name...**, type **rin**, **OK**.
4.	Does this record have a Note?	Click the **Notes/History tab**, if necessary. Yes there are two notes.
5.	We wrote a note about someone who goes sailing every weekend, now we can't remember who it was. Can you find the contact? Hint: Lookup the record that has a Note containing the word **sail**.	**Lookup**, **K**eyword **Search...**, type **sail**, be sure that the **Notes/History** check box is the only box enabled, **Fin**d **Now**. Bogie! Notice that ACT! found the word **sails** (a form of **sail**).
6.	Close the **Keyword Search** dialog box.	**C**l**ose**

☞ *Each time you create a Note for a contact, the Note is displayed at the top of the **Notes/History** list. This way, the most recent entries are the most readily accessible.*

Review: *Working With Your Contacts*

Try It...

1.	Lassie is working with the company Woof Woof Productions. You can't look her up by first name. Correct that.	
2.	We have a special marketing program aimed at Assistants. Lookup everyone in the database who has an Assistant.	
3.	Once you have the list, display the contacts (who have Assistants) in Contact List view. Add the Assistant column to the view. Rearrange the columns if you like.	
4.	How could we tell what Christmas presents we've given in the past?	
5.	Which month has more birthdays…May or September?	
6.	Lookup I.M.'s record and enter a note regarding his goals for next year (whatever you like).	

Scheduling Your Day

To understand how to get your day and your life organized with ACT!, you will:

☑ Learn to schedule simple activities.

☑ Utilize the Task List view to organize your day.

☑ Review all of the features packed in the Calendar view windows.

☑ Record the results of your interactions with your contacts.

☑ Understand how the History feature can be used to document your conversations.

ACT!

Activities

Yet another daily use of ACT! is to keep track of your schedule. Each item in your schedule is called an **activity**. An activity, in ACT!, can be any one of three things:

1. **A Call**

2. **A Meeting**

3. **A To-do**

When you schedule an activity, you usually schedule it with (or for) a contact in your database.

✔ It is seldom, for example, that you call yourself, or schedule a time to meet with yourself.

✔ While To-Do's are usually scheduled for you to perform, don't you usually perform them for someone else?

Calls, Meetings, and To-dos

Although the performance of each of these activities is quite different, they are all scheduled the same way. The only difference is which menu, keystroke, or icon you use to begin them.

Menu Option	Keyboard	Toolbar Icon
Contact, Schedule Call	**[Ctrl+L]**	
Contact, Schedule Meeting	**[Ctrl+M]**	
Contact, Schedule To-do	**[Ctrl+T]**	

The same dialog box is used to schedule each activity type. In fact, it is quite easy to change one activity type to another at any point. For example, if you want to change a call to a meeting or vice versa, you can do it with very little effort.

Let's start with creating a simple activity (we'll review the more advanced options in the next chapter.)

...schedule a simple activity

How To...

1. Lookup the contact whom the activity concerns.

You may associate some activities with your My Record, but most will be related to specific people in your database.

2. Choose the appropriate option from the **Contact** menu,
   or
   click the necessary toolbar icon,
   or
   press **[Ctrl]+** the corresponding key on the keyboard.

The **Schedule Activity** dialog box appears.

The activity type you selected is displayed under **Activity type:**. If you wish, you can click the drop-down arrow and change to a different type of activity.

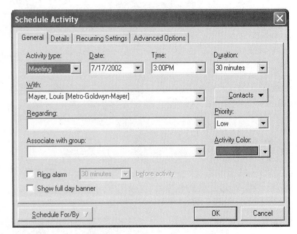

3. Select a **Date:**

Normally, the current date is displayed. To choose a different date, click the drop-down list button, then click the desired date.

To view a different month or year in this calendar, click the arrows to the left or right of the month indicator as shown in the illustration above.

You may also type dates directly into the **Date:** box.

ACT!

4. Select a **Time:**

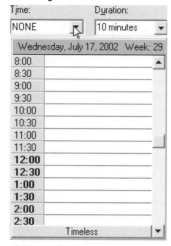

By default, the current time is displayed. To choose a different time, click the drop-down arrow. A time line appears.

☞ *If you don't want to assign a particular time for the activity, click the **Timeless** button at the bottom of the list. To-dos are often timeless activities*

Each hour is divided into two 30-minute intervals. Click the bar next to the time when the activity is to begin. If you like, you can drag over the appropriate number of bars to block off the duration of the activity (for example, drag over 4 bars for a 2 hour meeting).

5. If necessary, specify a **Duration:**.

If you estimate that the activity will last longer (or shorter) than the amount of time shown, click the down arrow and choose a different amount from the predefined times. You can also specify a duration by typing directly into the box. If an activity is planned for 4 and a half hours, you would type **4.5 hours** or **4 hrs 30 min** in the box.

6. Specify what the activity is **Regarding:**

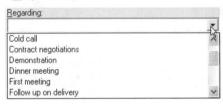

You can type anything, but you can also click the drop-down arrow to select from a list of common reasons.

☞ *If there is a particular activity you often schedule that's not on the list, scroll to the bottom of the list, click **Edit list... Add...**, type the activity, **OK**.*

7. Click the **Details** tab to enter any details that relate to the activity. You can enter as much as you like or cut and paste text from another application into this box (maybe information the contact sent you in an e-mail).

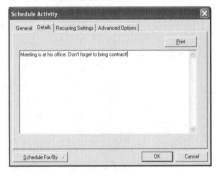

☞ *Notice there is a **Print** button on the **Details** tab, for printing out any details you want to take along.*

8. **OK**

We know there are other features, but let's keep it simple for now.

9. If you accidentally schedule an activity that conflicts with a pre-existing activity, the **Conflict Alert** dialog box appears. Click **Accept** to schedule the activity anyway or **Reschedule** to reset the time or date of the new activity.

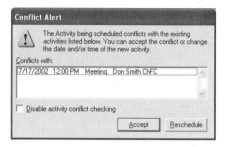

 *Feel free to type information directly into any or all of the entry boxes in the **Schedule Activity** dialog box. The drop-down lists are only a convenience. For example, you can also enter a specific meeting time (such as airline flight times, since their scheduled times may not fall exactly on the half hour).*

 *Right-click anywhere on the background of the Contact window, point to **Schedule**, and from the submenu, click on **Call...**, **Meeting...**, or **To-do...** to open the **Schedule Activity** dialog box.*

When you schedule an activity, it appears in the **Activities** tab of the Contact window. Activities appear in chronological order with the oldest activities displayed first (helps you catch up).

When Details have been entered for an activity, an icon appears in the Details column on the Activities tab. To view the details only, double-click the looking-glass icon. The **Schedule Activity** dialog box opens, with the **Details** tab displayed.

Practice: *Meeting With Mayer*

Step	What to do	How to do it/Comments
1.	Lookup the record for **Louis B. Mayer**.	Choose **Lookup, Last Name...**, type **may**, and click **OK**.
2.	Schedule a meeting.	Choose **Contact, Schedule Meeting**, or click the Meeting toolbar button, or press **[Ctrl+M]**.
3.	Schedule the meeting for this Friday (if today is Friday, schedule it for next Friday).	Click the list button for the **Date:** and click Friday's date. If you need to view next month, click the next month arrow at the top right of the calendar.
4.	The meeting is to last from 3:00 until 4:00 PM.	Click the list button for **Time:** and drag down over 2 bars starting with **3:00** (the hour between **3:00** and **4:00**).
5.	Select **Contract negotiations** as the reason for the meeting.	Click the drop-down arrow for **Regarding:** and select the phrase.
6.	Type the following on the **Details** tab: **Meeting is at his office.**	Click the **Details** tab and type.
7.	Save the activity.	Click **OK**.
8.	View the meeting on the Contact screen.	If necessary, display the **Activities** layout tab. The meeting should be displayed there.
9.	View the meeting Details.	Double-click the icon in the Details column.
10.	Close the **Schedule Activity** dialog box.	**OK**

Try It...

The Task List

When you schedule an activity with one or more contacts, that activity appears on the Activities layout tab of their contact record along with any other activities you have scheduled for that contact. This works fine, when you want to know what activities you have pending for one person. This is *not* too effective, however, if you need to see a comprehensive list of all tasks for all contacts.

The ACT! **Task List** provides just such a list.

✔ The **Task List** is similar to the **Activities** layout tab, but it displays a listing of pending activities for *every contact* in your database.

✔ You can apply a filter to display only those dates or activity types or priorities you wish to see at any given time.

✔ If you are sharing a database, you can also filter the display of activities to only show your own activities or you can display the name of the user for whom the activity is scheduled.

...view the Task List

1. Choose **View, Task List**

    or
click Task List on View Bar
    or
press **[F7]**.

2. Filter as desired.

The Task List screen appears:

Filtering the Task List

By default, the Filter area of the Task List window is displayed. If the Filter area is not displayed, click the **Filter** button to display it.

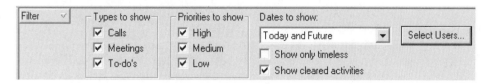

 You can also click the Filter icon on the toolbar to display a dialog box with the same options.

There are quite a few options available to filter the Task List. For example, to only work with your things to do for the day, in the **Types to show** you may want to uncheck Meetings (they will still appear on your calendar).

If you are a very structured person and have classified your activities by High, Medium, or Low **Priorities**, you can decide to only display the High priorities for days when your time is at a minimum.

The **Dates to show:** feature will allow you to quickly filter for specific pre-defined time frames of **Today** (for focusing on what you have to handle today), **Past dates** (for catching up on old items), **Today and Future** (for getting an overview of things to come), **Date Range...** (for specifying a specific time period that you need to check to see if a vacation might be possible) or **All dates** (for making yourself feel overwhelmed).

If you derive a sense of accomplishment from seeing your list of "Things to Do" with lines drawn through the completed activities, then leaving the check in **Show cleared activities** will be your cup of tea. The **Show only timeless** would have a similar effect of excluding Meetings from the display. It would also remove scheduled conference calls from the list as well.

Finally, you can also filter your Task List by users (people in your company who maintain their calendars in ACT!) by clicking on the **Select Users...** button. The default for ACT! is to display **All users**. If you wish to display only your activities, click on the **Selected users** options and then click on your name. In fact, you can show any combination of tasks belonging to other members of your staff (e.g. only yours and your

assistant's list.). Click on the name of each person's activities you wish to display. Click on their name again to unselect it.

 ACT! will only remember your User list selections for the current ACT! session. After exiting and re-opening ACT!, the Selected users filter will only display your personal calendar

If the filter area is displayed, you can easily see the combination of filters that have been selected. However, if the filter area is closed (with only the Filter button displayed), you can quickly verify the time frame by reviewing the Status Bar at the bottom of the screen. The total number (along with the associated breakdown) of activities is displayed.

Today and Future: 19 Activities - 3 Calls, 12 Meetings, 4 To-do's.

*To view more information about the contact before you call, select the record by clicking on the row header, right-click, **Go to Contact**. You could also create a lookup of all contacts displayed in the Task List by right-clicking anywhere and selecting **Create Lookup**.*

Once you have filtered the Task List to display the activities you want to work with, you can work straight from the Task List window or you can create a lookup of all contacts associated with the filtered list by clicking on the **Create Lookup** icon on the toolbar. The contacts are displayed in Contacts view where you can work with each contact one at a time as you move through your list.

You can also print out the filtered list by selecting **File, Print Task List** or by clicking the Print icon at the top of the window.

Scheduled For

If you work in a multi-user environment, it is difficult to look at the Calendar to see who is where among your team members except by filtering the Calendar…user by user. The Task List (as well as the **Activities** tab) allows you to add the Scheduled For column to display the User for whom the activity is scheduled. Right-click in the view and select **Add Columns to View...** from the shortcut menu. Select **Scheduled For** from the **Add Columns** list and click **Add**. Unfortunately it is not a clickable column, so you cannot sort the list by User.

If you wanted to work in Task List view, it would also be great to see the Contact's Phone number. Follow the same procedure to insert it onto the Task List view. Columns displayed in the Task List window will print out on the **File, Print Task List** report.

ACT! remembers the filters you have applied (except for multiple selected users) and will use them the next time you display the Task List.

Practice: *Viewing the Task List*

Step	What to do	How to do it/Comments
1.	View the **Task List** and add the Scheduled For column.	Choose **View, Task List**, or click the Task List icon on the View Bar.
2.	Use the Filter area to view the activities scheduled for Today only.	If the Filter area is not displayed, click the **Filter** button to display it. Select **Today** from the **Dates to show:** list.
3.	View the activities for all past dates.	Display the **Dates to show** list and choose **Past dates** .
4.	Create a Lookup of all contacts with these overdue activities.	Click the Create Lookup icon. *You can also right-click anywhere in the Task List view and select Create Lookup.*
5.	Return to the Task List, display everything, and experiment with some of the check boxes in the Filter area to hide or show certain types and priorities of activities.	Click the Task List icon. Place checks in all of the check boxes except **Show only timeless**, and choose **All** from the **Dates to show:** list. You can customize this list as much as you want.
6.	Hide the filter area.	Click the **Filter** button to hide the filter area.
7.	Select two activities and display only the contacts associated with those two activities.	Click on the row header of the first activity to select it, hold the **[Ctrl]** key down while you click on the second, right-click and select **Go to Contact**.

Try It...

Task List vs. Calendar

Actually the **Calendar** and the **Task List** display the very same activities…they just display them in a different way (similar to the way that the **Contacts** view and the **Contact List** view display the same contacts, only in a different format).

If your day is primarily task oriented (making phone calls, handling to-dos, etc.) you may want to work in the **Task List** view. However, if your day is more scheduled with meeting times, you may want to work in one of the **Calendar** views.

Using the Calendar

A good way to start each day is to check your Calendar (or your Task List). When you schedule activities in ACT!, they are recorded in the **Activities** layout tab for the contact the activity concerns. You can, of course, view all activities using the **Task List**, but to *really* get a clear view of what you have scheduled for today, this week, or this month, a calendar view is the way to go. You can view your calendar by three different time periods . . . by day, by week, or by month. These views are displayed using the Calendar View buttons on the View Bar.

Daily Calendar

Weekly Calendar

Monthly Calendar

How To…

…view the Daily calendar

1.   Click the Daily Calendar button on the View Bar

     or

     press [**Shift+F5**].

Daily Calendar

The Daily Calendar view appears.

The **Daily Calendar** shows your schedule in two ways. A "time line" view is displayed on the left of the window and a Task List pane is displayed on the right under the mini-calendar. Timeless activities will not display on the time line, only in the Task List pane (observe the Call and To-do shown here for **Edward G.** and **Ginger**).

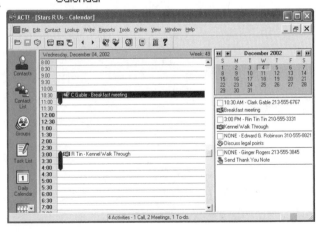

*You can also display the calendar window from the menu by choosing **View, Calendar**. A submenu appears from which you may choose to view the **Daily**, **Weekly**, or **Monthly** Calendars.*

...view the Week calendar

1.   Click the Weekly
      Calendar button on the
      View Bar

           or

      press **[F3]**.

Weekly
Calendar

The Weekly Calendar view
appears.

The Weekly Calendar
shows you the whole
week in time line view.
Activities are displayed
as they are in the day
view, but in less detail.
The Task List pane at
the right of the window
displays tasks for the
currently selected day.
To display the tasks
for any day on the
calendar, click
anywhere in the time
line for that day.

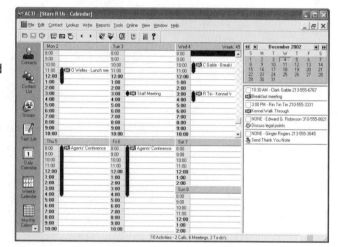

...view the Month calendar

1.   Click the Monthly
      Calendar icon on the
      View Bar

           or

      press **[F5]**.

Monthly
Calendar

The Monthly Calendar view
appears.

The Month view of the Calendar shows... well, the *month*. Activities (other than timeless) will display (with very little detail) on the day they occur. To display the Task List pane for any day, click that day in the Month calendar. All the day's activities appear in the Task List pane at the right.

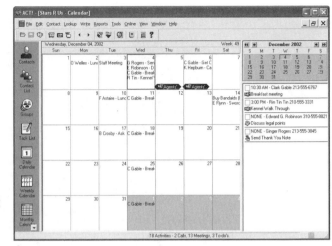

 At the bottom of each Calendar window, the Status Bar displays the total count of scheduled activities for the time period displayed. (If the month is displayed, the totals are for the month...if the week is displayed, the totals are for the week.)

Calendar Pop-ups

On Calendar views, if you move the mouse pointer over an activity in the Calendar Window (or the activity icon in the Task List Pane), a pop-up window will display showing the basic activity information. Not only does the Regarding and Contact information display, but you can also now see the Company name, the actual starting time, duration, and the first three lines of the Details.

Note in the example to the right that it "appears" on the calendar to be a 3:00 appointment, when in reality, the actual time is 3:30. Also note that you can only see the first three lines of the Details section. The ellipsis (...) at the bottom of the pop-up screen lets you know that more details can be found when you double-click the activity to open it.

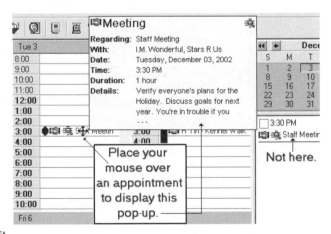

☞ *Calendar pop-ups for private activities display only for the user the activity is scheduled for.*

To disable calendar pop-ups, click **Edit, Preferences**, click on the **Calendars** tab, remove the check from **Enable calendar pop-ups**, **OK**.

Navigating Tips for the Calendar Views

In the upper-right corner of all three calendars is a small calendar displaying the current month (unless you change it, of course). Today's date appears in red, and the selected date has a box around it.

✔ You can change the current date in any of the calendars by clicking the desired date in this one-month mini-calendar.

✔ You can also view the next or previous month or year by clicking the navigation buttons at the top of the one-month mini-calendar.

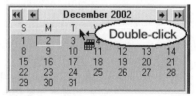

✔ When in a calendar view, buttons on the toolbar at the top of the screen can also assist your "movements through time." These buttons are sensitive to the type of calendar you are viewing (admit it, we could all stand a little more sensitivity in our lives). In the Daily Calendar view, click a button to see the next or previous day. In the Weekly Calendar view, the buttons move to the next or previous week. In the Monthly Calendar view, buttons display the next or previous month.

✔ The one month mini-calendar can also be used to display the different views of the calendar window. Double-click any day to display that day in the Daily Calendar view. Double-click the weekday letters at the top of the mini-calendar to display the current week in Weekly Calendar view. Double-click the month name on the mini-calendar to display the Monthly Calendar view.

One more trick! If you right-click the month title bar at the top of the mini-calendar, a list will display to help you quickly move to one of the previous or following months, as well as to "Today."

Practice: *Viewing the Calendar(s)*

Try It...

Step	What to do	How to do it/Comments
1.	View the calendar for this week.	Click the Weekly Calendar icon.
2.	Switch to the Day calendar.	Click the Daily Calendar icon or press **[Shift+F5]**.
3.	Display the daily calendar for yesterday.	Click yesterday's date on the mini-calendar.
4.	View next Month's calendar.	Click the Monthly Calendar icon and then click the **Next** navigation button.
5.	Return to today.	Right-click the Month title bar on the mini-calendar and click **Today**. Notice that the Calendar view does not change to the Daily Calendar view. It only displays Today on the Monthly Calendar view.
6.	View the December 2002 Calendar and Lookup all the contacts that were scheduled for the month.	Navigate to the December 2002 calendar. Right-click anywhere and select **Create Lookup** or click the icon.

Try It...

Step	What to do	How to do it/Comments
7.	Display the week of December 2nd in the Weekly Calendar view.	Click on December 2 in the mini-calendar. Then either click on the Weekly Calendar view icon or double-click the weekday letters at the top of the mini-calendar to display the week in Weekly Calendar view
8.	Point to several of the appointments to view the calendar pop-ups.	
9.	Change to the Daily View and test the Calendar Pop-ups.	Click on the Daily Calendar view and navigate to a day with activities on the Calendar time line.
10.	Click the Monthly View icon to return to the Month calendar. Notice that the same month is still displayed.	The calendar stays on the month you last displayed unless you close the calendar window. Monthly Calendar

Clearing Activities

You "clear" an activity when it is completed. After you mark the activity as completed, it is cleared from the **Activities** tab and recorded in the **Notes/History** tab where the date and time it was completed displays along with other information about its completion.

There are three places you can clear any activity: in the Contact's **Activities** tab, in the **Task List** view or in one of the **Calendar** views.

...clear an activity from the Task List or the Activities tab

How To...

1. Display the activity in the **Task List** view or on the Contact's **Activities** tab.

   Click the **Task List** button on the View Bar or click the **Activities** tab in the Contact view.

   Task List

2. Click in the check mark column next to the activity that you want to clear.

    *You can also select the activity by clicking on the gray square to the left of the activity, then right-click, **Clear Activity...** or press [Ctrl+D].*

   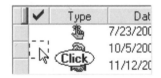

The **Date:** and **Time:** that the activity will show as cleared will display as today...however, you can change it before clearing the activity (in case you are catching up with your work and you really completed this activity earlier this week).

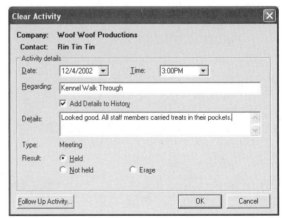

3. Choose an activity result. The **Result:** options depend on the activity type. Clearing a call provides a different set of choices than Meetings or To-do's:

Choose the result that best describes how the activity ended.

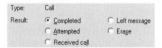

4. If you want any Details to appear in History for the contact, verify that the **Add Details to History** option is checked and enter or modify the **Details** section of the dialog box.

Type any new details of the customer contact or modify existing details, if necessary. You can type as much as you like here. "I said this and he said that and promised to do this…"

5. To schedule a follow up activity, click **Follow Up Activity...** and a new activity dialog box is displayed for the same contact as the one you are clearing with the same **Regarding** line.

While scheduling a follow up is an optional step, we are certain you recognize the importance of keeping the lines of communication open with your contacts. Scheduling a follow up activity now assures you will not forget later.

6. Click **OK**.

The activity is now cleared from the list and recorded to the **Notes/History** tab. If you scheduled a follow up, it will be displayed in the **Activities** tab.

 *When you clear an activity, you do more than just remove it from the Activities list. The fact that the activity was completed, along with the **Result** you chose, is recorded in the **Notes/History** tab for that contact as a History item. This History information can be incorporated into reports and used to help you analyze your work patterns and efficiency.*

If you work in a Calendar view more than the Task List view, no problem. In any Calendar view, an activity list for the selected day will appear to the right of the calendar (the Task List pane below the mini-calendar). At the left of each activity there is a check box.

44	←	July 2002	→	►►
S	M	T	W	T	F	S
	1	2	3	4	5	6
7	8	9	10	11	12	13
14	15	16	17	18	19	20
21	22	23	24	25	26	27
28	29	30	31			

☐ 9:30 AM - James Cagney 310-555
▨ Breakfast meeting

...clear activities from a Calendar view

1. Display the day that contains the activity you want to clear.

   All activities scheduled for that day appear in the Task List pane to the right.

2. Click the check box to the left of the activity.

    ☐ 9:00 AM - C ▨ Breakfast m

   The **Clear Activity** dialog box appears.

3. Choose the appropriate result.

4. **OK**

   The activity is cleared.

*You can also right-click an activity on a Calendar and choose **Clear Activity...** from the shortcut menu.*

Practice: *Clearing Stuff*

Step	What to do	How to do it/Comments
1.	Display the December 2001 calendar.	
2.	You forgot to clear the Lunch meeting with **Orson** on December 6th. Don't forget to add some Details about contract negotiations.	In Calendar view, click the check box to the left of the activity. Put a check in the **Add Details to History** and type some notes in the Details section. **OK**
3.	Lookup Orson Welles' contact record and observe the **Activities** and the **Notes/History** tabs.	Right-click the Lunch meeting with Orson and select **Go to Contact.** There are no new activities scheduled for Orson. The **Notes/History** tab displays the completed meeting details.

Step	What to do	How to do it/Comments
4.	View all activities on the **Task List**. Clear the call scheduled for **Katherine Hepburn** on December 6th. (You had some extra time today and you called her.)	Click the Task List icon. Click in the check mark column to the left of the activity.
	✔ Mark the call result as completed,	Choose **Completed**, from the **Result:** options. Click **Follow Up Activity…**.
	✔ Notice that regardless of when the activity was scheduled for, it will record the activity as completed today, and	Be sure to change the **Activity type:** to **Meeting**. Change the date and time as specified. **OK**
	✔ Schedule a follow up lunch with her for next Tuesday afternoon at 1:00.	
5.	Lookup **Katherine Hepburn's** contact record and observe the **Activities** and the **Notes/History** tabs.	ACT! cleared the call and added the lunch meeting. The completed call is now recorded in the **Notes/History** tab.
6.	While you are on Katherine's record, clear the Presentation meeting scheduled for 12/11. That meeting was not held. Notice how the activity is recorded in **Notes/History** tab.	Click in the checkmark column to the left of the meeting to clear it. Mark the Result: as **Not held**. ☞ *If you double-click the activity by mistake and the Schedule Activity dialog displays, click Cancel.*

☞ *Cleared activities can be displayed in the Task List or Calendar views. Click on the Filter icon (found on both the Task List and Calendar toolbars) to put a checkmark in **Show cleared activities**. Cleared activities can display with a line drawn through them or grayed out to note their cleared status. This is another one of those Preferences things. **Edit, Preferences**, click on the **Scheduling** tab if necessary, click on the **Gray** or **Strikeout** option, **OK**.*

Deleting a Note or History

As you do more and more in ACT!, history can get pretty cluttered. It's often helpful to "clean house" occasionally by removing unimportant items from the **Notes/History** section.

To remove an item from the **Notes/History** tab, select it by clicking its icon and press **[Delete]** on your keyboard. Click **Yes** to confirm the deletion.

 *You can also right-click the **History** or the **Note** icon and choose **Delete Selected** from the shortcut menu.*

Recording an Unscheduled Activity to History

It feels great to mark those activities as completed and watch your list get shorter. However, sometimes you just decide to call someone on the spur of the moment. Perhaps a regular client calls you to ask about a product. Since you did not schedule the call, there is no activity to clear and thus no History of the call will be automatically recorded. Rather than creating and then clearing an activity, you can just record the call directly into History.

...record a History entry

1. Lookup the contact for whom you want to record History.

2. **Contact, Record History...**

 *You can also right-click anywhere on the Contact screen and choose **Record History...***

 *Or, you can press **[Ctrl+H]** to display the **Record History** dialog box.*

[Ctrl+H] is our favorite method, but to each his own.

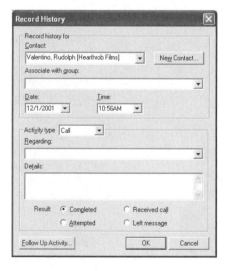

3. Change the **Activity type** if necessary.

By default the **Activity type** will be a "Call". However, if you have any uncleared activities, the **Record History** dialog will be populated with information from the oldest uncleared activity. You can always change the information in the dialog.

4. Change the **Date:** and **Time:** if necessary.

5. Enter something in the **Regarding:** area.

Remember, you are recording something you have done, not something you need to do.

6. Type any pertinent **Details**. Details should be considered the same as Notes.

Click in the box and type as much as you like in this area. It scrolls forever if need be!

7. Select a **Result:**

8. Schedule a **Follow Up Activity...** if desired.

9. Click **OK**.

A History is added to the **Notes/History** tab for the contact.

Practice: *Making History*

Step	What to do	How to do it/Comments
1.	Lookup the record for **Rudolf Valentino**.	**Lookup, First Name...,** type **rud, OK**.
2.	Record the fact that he called and wants to sign a contract.	Hot dog!!!!!! Press **[Ctrl+H]**. The default **Activity type:** is **Call**. **[Tab]** to the **Regarding:** box and type **He wants to sign a contract**. Click **Received call** in the **Result:** area. Click **OK**.
3.	Verify the item in the **Notes/History** tab.	Click the **Notes/History** tab, if necessary.

Try it...

Recording History to Multiple Contacts

Sometimes you meet with several people at the same time, and the results of the meeting are all the same. Consequently you want the same results to display in everyone's **Notes/History** tab...you just don't want to type it more than once!

...record a History entry for multiple contacts

How To...

1. In **Contact List** view, switch to Tag Mode and select all contacts for whom you wish to record the same history. Select **Lookup Tagged**.

   Contact List

   Create a lookup of the contacts for whom you want to record the same history. Any contact that has a **+** will have the history recorded.

2. Press **[Ctrl+H]**.

   Notice that the words **MULTIPLE CONTACTS** display in the top of the Record History dialog box.

3. Fill in the Record History as you normally would and click **OK**.

   The same history will be recorded on all selected contacts.

Practice: **Director's Association Meeting**

Try It...

Step	What to do	How to do it/Comments
1.	There was a Director's Association meeting (they all have an ID/Status of Director). Everyone but George Cukor was there. Record in history for the others that "Members Voted to Raise Dues"	In **Contact List** view, **Lookup**, **ID/Status**, enter "director", **OK**. Select George Cukor and click **Omit Tagged**. Now click **Tag All** to select the remaining names. Press **[Ctrl+H]**. In **Regarding:** type "Members Voted to Raise Dues". Change **Activity type** to **Meeting**. Click **OK**
2.	Switch to Contact view and verify that the history was recorded on each Director's **Notes/History** tab.	

History vs. Notes

If you ran into Victor Fleming at the club and he told you about a new picture he was thinking about, should you record the results of that meeting in a Note (click on the **Insert Note** button) or with History (press **[Ctrl+H]**)?

Notes are great for recording general information about a contact, their preferences, how they like to handle invoicing, what they thought about their last movie, etc.

If information you want to enter in the contact's record is date specific…you talked with them at the club, you agreed to general contract principles over the phone, you sent them roses…that information should be recorded as a History.

While both Notes and Histories display a date when you insert them, History entries will change the system fields on the **Status** tab…Notes won't. This becomes very important when you want to do date lookups to generate reports from your ACT! database.

Last Reach	8/15/2002	Create Date	8/4/1999
Last Meeting	7/4/2002	Edit Date	8/15/2002
Last Attempt		Merge Date	11/20/2001
Public/Private	Public	Letter Date	7/16/2002
Record Creator	Pal Friday		
Record Manager	I.M. Wonderful		

✔ Every time you clear a scheduled activity, both the appropriate system field and the Edit Date field are updated.

✔ Every time you enter a history (using **[Ctrl+H]** or right-click, **Record History…**), the appropriate system field as well as the Edit Date field is updated.

✔ Every time you enter a Note (**Insert Note**), none of the system fields are updated.

☞ *If you want to lookup every contact you have met with over a specific time period, it would be impossible to do if all you enter into the database is notes. A Note doesn't indicate how you gathered the information…was it a meeting or did you just speak with them on the phone? Using the Record History feature allows you to record the nature of the contact as well as the details (notes) of the interaction.*

Try It...

Step	What to do	How to do it/Comments
1.	Lookup Victor Fleming and view the system fields on the **Status** tab.	(The Status tab is on the Contact Layout 800x600 Layout.) Haven't had much activity with Victor in the last few years.
2.	Insert a note about the meeting.	On the **Notes/History** tab, click **Insert Note**.
3.	Did any of the system field dates change on the **Status** tab?	No
4.	Use the history feature to record your "Chance meeting at the club" and enter some notes about your conversation in the Details section of the History dialog.	**[Ctrl+H]** to open the History dialog. Change the **Activity type** from Call to Meeting. In the **Regarding:** field type "Chance meeting at the club". Type your notes in the **Details:** section. Click **OK**.
5.	Did the system field dates change on the **Status** tab?	Yes!!! Both the Last Meeting and the Edit Date now have today's date entered in them.

Adding the History Icon to the Toolbar

The Record History feature is just too cool not to have its own icon. Wait it does have one (just not on the Standard Tool bar.) ACT! menu commands can be added to the toolbar. So let's add it!

...add the Record History icon to the Standard Toolbar

1. **Tools, Customize Contacts Window...**	The **Customize ACT! Contacts Window** dialog box displays.

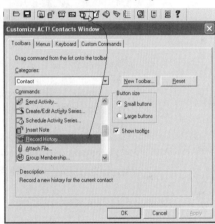

2. Click the drop-down arrow for **Categories:** and change it from **File** to **Contact**.

3. In the **Commands:** section, scroll to **Record History...** and click on it.

4. Drag it to the toolbar where you want it to be displayed and drop it.

5. Click **OK**.

Practice: Add the Toolbar Icon

Step	What to do	How to do it/Comments
1.	Add the Record History icon to your toolbar.	Follow the procedure above.
2.	William Holden called and wants us to represent him. Hotdog, we're good! Use your new Record History icon to record the call.	Lookup Bill's record. Click the Record History icon. In the **Regarding:** section type "New Client". Click **Received call**. **OK**

Activity Data Mining

You've seen the way that ACT! records history on the Status tab. In fact, ACT! keeps track of *every* change you make on a contact's record...any field changes, any additions (or completions) of planned activities, any notes inserted, any opportunities modified. ACT! even makes note of those times that you go back to edit a Note.

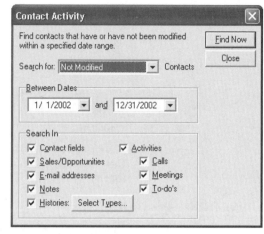

Since ACT! keeps track of it, you can perform a lookup for contacts that either have or have not been modified within a specified date range. You can even specify the types of changes you want to include in your lookup. You could look up any Contacts whose Sales Opportunities had changed in the last 30 days, any Contact that had a Note entered (or edited) in the last quarter, any Contact whose record wasn't touched in 2002 (as displayed in the example above).

...lookup contact activity

1. **Lookup, Contact Activity**

2. Select **Modified** or **Not Modified**

    Modified will display all Contacts that have had some activity posted to their record within the specified date range. **Not Modified** displays the list of lost prospects or unhappy customers...just kidding...but it might be close.

3. Select the beginning and ending dates for your date range search.

     *If you selected **Not Modified** in the previous step, the ending date has already been changed to the current date and it will be grayed out so that you can't change it.*

4. Select the areas of the Contact record you want to search for changes (or lack thereof).

    See an explanation of the **Search In** criteria on the next page.

5. **F̱ind Now**

A progress bar appears as ACT! identifies the records that match your search criteria.

The Contacts are displayed in Contact List view.

Search In Criteria

C̱ontact fields checks for changes to any field in the Contact record, excluding the e-mail address field.

S̱ales/Opportunities searches for changes made to any Sales Opportunities.

E̱-mail addresses looks for changes to e-mail addresses.

Ṉotes locates all Contact records that contain one or more notes that were entered or even edited during the specified time period.

H̱istories: or **Select Typﬦes...** narrows the search to those records with specific types of histories. Clicking on either of these options will display the **Select History Types** dialog box. From there you can select the specific types of histories to search for changes or additions (Attachments, E-mail Attachment, Call Attempted, Call Completed, Call Left Message, Call Received, Closed/Won Sale, Lost Sale, Contact Deleted, Letter Sent, E-mail Sent, Fax Sent, Meeting Held, Meeting Not Held, To-do Done, To-do Not Done, Time, All Others).

Unchecking the **A̱ctivities** option, unchecks the three types of activities beneath it (**C̱alls, M̱eetings, Ṯo-do's**). An activity, by its definition, is an uncleared event. Requesting a search on any of the activities, will search for an activity that was edited, entered, or cleared during the date range specified.

Practice: *Who has been slipping through the cracks?*

Try It...

Step	What to do	How to do it/Comments
1.	Who haven't we had any contact with in over a year?	**Lookup, Contact Activity,** select **Not Modified**, change the beginning date to a year ago. Click **Find Now**.
2.	Who have we had meetings with in the last 2 years.	**Lookup, Contact Activity,** change the beginning date to 2 years ago. Uncheck every **Search In** option. Click **Select Types…** , change to **Only the selected types below** and click **Deselect All**. Scroll to locate **Meeting Held** and select the option. Click **OK**. Click **Find Now**.

Review: *Scheduling Your Day*

Try It...

1.	Schedule a call to Busby next week to see if Ruby is still with him.
2.	You had that conversation with Spencer yesterday about his next movie with Katherine (thank goodness she has talked him into using our agency for the contract) Clear the activity (use whichever view you like to clear it).
3.	You sent roses to your employee Pal Friday in appreciation for all the work. Record it in history on Pal's record.
4.	Add phone numbers to your task list.
5.	Check out who we've written notes for this week.

Advanced Scheduling

Since keeping track of our schedules is sometimes not that straight forward, we will review all of the advanced scheduling options that ACT! offers. You will:

☑ Learn to make changes to activities that have already been scheduled.

☑ Review the General and Advanced Scheduling Options

☑ Understand the intricacies of scheduling recurring activities.

☑ Print your calendar (sometimes you just have to have it on paper).

☑ Schedule a series of activities with just a few clicks.

☑ Discover some amazing uses of SideACT!

Modifying Scheduled Activities

More than likely, a typical day for you includes changing appointments that are already on your Calendar. Schedules change. It's a fact of life. Sometimes a change is a good thing (your tax audit has been canceled). Sometimes it's not so good (the initial meeting with a new client has been set back a week). In either case, ACT! makes it easy to rearrange your scheduled activities. You can change an activity a number of ways.

...modify an activity in List View

1. Display the scheduled activity that you wish to modify in the Contact's **Activities** tab or in the **Task List** view.

   Usually activities are sorted by date.

2. Click the element of the activity you want to change.

   If you want to change the date, for example, click the current activity date. A box appears around the item and a drop-down button appears.

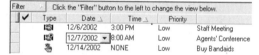

3. Change the element.

   Type the new information or click the drop-down arrow and choose from the list or calendar that displays.

☞ *If you work in a multi-user environment, you can't tell by looking at the activities who they are scheduled for unless you display the **Scheduled For** column. The **Scheduled For** column display the User for whom the activity is scheduled. To display the column, right-click in the view and select **Add Columns to View...** from the shortcut menu. Select **Scheduled For** from the **Add Columns** list and click **Add**.*

You can also edit the activity by opening the Schedule dialog box (the view you used to enter the activity in the first place).

...modify an activity from the Schedule Activity dialog box

1. Locate the activity you want to modify.

    Find the date on the Calendar where the activity appears.

2. If you are in one of the **Calendar** views, you can double-click anywhere on the activity to display the **Schedule Activity** dialog box.

    If you are on the Contact's **A**ctivities tab or in the **Task List**, point to the gray "row header" box that Double-click ─⟨ ⟩ appears to the left of each item in any ACT! list and double-click to display the dialog box.

Filter	Click the "Filter" button to the left to change the view
✔	Type	Date △	Time △	Priority
	✉	12/6/2002	3:00 PM	Low
	✉	12/13/2002	8:00 AM	Low
	✋	12/14/2002	NONE	Low

    *You can also right-click an activity and choose **R**eschedule Activity... from the shortcut menu.*

    The **Schedule Activity** dialog box displays.

3. Make the necessary changes.

    You may change any or all options.

4. **OK**

☞ *If you modify a recurring activity (we will discus these starting on page 121), ACT! displays a dialog box asking if you want to change just this instance or all of the activities originally scheduled. Click **Instance** to change just this one activity or **All** to change all of the later activities as well.*

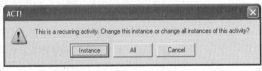

Practice: *Changes, Changes, Changes*

Step	What to do	How to do it/Comments
1.	Display the Task List.	**View**, **Task List**, or click the Task List icon.
2.	Change the date of the **Dorothy Lamour** call to next Monday.	Click the date for her call (a box appears around it with a down button to its right). Click the drop-down button and click next Monday's date in the calendar.
3.	Change the time of the Douglas Fairbanks' Breakfast meeting (11/12/2002) to one hour earlier.	Click the entry for his meeting in the **Time** column. Click the drop-down arrow and change the appointment to an hour earlier.
4.	Edit the phone call we had planned to James Cagney on 1/20/2003.	In the **Activities** tab, double-click the gray row header to the left of the activity.
	Change the "Call" to a "Meeting" for the same date at 1:00PM.	Click the drop-down for **Activity type:** and select Meeting.
	Add to the details section: "Edward G. has already accepted a part in the movie."	Click the Details tab. Click at the end of the existing sentence. Type the new text and click **OK**.

If you are in one of the Calendar views and you need to move an activity to a different day, you can also drag the activity to a different day on the mini-calendar. All other Activity details (including Time) will be maintained. Press [F4] to display a 3-month mini-calendar.

Scheduling-General Tab

In the previous section we focused on very basic scheduling and clearing of activities. However, much of our scheduling these days seems to be anything but basic. There are other options you can choose in the Scheduling tab. Let's review them now.

Scheduling for Multiple Contacts

Sometimes it seems that our meetings are never one-on-one any more...it's all about committees. No problem (at least for ACT!). You can schedule an activity for multiple contacts, just by adding them to the list.

...schedule a multi-contact activity

1. Lookup the first contact and create the activity. Don't click **OK** yet.

Create the activity (page 73) as you would for the one contact: set type; time; duration; etc.

2. Click the **Contacts** ▼ button and choose **Select Contacts....**

The **Contacts** ▼ button appears to the right of the **With** box in the **Schedule Activity** dialog box. The **Select Contacts** dialog box is displayed:

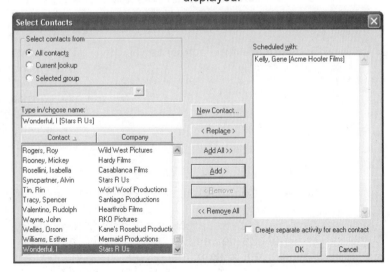

3. Locate the first additional contact, select the name, and choose **Add >**.

    ☞ *You can locate the name more quickly by typing the last name in the **Type in/choose name:** box.*

    Repeat until all desired contacts have been added to the list.

    The name is added to the **Scheduled with:** list on the right of the dialog box.

4. Check or uncheck **Create separate activity for each contact** as desired.

    Click **OK** to return to the **Schedule Activity** dialog box.

    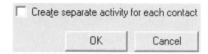

    When a single activity is scheduled for multiple contacts, you will see the name of the first contact (the first one alphabetically) followed by an ellipsis (...).

    ☞ *When this appears, the only way to view or edit the names is by editing the activity and accessing the **Select Contacts** dialog box (step 2 in this procedure).*

5. Complete the activity as you normally would.

    The scheduled activity will display in each contact's **Activities** tab. Depending upon whether or not you checked **Create separate...** in step 4, one or multiple instances of the activity will display in the Calendar and Task List views.

The **Select Contacts** dialog box contains a number of useful options:

✔ If you perform a lookup that displays everyone you want for the particular activity, you can choose **Current lookup** from the options at the top left of the dialog box to display a list of only those contacts in the lookup. You can then click **Add All>>** to add the entire lookup to your list instantly.

✔ In the header, click the column header name **Contact** or **Company** and
you will sort the list by that
column in ascending order.
(Click the same header again to
sort in descending order.) The triangle that appears to the right of the
column name indicates the list is sorted by that field. If several contacts
from a specific company will attend, it's easier to select them if you sort by
Company.

Contact △	Company
Robinson, Edward	Tough Guy Productions

✔ Type the last name of the entry you
are looking for in the **Type
in/choose name:** text box at the
top of the list and the list will be
searched for you. The more you
type, the more specific the search.
Be sure to sort by the column you
wish to search first. If you sorted by
Company, you can type the company name in this field.

Type in/choose name:

Rogers, Ginger [Beautymark Films]

Contact △	Company
Robinson, Edward	Tough Guy Productions
Rogers, Ginger	Beautymark Films
Rogers, Roy	Wild West Pictures
Rooney, Mickey	Hardy Films
Rooney, Micky	Hardy Films
Syncpartner, Alvin	Stars R Us

✔ When you schedule a multiple contact activity, by default you create only
one activity. When the activity is
complete, you need only to clear it
once to clear it for all contacts. This
works well for meetings where all of
the contacts in the list attend.

☐ Create separate activity for each contact

OK	Cancel

If you click the **Create separate activity for each contact** check box,
you create a series of individual activities, each of which have to be
cleared separately. This works well for activities such as follow-up calls to
each contact after a marketing campaign or trade show, where you want
to clear each call as it is completed.

 *If you can create a lookup of the contacts for whom to schedule the
activity, display the list in **Contact List** view. In **Tag Mode**, click **Tag All**,
then right-click, select **Schedule...**, and select the activity type.
Schedule the activity as usual.
Notice that the **With:** box
displays the first name with
the ... after indicating that the
activity has been scheduled
for multiple contacts. ACT! will
schedule a single activity for the selected contacts.*

Activity type:	Date:	Time:
Meeting ▼	7/20/2002 ▼	2:00PM ▼

With:

Gene Kelly ... ▼

Try It...

Step	What to do	How to do it/Comments
1.	Lookup **Gene Kelly** and schedule a meeting for next Monday at 3:00PM for 1 hour. Add **Fred Astaire, Ginger Rogers,** and **Cyd Charisse** to the list of attendees. Enter **Athlete's Foot Prevention** in the **Regarding** box and complete the activity.	Lookup Gene, click the **Schedule Meeting** icon and schedule this as you would any activity. Click the **Contacts** ▼ button and choose **Select Contacts....** Type **ast,** (Fred should be highlighted), click **Add>.** Type **rog** to highlight **Rogers,** click **Add>,** and then type **char** and click **Add>** for Cyd. Verify that **Create separate activities...** is not checked. **OK.** Type **Athlete's Foot Prevention** in the **Regarding:** box and click **OK.**
2.	In one of the Calendar or Task List views, observe the **With:** box.	The box is gray, (you must now edit the activity and use the **Contacts** ▼ button to change or view the meeting attendees). **Fred Astaire...** is displayed. The ellipsis (...) after his name indicates multiple attendees. Fred displays because his name is first alphabetically (even though you started with Gene Kelly.)
3.	Lookup each attendee and confirm that the meeting appears on each of their **Activities** tabs.	Of course it does.

Priorities

When you are scheduling any activity in ACT!, you can specify a **Priority:** of **High, Medium**, or **Low** on the General tab.

✔ Setting a priority for an activity causes that activity to appear in a particular color on ACT! Task Lists and Calendars. Normally, Low priority activities appear in dark gray or black, Medium in blue, and High in red.

✔ The Task List and Calendar views can be filtered to display only specified levels of Priority.

✔ The Task List can be sorted and printed by Priority assignment.

Like many options available to you in ACT!, using the Priority feature is your choice. Some users are happy to allow the default (Low) to be assigned to all activities, while others like to segregate activities by their importance. Play with it and see what works best for you.

Practice: How important is it?

Step	What to do	How to do it/Comments
1.	Change the priority of the Edward G. Robinson meeting (12/4/2002) to High.	Click the entry for his meeting in the **Priority** column. Click the drop-down arrow and choose **High**. Note the color change.

Try It...

Activity Colors

We have already observed that different priorities are associated with different colors. However, when scheduling any activity, you can manually change the color by clicking the down arrow for <u>A</u>ctivity color: (on the General tab) and clicking the color you want.

Activity Color:

✔ Some users like to classify the activity type by color. Prospecting calls are in (cold) blue, follow-up calls are in (warm) maroon, closing the deal calls are in (money) green, etc.

✔ If there are not many login users in your company, each employee may want to choose a color as their signature color for their activities. That way when you view all users on the shared Calendar or Task List, you can tell quickly by the color of the activity to whom it belongs.

☞ *Changing the color of an activity over-rides the color for the selected priority and it becomes the new default until you change it again. For example: You change the color of an activity to green. If you also set the priority of that item to High, then from that point on, any activity whose priority you set to High is green (until **you** change it again). In other words, you can change colors manually each time you create them to color code your activities, **or** you can let the priority option color code them for you.*

Show Full Day Banner

This option affects the way an activity looks when viewed in the **Monthly Calendar**. You can select this option when you schedule the activity (on the General tab). The full day banner displays at the bottom of the date box in the Monthly Calendar view only, as illustrated here.

Alarms

When your activities are scheduled for a particular time, you can set an alarm to remind you of them. No matter what you're doing in Windows, an alarm flashes to alert you to the imminent activity.

✔ For an alarm to go off, ACT! needs to be running, but it can be minimized or running in the background behind other applications you may be using.

✔ If an alarm is missed because your computer is shut down (or it's on but ACT! is not running), the alarm displays as soon as you open the database in ACT!.

...set an alarm

How To...

1. Schedule the activity for which you want to set an alarm. Set activity options as you normally would.

   Perform this task as you normally would (page 73) . Alarms can be set for Meetings, Calls, or To-Do's.

2. Click the **Ring alarm** check box.

   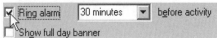

   There must be a check in the box in order for the alarm to go off.

3. Change the lead time for the alarm in the **before activity** box, if desired.

   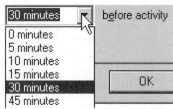

   If you want to set a different amount of time before the activity that the alarm is to go off, click the drop-down arrow, and choose a different option. If none of the options are what you want, type the lead time in the box. When you enter lead time manually, type it like you see it in the list. Example: to set a lead time of 10 days, type **10 days**.

4. **OK**

Practice: *Shopping with Audrey*

Step	What to do	How to do it/Comments
1.	Lookup the record for **Audrey Hepburn**.	**Lookup, Last Name...,** type **hep**, **OK**. It found two Hepburns (Audrey and Katherine).
2.	Schedule a meeting for today.	Click Schedule Meeting icon.
	Set the time of the meeting for about 15 minutes from now.	By default, today's date is already displayed in the **Date:** box. **[Tab]** to or click in the **Time:** box. Enter a time that's 15 minutes from now.
	The meeting will last 6 hours.	6 hours is not an option in **Duration:** so you'll have to type it.
	The reason for the meeting? Shopping at Tiffany's	In the **Regarding:** section type "Shopping at Tiffany's"
	Set the alarm to go off 5 minutes before the meeting so you won't be late.	Click the **Ring alarm** check box. Specify **5 minutes** in the **before activity** list box.
	Make the activity show as a full day banner in the Monthly Calendar. While you're at it, change the color of the activity to green (this trip could cost you) and add Details of "Ask for Edward".	Click the **Show full day banner** check box and click in **Activity color:** to change the color to green. Click the Details tab to add the note. **OK**
3.	View the activity in the Monthly Calendar. Do you see the Full day banner?	Click on the Monthly Calendar view. Monthly Calendar

Try It...

☞ *Now that you've scheduled the call, the alarm should go off in about 10 minutes (assuming that the internal clock in your computer is correct). When the alarm goes off, we'll stop and take a look at the various ways to respond. Turn to the exercise on page 114 when you see the alarm. For now, let's talk about a couple of other options in the **Schedule Activity** dialog box that may be helpful to you.*

Responding to an Alarm

When an alarm goes off in ACT!, the **Alarms** dialog box appears.

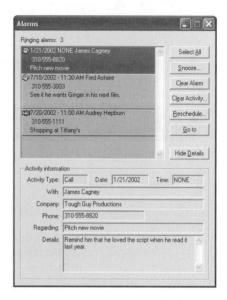

Each alarm displays all sorts of helpful information, including the Activity Type that the alarm represents, the Date, Time, Contact name, Company name, Phone number, description of the activity, and any Details. If you have more than one alarm going off, they appear in chronological order in the **Ringing alarms:** box. You can deal with one alarm at a time, or select them all and handle them in one "fell swoop." (Now if someone could just tell us what a "swoop" is and why we would want to "fell" it, we would never ask for another thing.)

When you see an alarm, respond in one of the following ways:

Select All　　Click this when you're short on time and want to handle multiple alarms quickly. A highlight appears over all alarms and the command you choose next affects them all.

Snooze...　　The **Snooze Alarm** dialog box appears in which you may set the alarm to go off again at a later time. Select the amount of time to delay, click **OK**.

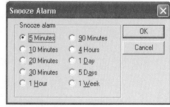

Clear Alarm　　Turns off the alarm for today only, but leaves the activity on your calendar.

Clear Activity... Displays the Clear Activity dialog box for the associated activity. From here, you can tell ACT! whether or not the activity was completed, or if you at least tried to complete it. See the section on Clearing Activities (page 88).

Reschedule... Displays the **Schedule Activity** dialog box. From there, you can make changes to the date, time, or any other option.

Go to　　Goes to the highlighted contact so that you can get more information on the contact before you complete the activity.

Hide <u>D</u>etails/Show <u>D</u>etails   Collapse or display the **Activity information** section of the Alarms dialog.

 *Notice that you can minimize this **Alarms** window while you handle the alarms, one at a time.*

Practice: *Responding to an Alarm*

Step	What to do	How to do it/Comments
1.	When the alarm for the Audrey Hepburn meeting goes off, view the **Alarms** dialog box.	Click **Show <u>D</u>etails** button if necessary to display the Activity Information at the bottom of the Alarms dialog box.
2.	Snooze the alarm for 10 minutes.	Click **<u>S</u>nooze...**, choose **<u>1</u>0 Minutes**, and click **OK**. The alarm goes away, but it will be back.
3.	When the alarm goes off again, clear the Alarm.	Don't clear the activity, just the alarm. Click **C<u>l</u>ear Alarm**.
4.	When you clear the alarm (not the activity), does the activity still appear on the contacts' **Activities** tab?	The activity stays there until you clear it. Clearing an alarm is not the same as clearing an activity.

If you don't get around to clearing the activity today, the alarm will go off again tomorrow. |
| 5. | When it comes up tomorrow, you can clear the activity. | |

 Don't overdo a good thing. Alarms are to be used for important activities… 10 minutes before an important conference call, 7 days before an anniversary date to remind you to buy a gift, at 5:15 every Tuesday so you can make it home in time to take your son to piano lessons. If you put an alarm on everything, then the purpose of alarms gets lost…no activity is any more important or time sensitive than the others. Get in the habit of checking the Calendar or Task List to see what's up for the day. Change your Edit, Preferences if necessary to roll-over your calls and to-dos. Besides, alarms take up system resources, always checking to see if it is time to ring yet, and they can also have some impact on your Palm Pilot battery life.

SideACT! Alarms

If ACT! is open, the regular Alarms feature works great to notify you of important meetings. However, what if you haven't opened ACT! yet today (say it isn't so...). The Alarms feature in ACT! only works if ACT! is open.

Lucky for us that ACT! ships with another small program called SideACT! that can run outside of ACT! and let us know that it is time to leave for that appointment. (It does a few other things as well, but we won't get to that until a few more pages.)

SideACT! can monitor up to three databases for activity alarms when ACT! is closed. However, SideACT! must be either in your system tray each time you start Windows or open/minimized for the alarm to operate.

 *To verify that SideACT! starts each time your PC starts, click **Start, All Programs**, point to the **Startup** folder and verify that **SideACT!** is listed. If it isn't, you can change that setting from within SideACT! Open SideACT!, click **Edit, Preferences...** and put a check beside the **Add SideACT! to Windows Taskbar** option, **OK**.*

...set up alarm notification when ACT! is closed

How To...

1. **Tools, SideACT! Alarms Setup**

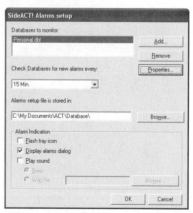

2. Click **Add...** to enter a database to monitor for alarms.

3. Select the database to monitor and click **Open**.

    If you have assigned a password or if the database is a multi-user database, you will be prompted for the user name and password.

   If it is a multi-user database, the user name you enter will indicate to SideACT! whose alarms you wish to display.

4. Repeat steps 2 and 3 for each additional database...up to three.

You can display the **Properties...** of the selected database to verify its path or the user name whose calendar is monitored. You cannot edit the properties (just **Remove** and start all over if necessary).

5. From the **Check Databases for new alarms every:** drop-down list, select how often you want SideACT! to search the ACT! database(s) for alarms.

You may only select from the available time intervals of 15 Min., 30 Min., 45 Min., 1 Hour or 2 Hours.

6. Leave the **Display alarms dialog** box checked and select one of the other alarm notification methods if desired.

☞ *If you don't leave Display alarms dialog checked, you won't know what alarm is ringing!*

Flash tray icon flashes the SideACT! icon in the lower right corner of the screen.

Display alarms dialog displays the SideACT! Alarms dialog box on the screen (see below).

Play sound activates a **Beep** or selected **Wav file:** for your alarm. You can browse to locate a Wav file. The Wav file will play before the Alarms dialog displays.

7. **OK**

☞ *The SideACT! alarm dialog is an abbreviated version of the ACT! alarm dialog. The SideACT! Alarm doesn't allow you to **Clear Activity** or **Reschedule**. Use the **Go to Contact** option to open the associated ACT! database (listed at the bottom of the dialog) to complete or reschedule the alarmed activity.*

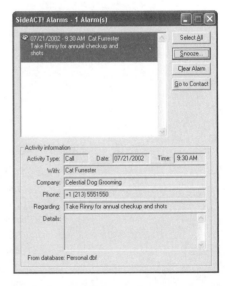

Practice: *Setting Up Alarms*

Step	What to do	How to do it/Comments
1.	Setup the SideACT! alarm to monitor the "Personal" database every 15 minutes.	**Tools, SideACT! Alarms Setup**, click **Add...**, select the "Personal" database and click **Open**.
2.	If you like, you can add a WAV file to the notification.	Windows comes with a few WAV files. To find them, click on **Start**, **Search** (of Find), **All files and folders**, enter " *.WAV ", click **Search**. Double-click some of the sounds to find out which ones you like. Make a note of their location and name and insert that into the SideACT! Alarms Setup dialog.
3.	When you are finished working in this Study Guide for the day and close ACT!, an alarm will go off.	When the SideACT!! alarm displays, select **Go to Contact.** When the Personal database opens, clear the activity and close ACT!.

Try It...

ACT!

Scheduling Activities for Other Login Users

When you share an ACT! database with other login users in your company, you may find yourself in the enviable position of assigning tasks to other ACT! users. (Hey, it's better than having them assigned to *you*.) Each user of the shared database has their own task list and calendar.

ACT! allows one user of a shared database to create activities for another user. When this is done, the activity shows up in the assignee's calendar.

...schedule an activity for someone else in your company

1. Create the activity as you normally would.

Lookup the contact for whom you want to schedule the activity. **Example:** You're setting up lunch with Queen Elizabeth for a fellow employee named Elmer. Lookup "Liz" (we're old friends), *not* Elmer.

2. Click the **Schedule For/By** button at the bottom of the activity dialog box.

Schedule For/By ▽

The dialog box grows to display two more fields: **Scheduled for:** and **Scheduled by:**

Once displayed, these two additional fields (**Scheduled for:** and **Scheduled by**) will display in the **Schedule Activity** dialog when you schedule new activities, until you turn them off.

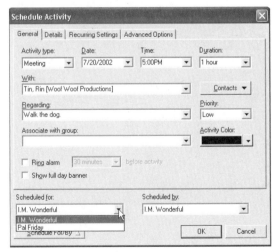

3.

From the **Scheduled for:** list, choose user for whom you want to assign this activity.

4. Click **OK** when you are done.

 *You can return the Schedule Activity dialog box to its original state (when it was smaller) by clicking the **Schedule For/By** button a second time.*

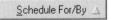

Practice: *Getting the monkey off your back*

Try It...

Step	What to do	How to do it/Comments
1.	Wow, you've got so much to do this week. Let's off load a few things to your assistant Pal.	Pal Friday works for Stars R Us and is a login user.
2.	Looking at your Task List, it seems there are at least two things we could ask Pal to do for us… ✔ Buy Band aids and ✔ Kennel Walk Through scheduled with Rin Tin Tin.	Open the Task List view. Double-click the row header for the first activity to modify it. Click the **Schedule For/By** button at the bottom of the activity dialog box to display the extra fields (if necessary). Click the **Schedule for:** drop down and change to Pal. **OK** Repeat for the second activity.
3.	View the Task List	Did anything change?

Filtering the Calendar and Task List Views

When more than one user shares your database, activities scheduled for all logon users in the database show up on the Calendars and the Task List views. While you may want to occasionally view the activities of a colleague, you will usually want to filter the Task List and Calendar views to only display your own activities.

...filter the calendar or task list for a User

How To...

1.	In the Calendar or Task List views, click the Filter icon on the toolbar at the top of the window.	The Filter dialog box displays.
2.	To display only your calendar, click **Selected users** first and then click on your name.	You can also click on more than one name (e.g. only yours and your assistant's calendar.)

3.   **OK**

Try It...

Step	What to do	How to do it/Comments
1.	Filter the Task List view to display only Pal's activities.	In Task List view, click the Filter icon. Click **Selected users** and click on Pal Friday. **OK**
2.	How many activities are on Pal's calendar?	She had a few already.
3.	View the Monthly Calendar.	Filtering the Task List does not filter the Calendar views. Monthly Calendar
4.	Filter the Calendar to only display *your* activities?	Click the Filter icon. Click **Selected users** and click on I.M. Wonderful. **OK**
5.	Switch to Weekly Calendar and check the filter.	The same filter is used for all Calendar views.
6.	Return to the Task List view and filter the Task List to only display *your* activities for Today (since all you can handle is what is on your plate for today…not so overwhelming anymore).	You will have to click on Pal to unselect the name. Click on I.M. Wonderful.\n\nFilter the dates to show to **Today**. **OK**

Scheduling-Recurring Activities

Some activities repeat over and over. You might wish to schedule a weekly staff meeting. Perhaps you wish to call on a contact once a month to assess their needs. Maybe there is someone with whom you want to close a deal and you want to bug them twice a week until they give up and agree with you. For any reason, if you wish to repeat an activity at regular (or irregular) intervals, ACT! can oblige.

...schedule a recurring activity

1.	Lookup the contact whom the recurring activity concerns.	If you meet with the same person each week, for example, look up that record.
2.	Display the **Schedule Activity** dialog box.	Choose to schedule a **Call, Meeting**, or **To-do** from the **Contact** menu or click the appropriate icon on the toolbar.
3.	Choose the date, time, and duration (as necessary) for the first of the recurring activities. Fill out the regarding line and set options (like alarms, colors, etc.) as necessary.	Set up the first activity as you would any single activity. The recurring activities will have the same settings and options. Only the dates change.
4.	Click the **Recurring Settings** tab.	The **Recurring Settings** tab of the dialog box appears.
5.	Choose whether the activity repeats **Daily, Weekly, Monthly, Yearly**, or if you wish to define a **Custom** recurrence.	

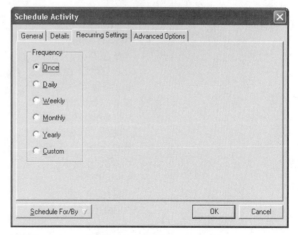

6.	Choose the options that define how often and for how long the activity will repeat.	We will discuss these options next.

7. When you have completed
choosing any other options for the
activity, click **OK**.

ACT! creates an identical activity
for each of the recurrence dates
you specified.

Each recurrence type--**Daily, Weekly, Monthly, Yearly** or **Custom**--has its own
set of options.

Daily In the **Every:**
box, specify how
many days there
will be between
each activity. In
the **Until:** box,
specify the date
the recurrences
will end. The
default is today.

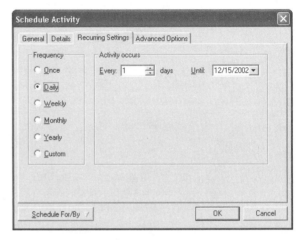

Example: If you
specify **3**, the
activity will occur
every 3rd day
until the date specified in the **Until** box is reached.

Weekly In the **Every:**
box, specify the
number of weeks
between each
occurrence of
the activity. In
the **Until:** box,
specify the date
the recurrences
will end. Use the
check boxes at
the bottom of the
dialog box to
specify the
day(s) it will
repeat each week.

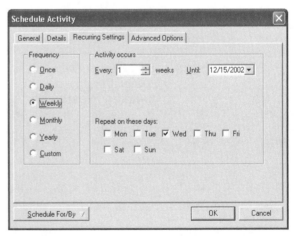

Example: You can schedule an activity to repeat on Monday,
Wednesday, and Friday every other week for the next 6 weeks.

Monthly   In the **Every:** box, specify the number of months between each occurrence of the activity. In the **Until:** box, specify the date the recurrences will end. You can now use the two sets of check boxes to specify what day or days of the month the activity will repeat.

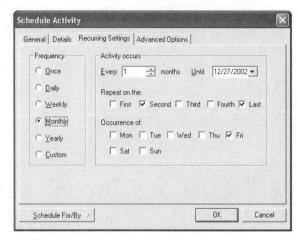

Example: You can schedule an activity that will occur on the second and last Friday of each month for the next three months.

Yearly   In the **Every:** box, specify the number of years between each occurrence of the activity. In the **Through:** box, specify the year in which the last activity will occur.

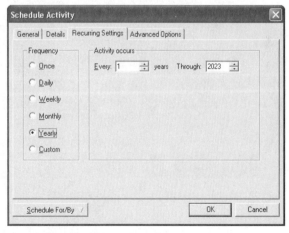

Example: You can schedule your birthday for the next twenty years (birthdays are important!).

Custom When none of
the other options
will do, use the
custom options
to make your
own sequence.
You will use the
Every: and the
Until: options as
you would with
any other
recurring activity.

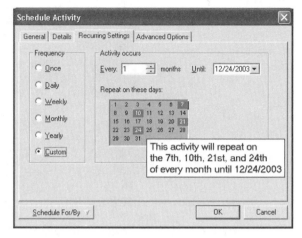

Click each day
you wish the
activity to occur. When you click a day, you select it. Click again to
de-select it.

One way or another, you are going to be able to schedule your activities when
you want, and as often as you want.

 *Recurring activities appear only once in the Task List and Activities
tab (even though you scheduled it for the next 20 years).
Recurring activities display a little arrow on the associated icon. After
you clear a recurring activity, the date for the next re-occurrence of the
activity will then display. However, all 40 occurrences will appear in the
Calendar.*

Practice: *Scheduling a Recurring Meeting*

Step	What to do	How to do it/Comments
1.	Lookup **Esther Williams**	Choose **Lookup, Last Name...,** type **wil**, click **OK**.
2.	Schedule an exercise class with her for next Wednesday from 9:00-10:00 AM. OK, we probably need to go more than once.	Click the Schedule Meeting icon. Click the list button for **Date:,** click next Wednesday, click the list button for **Time:** and drag over **9:00** through **10:00** AM, in the **Regarding:** area type: "Exercise Class".

Try It...

Step	What to do	How to do it/Comments
3.	Make the meeting recurring every week for the next two months. Change any other options as desired and click **OK**	Click the **Recurring Settings** dialog tab and choose **Weekly**. Be sure that **1** appears in the **Every**: box. Click the list button for **Until:** and click the **next month** button twice (to move ahead 2 months). Click the last Wednesday of the month. If necessary, click the **Wed** check box at the bottom of the dialog box to place a check in it, and remove the check from any other day's check box. Click **OK**.
4.	View the **Activities** tab for Esther. You'll see only the first of the exercise classes listed. View the Monthly Calendar to see how the classes display.	If you look closely, you'll see a small arrow on the meeting icon. This tells you that the meeting happens more than once.
5.	Clear next week's activity; you have a conflict and can't go.	Click in the check column to the left of the activity to display the **Clear Activity** dialog. Select **Not held. OK**
6.	On Esther's **Activities** tab, notice the next scheduled class date.	OH NO! Can't make that one either.
7.	OK, if you don't make the next one Esther will never believe you are serious. So reschedule the next class *only* for the 10:00-11:00 time slot. What happens when you click **OK**?	Double-click the gray row header to the left of the activity. Type **10a** in the **Time:** box and click **OK**. When you change one instance of a recurring meeting, ACT! warns you.
8.	Change only the selected **Instance**.	Click the **Instance** button. The remaining meetings (exercise classes) remain unaffected.

In the How to do it cell for Step 3, an embedded dialog shows:

Next Month

Until: 1/15/2003

January 2003

S	M	T	W	T	F	S
			1	2	3	4
5	6	7	8	9	10	11
12	13	14	15	16	17	18
19	20	21	22	23	24	25
26	27	28	29	30	31	

Advanced Options Tab

Public vs. Private Activities

If you share an ACT! database, other users can view the activities you have scheduled.

✔ If you don't want everybody knowing what you're up to, you can set up private activities.

✔ Private activities will display in *your* Task List and Calendar views as normal.

✔ However, when other users log in to the database (and they haven't filtered their Calendar or Task List views), your private activities appear on the Calendar, but the particulars of the activity (who the appointment is with or what it is regarding) are not displayed. In 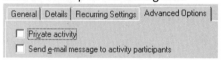 the example to the right, fellow employee Pal Friday has a private activity scheduled for 9:00. So, we know Pal is not available at 9:00 (we just don't know why).

✔ Private activities will not display in other users Task List view.

...specify an activity as private

1. While scheduling an activity, click on the **Advanced Options** tab.

   The **Schedule Activities** dialog box has four pages represented by the tabs at the top of the dialog box.

   | General | Details | Recurring Settings | Advanced Options |

   ☐ Private activity
   ☐ Send e-mail message to activity participants

2. Place a check in the **Private activity** attribute to hide the details from other login users.

3. Complete the activity as you normally would.

   This activity will not be viewable by anyone but you.

☞ *Private activities are only private if you are in a multi-user environment where each user logs in to the database file with a unique user login name.*

Sending an E-mail reminder

Also on the **Advanced Options** tab in the Scheduling dialog box, ACT! has included a handy check box that allows you to send an e-mail confirmation about the current activity to the contact(s) the activity is scheduled with.   This option requires two things:

1.   Your computer is set up to give you access to an e-mail system. This access could be through a network or a modem.

2.   ACT! has been configured to use that e-mail system. See page 180 for setting up your E-mail system to work with ACT! Until you tell ACT! which e-mail you use, it won't be able to use it. Hey... makes sense to us!

When you check the **Send e-mail message to activity participants'** option, an e-mail message is generated as soon as you click **OK** to complete the activity.

Whether the activity is with one or a dozen people, ACT! addresses the message to all participants. In fact, the message already contains all the necessary information but if you wish to add additional text, you may do so.   See page 184 for more details on sending and receiving e-mail in ACT! or page 180 for setting up your E-mail system to work with ACT!

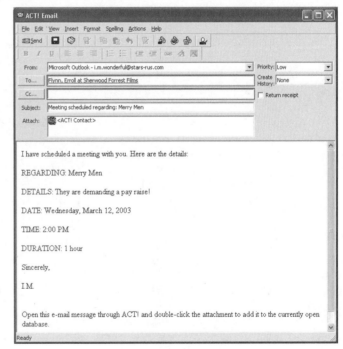

Scheduling Activities using the Calendar

When you need to schedule an activity for a particular day, you might find the calendar more convenient than the Contact window.

How To...

...schedule an activity from the calendar

1. Display the date of the activity on the calendar.

   Display the desired day in the calendar. You can use any calendar view, but we recommend Daily or Weekly view because you can pre-select the time and duration of the activity.

2. If you chose Daily or Weekly view, select the time and duration.

   If the activity is short, double-click the desired time slot. For longer activities, drag over the appropriate number of bars on the calendar.

   Schedule Activity dialog box appears.

☞ The **With**: box displays the name of the contact that is currently displayed in the Contact screen. Remember, you can use the drop-down list to change the contact if necessary.

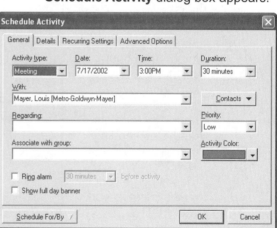

The correct **Date:**, **Time:**, and **Duration:** should already be displayed (if you selected them). You can change any of this information as necessary.

☞ *If you're scheduling a timeless activity, click the drop-down arrow for the* **Time:** *list and choose* **Timeless** *from the bottom of the time line.*

3. Fill out the remaining options as desired. Change the activity type, priority, alarm options, etc., as with any activity.

4. Click **OK.**

Practice: **Scheduling Activities from the Calendar**

Try It...

Step	What to do	How to do it/Comments
1.	Display next Monday in the Weekly Calendar view.	Click the Weekly Calendar icon and click on Monday of next week on the mini-calendar at the top right of the calendar window.
2.	Select the hour from 4:00 to 5:00 PM on Monday.	Click on the **4:00** bar and drag to **5:00** and release the mouse button. The **Schedule Activity** dialog box appears.
3.	Schedule a meeting.	If necessary, click the down arrow for **Activity type:** and choose **Meeting**. Notice that the date and time are correctly filled in for you.
4.	Select Spencer Tracy as the contact.	Click the drop-down list button to the right of the **With:** box, locate, and select **Tracy, Spencer**. *(Hint: once the list is displayed, press* **tr** *on your keyboard to jump to the first contact whose last name begins with* **Tr**.*)*
5.	Note that the meeting is to be a discussion of contract negotiations.	Display the drop-down list for **Regarding:** and choose **Contract negotiations.**
6.	Complete the scheduling.	Click **OK**.

Printing the Calendar

If you carry a brand-name paper calendar around with you (we don't want to drop names like "Franklin" or "Day Runner" or "Day Timer" so we won't mention them), ACT! has a terrific printing feature that allows you take your on-line calendar with you, even if your computer stays behind when you travel.

✔ The calendar print feature offers dozens of popular calendar layouts for the major paper planning calendars.

✔ Many companies offer pre-printed, pre-perforated calendar inserts designed for just this purpose.

✔ All you have to do is print using the appropriate format, punch out the pages, put them in your book, and you're off.

✔ If you prefer, there are plain paper options if all you need is a basic printout.

...print a calendar

1. View the calendar you want to print (day, week, or month).

   You can change your mind in the next step, but if you pre-select the view you want you won't need to change the options.

2. Choose **File, Print...**

   or

   click the **Print** icon

   or

   press **[Ctrl+P]**.

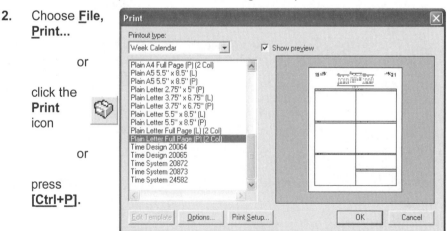

3. Select a **Printout type:**, if necessary (the active calendar view is assumed).

   If you want to change to a different calendar view, choose it from the **Printout type**: drop-down list. For each printout type, there is a different list of layouts listed below.

4. Select one of the paper forms (the last one you printed will still be selected.)

Click one of the choices in the list on the left. A preview of the paper appears on the right. If necessary, click the **Show preview** option to see how your activities will look on the selected paper type.

5. If you wish to filter the calendar or set additional print options, click the **Options...** button. The **Calendar Options** dialog box displays several customization options. Many people like to check the **Company name** option to print the company name next to the contact name.

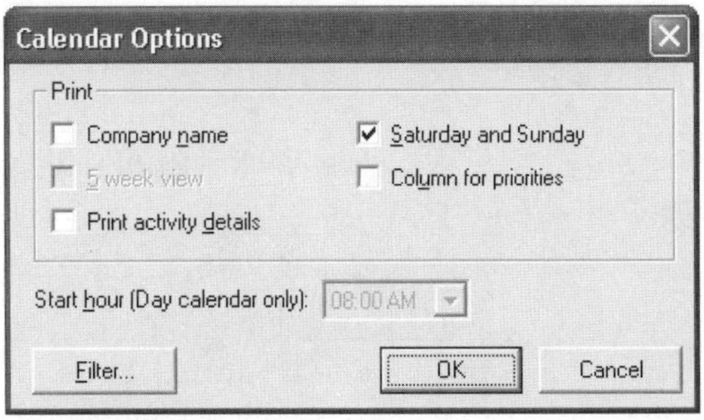

Calendar Options

Print
- [ ] Company name
- [ ] 5 week view
- [ ] Print activity details
- [x] Saturday and Sunday
- [ ] Column for priorities

Start hour (Day calendar only): [08:00 AM ▾]

[Filter...]   [OK]   [Cancel]

6. From the Calendar Options area, you can also click the **Filter...** button to filter dates, activity types, etc.

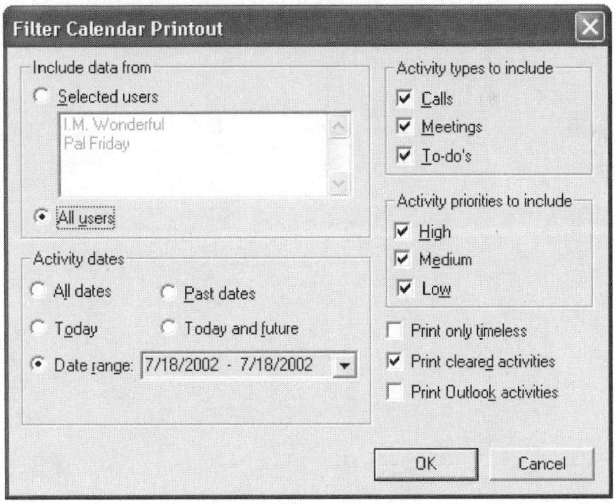

Filter Calendar Printout

Include data from
- ( ) Selected users
  - I.M. Wonderful
  - Pal Friday
- (•) All users

Activity dates
- ( ) All dates   ( ) Past dates
- ( ) Today   ( ) Today and future
- (•) Date range: 7/18/2002 - 7/18/2002 ▾

Activity types to include
- [x] Calls
- [x] Meetings
- [x] To-do's

Activity priorities to include
- [x] High
- [x] Medium
- [x] Low

- [ ] Print only timeless
- [x] Print cleared activities
- [ ] Print Outlook activities

[OK]   [Cancel]

7. After you have set any desired calendar and filter options, click **OK** until you return to the initial **Print** dialog box, then click **OK** once more.

Another **Print** dialog appears. This print dialog box allows you to control the printer itself, number of copies, etc..

8. Set print options as desired and click **OK**.

It always helps to be sure that your printer is on, properly connected, and loaded with paper before you print.

Try It...

Step	What to do	How to do it/Comments
1.	View next week's calendar, if necessary.	Click the Weekly Calendar icon on the View Bar and (if necessary) click any date that falls in next week on the small calendar box on the upper right.
2.	Display the **Print** dialog box.	**File, Print...,** or click the Print icon.
3.	Select **Plain Letter Full Page (P) (2 Col)**.	Scroll down in the list to find the plain paper option and click it.
4.	The **Options...** button will lead you to choices that affect what gets printed. Check to make sure that the Company name will be printed on the calendar along with all activities for I.M. Wonderful only.	Click **Options...** to display some basic choices. Be sure to select the **Company name** option. Click **Filter...** to display a filter dialog box. Make sure **Calls, Meetings**, and **To-do's** are checked. If the Calendars are filtered to only display I.M., then the default will be to print a calendar of only I.M.'s activities.
5.	Print the calendar.	**OK, OK, OK, Print** *(No... we're not getting impatient... You have to click 3 **OK** buttons to complete the printout.)*

Activity Series

You call a hot lead on Monday…you want to follow up the call with a letter on Wednesday…and another call on Friday. (That's the spirit, don't give them a moments rest!) Normally this would involve scheduling three separate activities. If this is a common scenario for you, you might want to create an **Activity Series**.

An Activity Series is a series of activities (we just love to state the obvious). This series of activities (all of them) is given a name and saved. When you are ready, you can schedule all the activities in the series with the current contact (or Current lookup) with only a few keystrokes.

…create an activity series

How To…

1. Choose **Contact, Create/Edit Activity Series…**.

2. Make sure **Create a new activity series** is the selected option (unless you want to edit an existing activity series that is).

The first **Activity Series Wizard** dialog box is displayed:

3. Click **Next >**.

The second **Activity Series Wizard** dialog box is displayed:

4. Choose **Start date** if you want to schedule a series of activities *beginning* on a specified date.

   Choose **Due date** if you want to schedule a series of activities *ending* on a specified date.

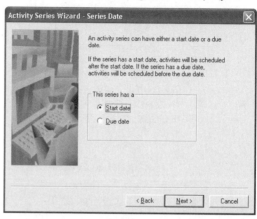

5. Click **Next >**.

The third **Activity Series Wizard** dialog box is displayed:

6. First define the first activity in the series using the controls in this dialog box. If this is the starting activity for a series you will probably want to schedule it 0 days after the **Start** date but a specific number of days **Before** the due date (depending on which option you chose in the previous dialog.

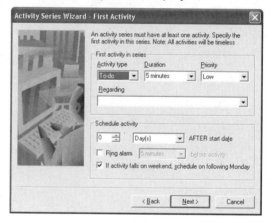

7.   Click **Next >**.

The fourth **Activity Series Wizard** dialog box is displayed:

8.   This grid eventually displays each of the activities in the series. This is also the screen that displays if you choose to edit an existing series.

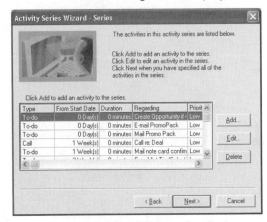

9.   To add the next activity, click **Add...**.

The **Add Activity** dialog is displayed:

10.   Fill out this dialog box for the next activity and click **OK**.

If you wish to add additional activities to the series, click **Add...** again and define the next, until you have the entire series defined.

11.   Click **Next >**.

The final **Activity Series Wizard** dialog box is displayed:

12. Give the series a meaningful name (hint: **Series1** is not a good name…try Prospect Follow Up).

Type a description of the series if you wish (this can be useful in identifying the purpose of the series later and is recommended).

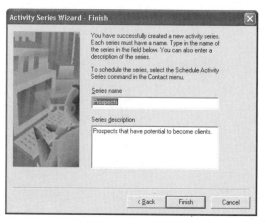

13. Click **Finish**.

You may now schedule activities based on this series.

Practice: *Create a Series*

	Step	What to do	How to do it/Comments
Try It…	1.	Begin a new activity series. Base the series on a **Start date**.	Choose **Contact, Create/Edit Activity Series…. Create a new activity series** option, click **Next>**, choose **Start date**, click **Next>**.
	2.	Make the first activity a To-do. Set the duration to timeless, and leave priority alone. The regarding is **Mail Promo Brochure**. The To-do should be scheduled 0 days after the start date (since it is the starting activity).	Change the **Activity type** to **To-do**, set the **Duration** to timeless, type **Mail Promo Brochure** as the **Regarding**, and click **Next >**.
	3.	Add a follow up call to the To-do for three days after.	Click **Add…**, change **Activity type** to **Call**, choose **Follow up** from the **Regarding** list, change the days after to **3 Day(s)** after the start date, and click **OK**.
	4.	Click **Next >** and name the activity series **Prospect**.	Replace the default **Series name** with **Prospect** and click **Finish**.

...use an activity series

How To...

1. If you wish to schedule a series for more than one Contact, perform a lookup. Choose **Contact, Schedule Activity Series...**.

   The **Schedule Activity Series** dialog box is displayed:

2. Select whether to schedule with **All contacts**, the **Current contact** or the **Current lookup**.

   Select a **Series start date** and

   Click the series you want under **Select activity series**. Note the **Series description** that displays at the bottom of the series list.

3. Click **Schedule**. You will be asked to confirm this series, read the confirmation box carefully and if it is correct click **Yes**.

   That's it. The activities are all scheduled for the specified Contact(s).

Practice: *Using a Series*

Try It...

Step	What to do	How to do it/Comments
1.	Schedule the **Prospect** series for **Mickey Rooney**. Begin the series next **Wednesday**.	Lookup **Mickey Rooney**. Choose **Contact, Schedule Activity Series...**, and select **Prospect** from the list (if necessary). Set the **Series start date** to next Wednesday, make sure the **Schedule activity series with** option is set to **Current contact**, and click **Schedule**. Click **Yes** to confirm.
2.	Observe Mr. Rooney's Activities list. When are the activities scheduled? Why is the second activity in the series set for **5** days after the original (instead of 3)?	Unless you turn the option off, an activity in a series that falls on the weekend is automatically shifted to the following Monday.

Roll Over

We know you're perfect. We know you make every call and perform every to-do exactly when they are due. But we are not you (more's the pity), and sometimes the time just slips away and we don't make the call or get the to-do done.

As long as the unfinished tasks remain on your schedule, they are associated with the day on which they were originally assigned and it is easy to loose track of them. (When we say "you," we mean "us." You're perfect!)

✔   If you wish, you can "roll over" these missed tasks so they always show up on the current day's calendar.

✔   You can choose to roll over calls, to-dos, meetings, or any combination of the three.

...cause activities to roll over

1.   **Edit Pr<u>e</u>ferences...**

 Or right-click just about anywhere and choose **Pr<u>e</u>ferences...** *from the shortcut menu.*

2.   Click the **Scheduling** tab.

By default, **Settings <u>f</u>or** will display the options for **Calls**.

3.   Click **Automatically r<u>o</u>ll over to today** option check-box.

If there is already a check in the box, that type of activity is already being rolled over.

4.   Click the drop-down list for **Settings <u>f</u>or** and change to **To-do's**.

Click **Automatically r<u>o</u>ll over to today** option check-box.

 You don't need to rollover Meetings. If they didn't happen yesterday, they sure won't rollover to today.

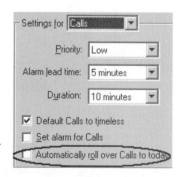

5.   Click **OK**.

The next time you open ACT! (and if any of the specified activities have "slipped by"), you are notified and asked if you want to roll them over to today.

☞ *While you are in Preferences you may also want to default your Calls and To-do's to timeless (who wants to schedule calls for 10:05 and 10:15, etc.) You can always select a time (as for a conference call), but by default they will be created with a Timeless designation.*

The next time you log on, the ACT! Reminders dialog will prompt you to roll over your activities. See…just a *few* activities got by us (among other things…)

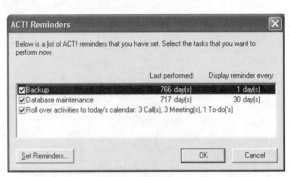

Practice: *Roll Over (Beethoven?)*

Try It…

Step	What to do	How to do it/Comments
1.	Display the **Task List** view. Observe the dates for the listed activities.	Click the Task List icon. If necessary, click the Filter button, choose **All dates** under **Dates to show**. Observe the dates on the activities if they are displayed. Several activities are overdue (*way overdue*).
2.	Turn roll over on for your calls and to-do's, but not meetings. ☞ *If the meeting didn't take place, it's not going to roll over to today!)*	**Edit Preferences...**, on the **Scheduling** tab, **Calls** displays in **Settings for**, click the **roll over** check-box. Click the drop-down arrow for **Settings for** and choose **To-do's** from the list, and click the **roll over** check-box again, and click **OK**.
3.	Close the **Stars R Us** database and then reopen it.	**File, Close** **File**, click the **1 Stars R Us** file at the bottom of the menu.
4.	Confirm the roll overs.	Click **OK** to bring the overdue activities to today's calendar.
5.	Observe your Task List.	Click the Task List icon. The overdue calls and to-do's are now due today.

Sharing Outlook and ACT! Activities

What if you work in a company where management uses the Outlook calendar for scheduling corporate meetings and activities and you and your sales staff use ACT!...you smile and say "No Problem!"

Setting up for exchanging activities is a two-part process. First we need to update both the ACT! and the Outlook calendars. Then we need to change the Calendar filter to display the Outlook activities.

...exchange Outlook and ACT! Calendars

1. In one of the Calendar views, click **Tools, Outlook Activities..., Update...**

    The **Update Calendars** dialog box is displayed.

2. Select the direction of the update...Outlook to ACT!, ACT! to Outlook, or both ways.

    Then select the date range to update.

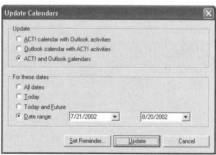

3. Click **Set Reminders...**

    Select how often you want to be reminded to update the calendars.

    OK

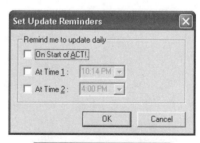

4. **Update**

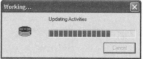

What, you say that the Outlook activities don't display on your calendar? Well, we did say that this was a two-step process.

...filtering the Calendar view to display Outlook activities

How To...

1. Click the Calendar filter icon. 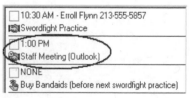 A new option displays.

2. Place a check in the **Show Outlook activities**.

3. **OK**

The ACT! calendar displays the Outlook activity with the designation of **(Outlook)** to the right of the regarding line. You *cannot* edit the Outlook activity in ACT!. The Calendar Pop-up will display the activity details (including location, end time, notes, etc.). You can also double-click it to display the information

The Outlook calendar displays the ACT! activity with the designation of **(ACT! Meeting)** or Phone Call or To-do to the right of the activity description. You *cannot* edit the ACT! activity in Outlook. You *can* double-click it to display additional information (end time, details, group association, etc.)

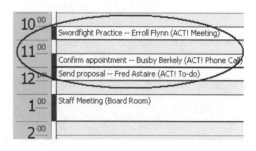

If you selected to update **On Start of _A_CT!**, the next time you start ACT!, the ACT! Reminders dialog will display to prompt you to update the calendars. Click **OK** to display the Update Calendars dialog box, then click **Update**.

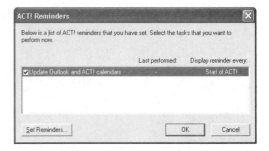

If you selected to update at a specific time, when the time is right, ACT! displays the Calendar Update Reminder dialog. Click **Yes** to display the Update Calendars dialog box, then click **Update**.

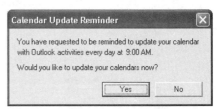

Practice: _Updating the Calendars_

Try It...

Step	What to do	How to do it/Comments
1.	If you use Outlook, setup ACT! following the two-step procedure above.	Otherwise go on to the next page.
2.	Play a little. You should have activities on your ACT! calendar for today if you just rolled over your activities from the previous practice. When you are finished, remove the activities from both calendars.	Click **Tools, _O_utlook Activities...**, **_R_emove All Activities..., OK**

SideACT!

SideACT! is a specialized program that installs on your computer along with ACT!. You can use SideACT! whether or not ACT! is running.

SideACT! is a quick access Task List that you can print. Although SideACT! does not associate an activity with a particular contact (as in your ACT! database), you can use SideACT! to record To-do's, Meetings, and Calls. You can change the order in the list, mark them as completed, or delete them. The advantage is speed and the ability to track miscellaneous tasks that really don't need to be recorded in ACT!.

...run SideACT!

How To...

1. You can access SideACT! from…
   the Windows desktop
   or
   the icon on the ACT! toolbar
   or
   clicking **Tools, SideACT!**
   or
   pressing **[Ctrl+Q]**

SideACT!

Practice: Run SideACT!

Try It...

Step	What to do	How to do it/Comments
1.	Run SideACT!. It is not necessary to exit ACT! to run SideACT!.	Double-click either the desktop icon or the SideACT! icon on the ACT! toolbar.
2.	Fast wasn't it? Leave the window displayed.	![My Tasks.SPD - SideACT! window with File, Edit, View, Item, Send to ACT!, Help menus; toolbar; "Type text here and press Enter" field; columns ✔, Item #, Regarding, Date, Type; Ready status bar]

Entering SideACT! Activities

Creating a quick To Do list in SideACT! is…well…quick!

…enter an activity in SideACT!

How To…

1. Type the text of the activity, and press **[Enter]**.

   Just start typing. Your text will replace the ***Type text here and press Enter*** label.

   When first entered, the date will be the current date and the type will be a To-do.

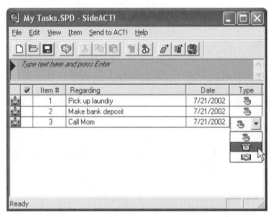

2. Repeat step 1 to add another activity to the list.

3. Edit the **Date** as necessary.

   Click the **Date** item for the activity, and edit the date as necessary.

4. Change the **Type** as necessary.

   Click the **Type** item to display a drop-down list of activity icons, choose the appropriate one.

5. To change the order…
   click the item number, backspace over the old and type a new number

   or

   click the row header to select it and drag it to its new position in the list order

   or

   click the row header to select it and press **[Ctrl+UpArrow]** or **[Ctrl+DownArrow]**

   Each item in SideACT! has a "button" to its left. If you click this button, you select its item.

   As you drag the item to a new position, the mouse pointer turns into a four-headed arrow and a dark line displays to show you where the item will be moved when you release the mouse button.

Clear a SideACT! Activity

You can clear an activity by clicking in the checkmark column. A line will appear through the activity to indicate that it is complete.

	✔	Item #	Regarding	Date
⟡		1	Pick up laundry	7/21/200
⟡	✔		~~Make bank deposit~~	~~7/21/200~~
⟡		2	Call Mom	7/21/200

 *In SideACT!'s Preferences (**Edit, Preferences**) you can indicate whether you want to move completed items to the bottom of the list or leave them where they are in the list when you mark them as complete.*

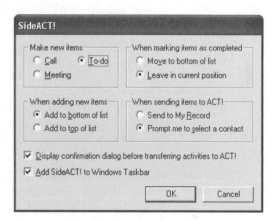

Practice: Getting Ready for the Trip

Step	What to do	How to do it/Comments
1.	Let's create a list of things we have to do before leaving for vacation. Pickup laundry	Type **Pickup laundry** and press **[Enter]**.
2.	Make a bank deposit	Type and press **[Enter]**.
3.	Ask neighbor to get mail	
4.	Mail Gable proposal.	
5.	Better move that last one to the top of the list...or no vacation.	Select Item # 4 and drag it to the top of the list.
6.	You just got back from the bank. Mark that item as completed.	Click in the checkmark column to the left of the Item # to mark as complete.

Try It...

Dragging SideACT! items to ACT!

If you would like to copy the SideACT! activity to your ACT! database, there are icons at the top of the SideACT! screen that allow you to Move or Copy the selected SideACT! item to ACT!. However, it is easier to just drag the item there.

Move
Copy

...drag SideACT! activities to ACT!

1. In ACT!, lookup the contact with whom you want to associate the SideACT! item.

2. Open SideACT! Open SideACT! so that it is in front of ACT.

3. Click on the button to the left of the SideACT! item you want to copy to the contact and drag it onto the ACT! database. You can drag it anywhere to the ACT! screen.

4. When the mouse displays with a + sign, release the mouse button. The item is copied to the contact record.

☞ *If the SideACT! item has been marked as completed, it will be copied to the **Notes/History** tab. If it is still an active item, it will be copied to the contact's **Activity** tab and be displayed on the Calendar and the Task List views as an open item for the date that was listed in the SideACT! file.*

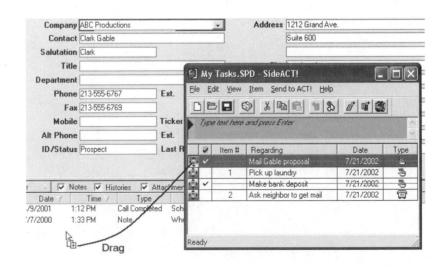

Practice: *SideACT! to ACT!*

Step	What to do	How to do it/Comments
1.	OK we finished mailing the Proposal to Clark. Mark it as completed. Let's copy it to the Stars R Us database to Clark Gable's Record so that we have a record of what date we sent the proposal over to him.	In SideACT!, click in the checkmark column to the left of the "Mail Clark proposal" item to complete it. Switch to or open the ACT! database and lookup Clark Gable. If ACT! is still open in the background, click on it's button on the Windows Taskbar. Now click on the SideACT! toolbar icon on the ACT! toolbar to display SideACT! in front of ACT! Select the item to transfer by clicking on the row header to the left and then drag it to the ACT! screen. When the mouse displays with a + sign, release the mouse.
2.	Notice the activity is copied to Clark's record as a "To-do Done".	How easy was that!

Try It...

SideACT! Scenarios

If you are a list maker, SideACT! might be your new best friend. SideACT! is like any other Windows program...you can save, print, or open a new file. So since you can save the file, you can have multiple SideACT! lists.

You could have a list of Sales Goals, Personal Things To-Do, Project Checklists, or Ideas for an Article you are writing. Think about it. If you are gathering ideas for an article you will be writing, a project you will be heading, a conference you will be arranging, etc., ideas seldom come at convenient times. You saw how fast SideACT! opened. If you start to use this handy little program to collect ideas, while you are working in 10 other things and another idea for the conference comes to you...open SideACT!, enter the idea, close SideACT!, get back to what you were doing in less than 15 seconds. How cool is that!

Practice: Create Your Goals List

Try It...

Step	What to do	How to do it/Comments
1.	Save your current SideACT! list if you like.	**File, Save**, give it a name (the default name is "My Tasks", click **Save**
2.	Create a new list named **Personal Goals**.	**File, New** **File, Save**, type "Personal Goals", click **Save**.
3.	Enter a few goals for the year and then close SideACT!	Enter a few goals. **File, Exit** or click the Close button. Your file is automatically saved for you.
4.	Open SideACT! again. Are your goals still there?	You should always have goals.
5.	Close SideACT!	

☞ *SideACT! has great appeal to some users. Others have no use for it. If you "don't get" SideACT!, and wish it would disappear from the taskbar, you can make it go away. Run SideACT!, choose* ***Edit, Preferences...,*** *remove the check from the* ***Add SideACT! to Windows Taskbar*** *check box, and click* ***OK****. The icon disappears from the system tray on the taskbar. You can still run SideACT! from the icon on ACT!'s toolbar.*

Actually we got carried away with the lists because we loved this feature so much, so we needed a quick way to open the different SideACT! files (other than open SideACT! and then click **File, Open**, click on the file, and click **Open**.) You could create shortcuts to the SideACT! file on your desktop, but we liked ACT!'s feature of Attachments better.

Attachments

You've created a Sales Goal list in SideACT! that you want to look at every morning before you hit the phones. You've created a PowerPoint presentation aimed at getting a specific client account. You've analyzed a contact's account using Excel and made some pricing changes accordingly. It is very important that you be able to view any of this information at the click of an icon. ACT! has you covered.

You can "attach" any file to a Contact. What we mean by "attach" is to create a shortcut to the file. This shortcut appears in the **Notes/History** tab.

...attach a file to a Contact

1.   Display or select the Contact for whom you want to attach a file.

If you are viewing the Contact List, you can double-click the Contact header at the left of the row. If you are viewing the Contacts screen, you're already there.

2.   Choose **Contact, Attach File...** from the menu.

The **Attach File** dialog box displays:

*You can also right-click any background area of the Contact screen and choose **Attach File...** from the shortcut menu.*

    *The keyboard shortcut for this action is **[Ctrl+I]**.*

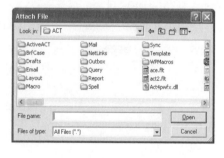

3.   Switch to the drive and folder where the file is stored, and select the file.

Select a file by clicking the icon to the left of the file name.

Selected File→ 1 Licenses and Registrations.doc
2001 Client Revenues.xls

4.   **Open**

A shortcut to the marked file(s)is added to the Notes/History list for that record.

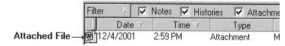

Attached File→ 12/4/2001   2:59 PM   Attachment   M

Once a file is attached, you can open the file whenever you need it.

...open an attached file

How To...

1. Display the Contact to whom the file is attached.

2. Display the **Notes/History** tab.

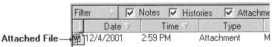

Attached File →

Filter	☑ Notes ☑ Histories ☑ Attachme	
	Date ⌄	Time ⌄	Type
12/4/2001	2:59 PM	Attachment	M

3. Double-click the icon for the desired attachment.

The file referred to by the shortcut opens the intended application.

☞ *It is important to note that while you can attach literally any file, you can only **open** those files that are associated with an available application. If you attach a document created in the ACT! word processor, it is opened into the ACT! word processor. If you attach a file created with Microsoft Excel, it is opened into Excel, and so on. If the system does not recognize the file type, you can't open it by double-clicking it.*

Practice: *Attaching Stuff*

Try It...

Step	What to do	How to do it/Comments
1.	Lookup **My Record**.	
2.	Attach the **Personal Goals** SideACT! file that you created in the last practice.	**[Ctrl+I]** to open the Attach File dialog box. By default, ACT! stores the SideACT! files in the ACT! Database folder… c:\my documents\act\database Find the file, click on it and click **Open**.
3.	Open the attached file to review your goals.	Double-click the shortcut to open SideACT! with your personal goals displayed. Imagine the possibilities!
4.	Close SideACT!	**File, Exit**

Note that if you are sharing the ACT! database on a network, other users also see the attachment icon in a Contact's record. However, if the file itself is stored on your c:\ drive or on your personal drive on the network, it displays as a History icon (instead of the expected jump arrow) and other users cannot open it by double-clicking the attachment icon. The file must be stored in a public drive and folder for others to have this type of access.

Filter		☑ Notes	☑ Histories	☑ Attachme
	Date /	Time /	Type	
Unavailable—📋	9/30/2002	1:41 PM	Attachment	Gi
Available—📋	9/30/2002	10:59 AM	Attachment	AC

Review: *Advanced Scheduling*

1.	Display next month's calendar.
2.	Select the second Wednesday morning breakfast meeting with Clark Gable.
3.	Open the **Schedule Activity** dialog box.
4.	Change the meeting time to 11:00 AM.
5.	Complete the change.
6.	Change only this instance of the recurring breakfast meeting.
7.	Did the meeting change on the calendar?
8.	Schedule your vacation for this year to last 5 days (or more). Make it an annual event for the next few years. This is definitely a full day banner kind of activity.

Try It...

Get It In Writing

To cement your relationships with your clients and produce reports that help you to be more productive, you will:

- ☑ Learn to create letters, memos, and faxes.

- ☑ Understand the differences between the ACT! word processor and Microsoft Word.

- ☑ Save, print and attach documents to Contact records.

- ☑ Create labels and envelopes for your Contacts

- ☑ Create custom templates for use with one or more Contacts.

- ☑ Practice using the Mail Merge Wizard

Creating Letters, Memos, and Faxes

Written communication with business contacts is one of the easiest things to neglect. A personal Note after a sales meeting can be an effective way of keeping your name in your client's mind, but the time it takes to address and write a Note can sometimes be more than you think you can spare. Fortunately, you are an ACT! user. ACT! can make the tedious work of writing letters almost effortless.

ACT! comes with its own word processing program, although you can use Microsoft Word if you prefer. When you write a letter, memo, or fax, ACT! opens your selected word processor program with the appropriate document template.

✔ A template is a pre-defined document. The document template contains special "place holders" that reads data from the current contact record and from your "My Record."

✔ When you use an ACT! template to create a new letter, memo or fax cover sheet, information like **Name** and **Address** is placed where the "place holders" were in the template.

✔ You end up with a document that is already addressed and "signed," all you have to do is type or modify the message itself and print it.

There are a world of word processing documents you can create with ACT!, and to make the basics even easier, three of the most common documents are already formatted for you: a letter, memo, and fax cover. It's just a matter of picking which one you want. Since we don't want to bore you with instructions for all three (the tasks are very similar), we'll just go over the procedure for creating a letter here. If you'd rather create a memo or fax cover, choose the one you want from the **Write** menu instead of **Letter**.

We will divide this process into 3 steps: creating, saving, and printing the letter.

...create a letter

1. Display the contact to whom you want to send a letter.

2. Choose **Write, Letter** from the menu
    or
    click the **Write Letter** toolbar icon.

    A Document window opens in your selected word processor with the date, name, address, etc. entered and formatted for you. If you are using the ACT! word processor, the insertion point is already positioned between the greeting and closing of the letter.

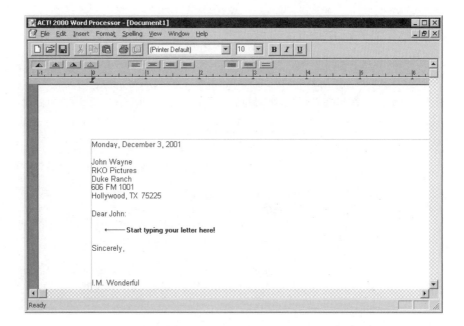

3. Type the body of the letter.

    For the procedure to save the document, see page 157. For the procedure to print the document, see page 158.

☞ *To return to the ACT! Contact window, you could close the Word Processing window by choosing **File, Exit** or by clicking the Close button on the window's title bar. You could also just click the ACT! button on the Windows task bar (which leaves the word processor open for fast access when you create a new document). Or you could just press **[Alt+Tab]** to switch back and forth between the ACT! database window and the Word Processor application.*

Click here to return to ACT!

ACT! Word Processor

The ACT! Word Processing window has its own menu bar which includes standard word processing features such as **formatting** and **spell check** (to use it, choose **Spelling, Check Document...**). ACT! provides many of the same features found in Microsoft Word. However ACT! cannot insert tables or columns in your document and has very limited graphics capabilities.

The toolbar in the ACT! Word Processing window contains
options for font style, size, and attributes such as Bold, Italic, and Underline.

| Times New Roman | ▼ | 10 | ▼ | **B** | *I* | <u>U</u> |

There are four tab buttons: Left, Center, Right, and Decimal-justified. To position a tab stop on the ruler,
click the button for the kind of tab you want and then click the desired position on the ruler. (The standard tab setup is left-justified tabs at one-inch intervals.)

There are four alignment buttons: Left, Centered, Right, and Justified. Select the paragraph(s) you
want to justify and click the desired button. (Left-justified is the default.)

There are three line spacing buttons: Single, 1.5, and Double. Select the lines of text and click the desired button
to change the spacing. (Single spacing is the default.)

Practice: *A Letter to The Duke*

Step	What to do	How to do it/Comments
1.	Lookup **John Wayne**.	Choose **Lookup, Last Name...**, type **way**, and click **OK**.
2.	Create a letter.	Choose **Write, Letter**, or click the Letter icon on the toolbar. 
3.	Observe the Word Processing window.	Is this cool or what?
4.	Type the body of the letter shown below.	
	I really liked your last film, especially the part where you got the bad guy. You seem to have a real knack for that. How is your horse? Let's get together soon to discuss your next project.	
5.	Spell check the letter, if you like and leave it displayed.	**Spelling, Check Document...** Follow the suggested prompts.

Try It...

Saving Documents

When you create a new contact in ACT!, the data is automatically saved. This is not the case with word processing documents. You must save them if you want to keep them on file for future reference.

...save a word processing file

How To...

1. Choose **File, Save or File, Save As...** from the menu.

   If you're saving a file for the first time, the **Save As** dialog box appears regardless of which option you choose.

   The word processor will automatically save to a folder named **Document**. Unless you have a specific reason not to, save your ACT! documents here.

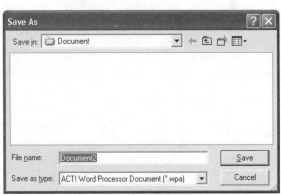

2. Type a **File name:**.

   File names can be alphanumeric and may contain up to 255 characters (including spaces).

3. Click **Save**.

   The document is saved in the **Document** folder.

[KB] *[Ctrl+S]* saves the document, *[F12]* displays the **Save As** dialog box.

Practice: *Saving the Letter*

Step	What to do	How to do it/Comments
1.	Open the **Save As** dialog box.	Choose **File**, **Save**, or **File**, **Save As....**
2.	Name the file: **Duke Next Project**.	Type **Duke Next Project** in the **File name:** box.
3.	Save the file.	Click **Save**.
4.	Observe the title bar of the Word Processing window.	**Duke Next Project** should appear somewhere on the title bar. You may also see a period and a three letter extension such as **.adt** or **.wpa**. These identify the letter as a Microsoft Word document or an ACT! Word Processor document respectively.
5.	Leave the document on the screen.	

Printing Documents

The process of printing a Word Processor document (as with most Windows applications) is not tough. You choose **File, Print...**, change any options you wish to change, and click **OK** (or **Print**).

However, when you print a document that started with an ACT! contact, something else happens besides printing.

...print a document

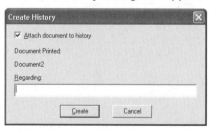

1. Choose **File**, **Print**, select any desired options, and click **OK**.

The document is sent to your printer and the **Create History** dialog box appears.

2. Type a phrase in the **Regarding:** box.

Type a few words that describe the subject of the document. This is the description that will display in the Regarding column on the contact's **Notes/History** tab.

3. Leave **Attach document to history** checked if you want to save the document and attach a shortcut to the document on the **Notes/History** tab of the contact's record.

You might uncheck the feature for something like a Fax Cover or a standard mail merge letter (no need to save).

4. Click **Create**.

If you haven't saved the document, leaving **Attach document to History** checked will display a **Save As** dialog box after you click **Create**. Type a **File name:** and click **Save**.

5. Once the file is saved and the History is created, you may be asked if you wish to print an envelope. If you do, click **OK**.

6. If you choose **OK**, another **Print** dialog box is displayed with a list of envelope sizes.

Don't be discouraged because no preview is available, envelopes tend to come in standard sizes. All you have to know is which one you have.

7. Select the appropriate envelope size (10 is what most companies use) and click **OK**, when the regular **Print** dialog box displays, click **OK**.

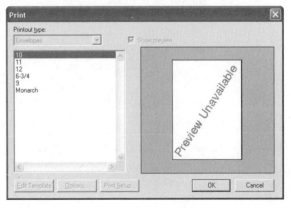

8. Choose the **Feed method** and indicate whether you feed envelopes **Face up** or **Face down**, click **OK**. (You will need to know how your printer handles envelopes.)

 Some printers go off-line and wait for you to manually feed the envelope. Others may feed from an envelope tray. If you are not familiar with how your printer handles envelopes, you may wish to consult the printer user's manual.

Attachment Review: When you write a letter, memo, etc. in ACT!, you are automatically asked if you want to attach the document to the Contact history. This prompt occurs when you print the document. Leaving the check-box checked automatically attaches that document to the Contact record. It is necessary to save the document for this to work.

✔ When you attach a document to History, it appears in the History list with a special icon.

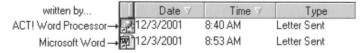

written by...		Date ▽	Time ▽	Type
ACT! Word Processor →		12/3/2001	8:40 AM	Letter Sent
Microsoft Word →		12/3/2001	8:53 AM	Letter Sent

✔ If you double-click the icon in the History list, you will open the document into the word processor (this does require the document to be saved to disk).

✔ The next time a client calls you and refers to a document you sent them, it will be no more than a couple of clicks away.

Practice: *Printing Wayne's Letter*

Try It...

Step	What to do	How to do it/Comments
1.	Display the **Print** dialog box. Observe the options.	Choose **File, Print...**
2.	Print the document.	Click **OK** to print the document. *(If you don't have access to a printer, you may get one or more error messages. Click **OK** or **Cancel** as appropriate to dismiss them.)* You should end up at the **Create History** dialog box.
3.	Create a history of the letter for this contact noting that it regards a **Future meeting**. Since you have already saved the document, you will not be prompted again. Do not print an envelope.	In the **Create History** dialog box, type **Future meeting**, make sure there's a check in the **Attach document to history** check box, click **Create**. When you are prompted to create an envelope, click **Cancel**.
4.	Close the Word Processor window.	Choose **File, Exit**, or click the **Close** button on the word processor title bar.
5.	If necessary, lookup John Wayne's record and view the **Notes/History** tab.	You should see the letter attached to John's record.
6.	Use the attachment icon to open the letter again.	Double-click the shortcut icon to the left of the **Future meeting** attachment.
7.	Close the Word Processor window again.	Choose **File, Exit**, or click the **Close** button on the title bar.

162 | ACT!

Choosing a Word Processor

When you install ACT! on your computer, a pretty good word processor is installed with it. The ACT! word processor is fully capable of meeting the majority of your word processing needs, but if you need some of the more advanced features of Microsoft Word (like columns, tables or graphics), you can use it instead. Naturally, you must have Word installed on your computer in order for ACT! to use it.

...choose a word processor

How To...

1. Choose **Edit, Preferences....**   The **Preferences** dialog box appears.

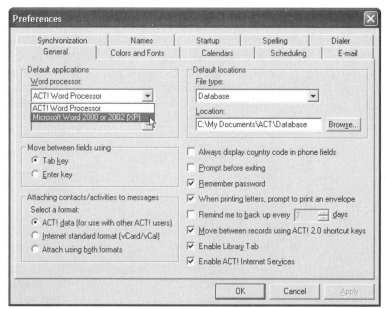

2. Click the **General** tab, if necessary.   The **General** tab is usually the first one displayed.

3. Select the **Word processor:** from the drop-down list.   A list of word processors supported by ACT! appears.

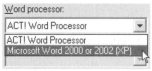

☞ *Other than its own Word Processor, ACT! supports Microsoft Word starting with version 2000 to the current version).*

4. Click **OK**.

☞ *While ACT! can work quite well with Word (provided you have one of the appropriate versions), unless you need the power that this high end word processor provides (such as tables, columns, or advanced graphics), we recommend you use the ACT! word processor. We think you will find it easy, fast, and reliable.*

Envelopes and Mailing Labels

When you print any Word Processor document, you have the opportunity to print an envelope. If you don't print the envelope right then, you can still do it later. In addition, you can print envelopes (or labels) for many contacts at once.

If you find mailing labels more efficient than printing directly on envelopes (and on many printers it is), you will find the process of printing sheets of mailing labels very simple.

...create envelopes or mailing labels

1. Perform a lookup that displays the contact(s) for whom you want to generate envelopes or mailing labels.

    If all of the contacts you want are in a group, view that group (see page 239).

2. Choose **File**, **Print...** , or press **[Ctrl+P]**.

    The **Print** dialog box appears. Note the **Printout type:** list in the top left corner.

3. Display the **Printout type:** drop-down list and choose **Envelopes** or **Labels** (or simply type an **E** to change to Envelopes or **L** to change to Labels).

    Print

    Printout type:

    | Address Book | ▼ | ☑ |

    Address Book
    Day Calendar
    Week Calendar
    Month Calendar
    Reports
    Labels
    Envelopes
    Day Runner 031-GL
    Day Runner 033-GL

4. A list of envelope or mailing label sizes appears from which you may choose.

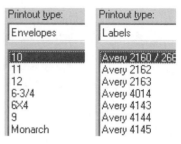

Printout type:	Printout type:
Envelopes	Labels
10	Avery 2160 / 26€
11	Avery 2162
12	Avery 2163
6-3/4	Avery 4014
6X4	Avery 4143
9	Avery 4144
Monarch	Avery 4145

5. Choose the desired envelope size or label number.

Click one of the choices in the list.

6. Click **OK**.

A **Run** dialog box appears.

The **Run Label** dialog box contains two tabs (one more tab than the **Run Envelope** dialog box).

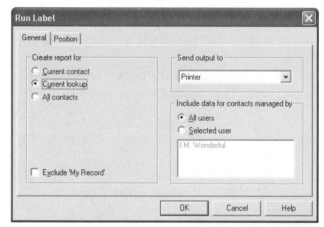

☞ *The **Position** tab for labels allows you to start printing on a specific column or row, thus allowing you to print partial sheets of labels.*

7. Choose the contact(s) to **Create report for.**

Current contact creates one envelope or label for the current contact.
Current lookup prints all contacts in the current lookup.
All contacts prints the entire database.

8. If you want to be included in the mailing, verify that there is no check in the **Exclude 'My Record'** option.

This option only affects the printing if your 'My Record' is actually in the current lookup.

9. If necessary, click the drop-down arrow and choose a **Send output to** option.

Printer sends the job directly to your printer without viewing it first.

Preview displays the printout in print preview so you can review it before printing.

10. Click **OK**.

Practice: *Creating an Envelope*

Try It...

Step	What to do	How to do it/Comments
1.	Lookup the record for **Van Johnson**.	Use any method you wish.
2.	Create and *preview* (don't print) an envelope. Use the number 10 size.	Choose **File, Print...** , or press **[Ctrl+P]**. Click the list button for **Printout type:** and choose **Envelopes**, confirm that **10** is selected, click **OK**. Choose **Current contact**, and **Preview**, click **OK**
3.	Whose return address is on the envelope? Why?	Once again, we illustrate the importance of the My Record.
4.	Close the Preview window.	Click the **Close** button on the preview toolbar bar.

Custom Templates

Mass mailings are a common marketing tool. You send the same letter over and over to different contacts in your database (such as a letter of introduction) or to a large number of people all at once (to notify them of a new product offering or perhaps to tell them all something that is of common interest.)

When you send the same letter, you want each receiver to think the letter was written just to them. You could open with a phrase like "Dear Valued Customer." Then make sure the letter contains no gender specific, or location specific terms.

However, a letter like this does not make your customer feel special! And if they don't feel special... well....

ACT! can create highly customized letters for individual contacts. In each of these cases, however, you have to type the body of the letter yourself.

> Generic Industrial Products
> AnyTown, NH 10000
>
> Dear Valued Customer,
>
> We wanted you to know just how much we appreciate your business, and hope you are finding our product(s) and service(s) adequate or better.
>
> On a personal note I really enjoyed our last visit. I hope the next time I visit your neck of the woods I hope you will have time to visit. Please call me if I can be of any service in any way. It is people like you that make my business what it is.
>
> Thank you
>
> George Generic

✔ Creating a customized letter for a large number of people involves creating a custom document template.

✔ In the document template, you type the text of the letter and insert place holders for those personal bits of information that make the letter personal (names, addresses, dates, etc.).

✔ Once the letter is created, you merge the letter with the contact records to whom you wish to send the letter. Each contact has a separate letter created for them.

✔ Each letter contains personal information about that particular contact. This information is placed where you positioned the place holders in the document template.

✔ The more information you keep on your contacts, the more personal you can make your letters.

Creating a Custom Document Template

Templates can be thought of as blue-prints that are used as a starting place for creating documents. They contain information like margin settings, line spacing, font selections, and so on. They also can contain text and field place holders as with a mail merge template.

Perhaps the most efficient way to create a new custom template is to modify a template that has already been created. We will approach the process from this perspective.

...create a new template from an existing document template

1. Choose **Write, Edit Document Template...** from the menu.

   The **Open** dialog box appears.

   ☞ *ACT! displays the contents of the **Template** folder automatically. These are not documents, they are Template files.*

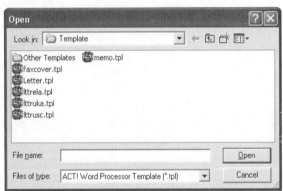

2. Select the template that is closest in style to what you want to do and click **Open**.

   If you are creating a letter, **"Letter"** is probably the best place to start, but if you are creating a memo or fax cover, to which to merge, you can choose them instead. The template opens into the word processor. The **Mail Merge Fields** dialog box is displayed in the Word Processor window.

All database fields are displayed in the **Field:** list, separated into 3 types:

Contact field-inserts a placeholder for data from the contact's record.

My Record field-inserts a placeholder for data from the current 'My Record' (this would allow other login users to use the same template)

or **Field label**-inserts the field label, not any data

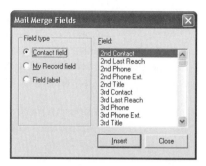

3. Choose **File, Save As...**, type a new name for the template, **Save**.

     If you are using Word as your word processor, the template name displays in quotes (e.g. "Thank you letter" or "Thank you letter.adt")

    Unless you want to modify the original template, always save it with a new unique name ... otherwise, you replace the original template. Do this BEFORE you edit your new template so you don't accidentally overwrite the basic template.

4. Type the body of the letter. Make note of where contact information should appear.

    Add the text you wish your letter/fax/memo to say where it belongs. Remember, you are going to send this document to many people.

5. Insert field place holders as necessary.

    Position the insertion point in the document, select the appropriate **Field type**, select the field to insert, and click **Insert**.

     *If the dialog box gets in your way, click the **Close** button. You can always re-display it (**Insert, ACT! Mail-Merge Fields...**)*

    When you want to include a piece of information from the contact database, position the insertion point in the template where the information will go, select the field that contains the information from the **Mail Merge Fields** dialog box, and click **Insert**. A place holder displays where the actual data will be when the merge is run.

6. Save and close the file.

    You are now ready to merge the template with one or many contact records.

Perhaps the most common mistake when creating mail merge templates involves failing to include spaces and punctuation around the place holders.

✔ If the content of the field would have spaces on either side, so should the place holder.

✔ If the field content ends the sentence, the place holder should have punctuation after it.

☞ *There are some sample templates in the **Other Templates** folder that you can use or edit. There are sample templates for birthday, anniversary, order confirmation, follow up, prospect, special offer and newsletter. There are even two templates for printing **envelopes** from the Write menu (instead of the File, Print menu option).*

Practice: *Creating a Custom Template*

Step	What to do	How to do it/Comments
1.	Edit the **Letter** document template. When the word processor displays, click it's maximize button.	Choose **Write, Edit Document Template...**, choose **Letter**, and click **Open**.
2.	Save the template as **Prospect**. *(You should always do this **before** you make any changes to the original template.)*	**File, Save As...** (don't choose **File, Save** or click the Save button), type **Prospect**, click **Save**.
3.	Observe the **Mail Merge Fields** dialog box. If it blocks your view of the letter, move it so it doesn't.	Point to the title bar of the box, hold down the left mouse button, and drag the box to a different spot.
4.	Type the following beneath the salutation: **Well** followed by a space.	The insertion point is already positioned for you. Press the **[Spacebar]** once after typing the word. You're going to insert a field after the space.
5.	Insert the **Salutation** field for the contact.	**Contact field** is already selected in the **Mail Merge Fields** dialog box. Scroll down in the list and select **Salutation**. Click **Insert**.

Try It...

Try It...

Step	What to do	How to do it/Comments
6.	Type the following: **, the time has come to talk about your current representation. Are you truly satisfied? I have several other clients in** and add a space.	Press the **[Spacebar]** after the word "in". You're going to insert another field at the end of the sentence.
7.	Insert the **City** field for the contact.	Scroll up in the **Mail Merge Fields** dialog box list, select **City, Insert**.
8.	Finish the letter with the following: **, and will be glad to provide you with their names and phone numbers so they can tell you just how happy they are with my services. You can reach me at** Have ACT! put in the phone number of the current My Record.	At the end of the paragraph insert the **Phone** field. Be sure to change the Field type to **My Record field** before inserting the field.
9.	Type a period after the My Record phone field. Save the template.	Click the Save button or choose **File, Save** to save the changes you just made.
10.	Exit the word processor.	

Merging the Template with the Current Contact

When your template is complete, you are ready to merge. You can merge it with the current contact's information or with an entire lookup.

...merge a custom template with the *current* Contact

1. Lookup the contact who will receive the letter.

2. **Write, Other Document...**, select the template, click **Open** — The merged letter displays in the word processor window.

Merging the Template with a Lookup

It is not a bad idea, before you do a large merge, to test the template with a small number of contacts just to see if you missed any spaces or placed any fields where they should not be.

...merge a custom template with a *lookup*

1. Perform a lookup that displays the contacts you wish to receive your letter.

2. Choose **Write, Mail Merge....**

 The **Mail Merge Wizard** starts.

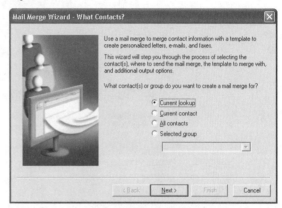

3. Select **What Contacts** you want to create the mail merge for and click **Next >**.

 You can merge the **Current lookup**, the **Current contact, All contacts** or a **Selected group**. Use the **Current contact** if you are testing the template.

4. Select the method of delivery in the **Send How?** option.

 You can merge directly to the **Printer**, send the letter as an **E-mail**, even **Fax** to all of the contacts in your lookup *(each contact must have a valid fax number and you must have a fax modem and appropriate fax software for this to*

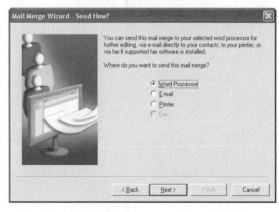

 work). If you are testing your merge, or if you want to review it before you actually send or print, choose **Word Processor**.

 Click **Next >**.

5. Click the **B**rowse… button to locate the template to use in the Mail Merge. Single-click a template with which to merge and click **Open**.

If you selected Word Processor, click **Finish**.

Otherwise click **N**ext >.

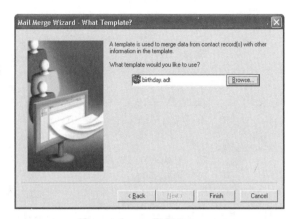

6. If you chose **E**-mail…

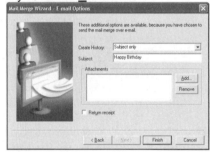

Select how you would like to **Create History:** for the mail merge (None, Subject only, Subject + Message, or Attach to Contact(s)),

Enter a **Subject:** for the e-mails,

Add… Attachments as desired,

Check the **Ret**u**rn receipt** if desired.

Finish

If you chose **P**rinter…

Enter what you would like to display in the **N**otes/**History** tab under **Regarding:** and then select the **Create history when sent** option (otherwise there is no point in entering a "Regarding" line).

Finish

 If you output to a printer, e-mail or fax, the documents are printed, faxed or sent and a history is created for each contact in the lookup. If you chose word processor, the documents are displayed in the word processor. One document is created for each contact in the lookup. A section break is placed between each letter. If all is as it should be, you can print from the word processor menu.

Practice: Caution, Merging Letters Ahead

Try It...

Step	What to do	How to do it/Comments
1.	Lookup all contacts with an **ID/Status** of Prospects.	**Lookup, ID/Status,** select 'Prospect' from the drop-down list, **OK**
2.	Merge the **Prospect** template with the active lookup, and display it in the word processor.	**Write, Mail Merge...,** choose **Current lookup** and click **Next>,** choose **Word Processor** and click **Next>,** use the **Browse...** button to select the **Prospect** letter you just created (if you didn't do the previous exercise, select any template), click **Finish.**
3.	View the results in your Word Processor.	Scroll down to view all of the letters. Notice how the inserted fields display the correct information for each contact in the body of the letter.
4.	Exit the word processor without saving your changes.	**File, Exit,** or click the Close button on the title bar. If you're prompted to save, click **No.**

*If you had printed the documents, a **Create History** dialog box would have displayed allowing you to add history to each record in the lookup. Whatever you type in the **Regarding:** box is what will be included in the **Notes/History** tab.*

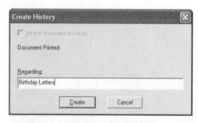

Depending upon the options you have selected in Edit, Preferences, you may also be asked to print Envelopes.

Hidden Text in Microsoft Word

If you are going to use Microsoft Word as your word processor for ACT!, you need to be aware that ACT! places a code (using the Hidden Text feature in Word) at the top of each ACT!/Word template.

Hidden text in Word is text that has been formatted with the Hidden attribute. This text will not print (unless you specifically tell Word otherwise) and will only display on the screen if you have non-printing characters displayed.

Before the template is merged with a contact, the code looks like this:

DatabaseID=[[DatabaseID]]|ContactID=[[ContactID]]|

After the template has been merge, the code appears like this:

DatabaseID=5259265A202058543E245820|ContactID=4A24332120202F26225 75720|

It is important that the hidden text is (or should be) at the top of each document template (that means no text, spaces or returns above it).

... display/hide non-printing characters

1. If non-printing characters are not displayed, click the **Show/Hide** button on the Word toolbar. ¶ This displays (and hides) non-printing characters (Hidden text is non-printing text).

2. To hide the non-printing characters, click the **Show/Hide** button again.

Practice: *Observing Hidden Template Text*

Try It...

Step	What to do	How to do it/Comments
1.	Make sure Word is being used as your ACT! word processor.	**Edit Preferences...** On the **General** tab, the **Word processor:** option should be set to **Microsoft Word 2000 or 2002(XP)**. If this is not the case, change it.
2.	Edit the basic **Letter** template.	**Write, Edit Document Template...**, choose **Letter** from the list of template files and click **Open**.
3.	Close the **Mail Merge Fields** dialog box and show the non-printing characters.	Show or hide non-printing characters by clicking the Show/Hide button on the Word toolbar.
4.	Observe the hidden text at the top of the document.	Regardless of how you may modify this template, this text must remain unedited and at the top of the document.
5.	Exit Word without saving changes.	We were just "window shopping."

So what's the point? The hidden text at the top of an Word template must not be altered or moved.

✔ This hidden text is used by ACT! to store information about the document's relationship with the Contact for whom the document was written.

✔ This information is used to create a history of the document creation, and is especially important for creating history of mail merges.

✔ If the hidden text is not located at the top of the document, ACT! cannot gather the information needed to record the document in the Contact history correctly.

✔ If this problem is not corrected on your document templates, it can cause corruption in the database. (We know it seems strange, but trust us...it happens!)

ACT!

Repairing Deleted Hidden Text

Problems most often occur when a user modifies an existing ACT! template and either deletes or places text in front of the hidden text. When this occurs you must fix it which, fortunately, is pretty simple.

...repair hidden text in an ACT! Word document template

How To...

1. Open the damaged template in Word. If the document contains any hidden text, select and delete it.

   Sometimes the hidden text can be accidentally repositioned elsewhere in the document. Don't try to move it back to the top, it's safer to get rid of it.

2. Return to ACT! and choose **File, New....** Select **Microsoft Word 2000 or 2002 (XP) Template** and click **OK**.

   A new, blank template is displayed. If non-printing characters are displayed, the hidden text shows at the top of the page.

3. Press **[Ctrl+A]**.

   This selects the entire document.

4. Choose **Edit, Copy** or the equivalent.

   Copy the data to the Windows Clipboard, then close the document.

5. Switch to the damaged template and press **[Ctrl+Home]**.

   This keystroke moves to the top of the document.

6. Choose **Edit, Paste** or the equivalent.

   Paste the copied data.

7. Save the template.

Practice: *Repairing Word Documents*

Step	What to do	How to do it/Comments
1.	Mail Merge "Corrupt Letter" to the Hoofers group and print the document.	Use the Mail Merge wizard to send the Corrupt Letter .
2.	Was history recorded on all records?	No
3.	Close the merged document and return to ACT!	**File, Close** and **[Alt+Tab]** back to ACT!
4.	Edit "Corrupt Letter" and repair the template.	Repair the template following the instructions above.
5.	Run the mail merge again and print.	
6.	Did the history record on all?	Yes

Review: *Getting It On Paper*

1.	Lookup contacts in our database that have May birthdays. Send them all the Birthday letter from all of us at Stars R Us ..\Other Templates\birthdayfromgroup.adt
2.	Edit the **Letter** template (save it as **Kitty**) to contain the following paragraph as the only paragraph in the body of the letter: **Since I know you are a big fan of Kitty Carlisle, I wanted to let you know about her celebrity roast next month. Call our office at *(insert you're My Record phone number here)* for details.**
3.	Lookup all contacts referred to us by Kitty Carlisle.
4.	Merge the **Kitty** template with the current lookup. You can preview on the screen (if you don't want to print).

Using E-mail

To understand how you can use the ACT! e-mail window as well as the Microsoft Outlook program with equal ease and efficiency, you will:

- ☑ Setup ACT! to work with your e-mail program

- ☑ Review the ACT! E-mail window

- ☑ Send and receive e-mail

- ☑ Create a new ACT! contact from an e-mail

- ☑ Attach e-mails to specific contacts or groups

- ☑ Learn the basics of designing an html template for e-mail merges.

- ☑ Understand the features that Outlook offers

You've Got Mail

E-Mail is becoming increasingly important in business. ACT! can make use of your existing e-mail system to send and receive messages directly from ACT!. You can integrate your existing e-mail program with ACT!, so that you can easily send and receive e-mail messages to and from contacts, record history of the contact, attach e-mail contents to a record, create a new ACT! record from an e-mail, e-mail merge announcements to your contacts and prospects (in color and with graphics, if you like), and so much more.

Setting Up Your E-mail System in ACT!

ACT! can work with quite a few e-mail systems to send e-mail to one of your contacts. ACT! supports Microsoft Outlook 2000-XP, Outlook Express 5.5 or later, Lotus Notes Mail 5.0 or later, Eudora, and Internet mail (*no, AOL or Hotmail is not in the list*).

If you normally use another e-mail (like GroupWise), you don't have to go out and buy another software to use ACT! and e-mail All you need is Internet access and a POP3 account. ACT! has a built-in SMTP/POP3 e-mail client that you can use to send and receive e-mail.

☞ *However, if you use an e-mail software other than Outlook or ACT!'s built-in e-mail client, some of ACT!'s e-mail features will not be available. For example, using other e-mail systems with ACT! will limit your messages and mail merges to plain text (no html).*

You probably already set up an e-mail system when you installed ACT!, however, let's look at the next section anyway to see how to configure it.

...set up and configure your e-mail system

1. **Edit, Preferences...,** click the **E-mail** tab.

    You may have already set up your e-mail when you first installed ACT! If an e-mail system is displayed as below, skip to step 4 to configure ACT!.

2. Click the **E-mail System Setup...** button. Put a check next to your e-mail system and click **Next>**.

    E-mail system
    Send e-mail to contacts using: | Microsoft Outlook ▼ | E-mail System Setup...

3. Fill out additional information as necessary and click **Finish.**

4. Click the **Composing Options...** button.

5. Select to **Send messages in: HTML** (for Outlook or ACT!) or **Plain Text** (for all other e-mail software or just because you like it better).

6. Leave the **Default priority** set to Normal. You can always change it for individual e-mails.

    (Change it to High only if you think Puff Daddy is a diet guru.)

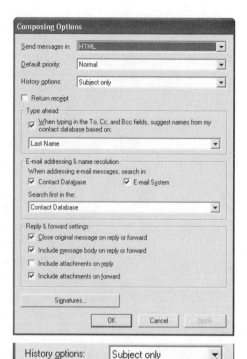

7. The **History options:** you select as a default will determine what is recorded to either a Contact record or the My Record (if the e-mail address is not found in ACT!).

    None would not record any history to the Contact's record (by default).

    Subject only records the Date, Time, Subject:, and Sender to the Contact's **Notes/History** tab.

    Subject +Message records the text of the message in addition to the info captured by the Subject only option. This option allows you to instantly view the text of the message and will be synced to remote users. (Your signature text is also included with the message.)

    Attach to Contact(s) saves a copy of the e-mail to the folder specified in Edit, Preferences, E-mail tab, Folder location and places a shortcut to the e-mail in the Contact's **Notes/History** tab. If the default folder is on your c:\ no other users can view the e-mail. If it is on a shared drive, others may be able to read the e-mail. Attachments do not sync.

8. Select the **Type ahead** default.

    When you enter a name in the To: field of a new e-mail, do you plan to enter the name starting with their Last Name, First Name, Company or their actual E-mail Address?

9.   In the **E-mail addressing & name resolution** section, specify if you want to search in the ACT! **Contact Database** as well as your defined **E-mail System** (such as Outlook)?

Also, select where you want ACT! to search for the e-mail address first...in your own database or in your E-mail system's address book.

10.   Change the **Reply & forward settings** options as desired.

11.   Click **Signatures...** to create one or more signatures for your e-mails.

☞   *Give each signature a descriptive name.*

   OK

Enter your **Signature text:** as desired.

☞   *Be sure to leave a blank line in front of your signature to separate it from the rest of your message.*

12.   **OK**

13.   Back in **Preferences**, you may want to put a check next to the **Empty Deleted Items folder on exit** option so that you don't have to manually delete the items.

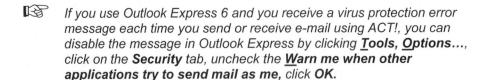

14.   In the **When connected notify me of new mail every __ minutes.** you may also want to increase the time interval for checking for new mail.

The default is every 3 minutes. Hey, do you really need to be that connected?

15.   **OK**

☞   *If you use Outlook Express 6 and you receive a virus protection error message each time you send or receive e-mail using ACT!, you can disable the message in Outlook Express by clicking **Tools, Options...**, click on the **Security** tab, uncheck the **Warn me when other applications try to send mail as me,** click **OK**.*

Practice: *Configure your e-mail*

Step	What to do	How to do it/Comments
1.	Enter your default signature.	**Edit, Preferences**, click **Composing Options** button, click **Signatures...**, enter your **Signature text:** as desired. **OK**
2.	Change the Preferences to your ...well...your preferences.	**OK OK**

Understanding the ACT! E-mail Window

ACT! has a separate e-mail window that displays when you click the **E-mail** button on the View Bar. While the Contact List, Groups, Task List, Calendar and Internet Services views open into windows inside the ACT! program, ACT! E-mail opens into it's own window with it's own button on the Windows Task Bar.

The E-mail window is divided into three panes: the Folder List, the Message Headers list and the Preview Pane. The Status Bar at the bottom of the window indicates the total number of messages and those that remain unread in the selected folder.

When you open **ACT! E-mail**, the Inbox for the E-mail System you selected displays your messages.

From this window you can read the

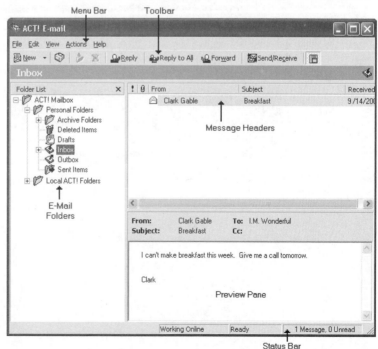

e-mails in your Inbox (or subfolders), create new e-mails, print a highlighted e-mail, move a selected e-mail to a different folder, delete an e-mail, Reply (or Reply to All), Forward, along with a few other amazing features.

Reading Your E-mail

This is so straight forward, it's almost too obvious to include in the book, however, we wanted to be sure you understand the Preview Pane options.

...read your e-mail from the ACT! E-mail Window

How To...

1. **View, E-mail** or click on the **E-mail** button

The **ACT! E-mail** window opens and displays the messages from your default e-mail system.

2. Select a message to view it in the Preview Pane

   or

   double-click it to open it into its own window.

 To hide the Preview Pane, click **View, Preview Pane** or click the **Toggle Preview Pane** icon.

 Of course you can always change the size of the Preview Pane by placing the mouse pointer over the middle splitter bar. When the mouse displays as a double-headed arrow. Click and drag the bar up or down.

Sending E-mail

There are actually three ways you can send an e-mail to an ACT! contact in your database and have that action recorded as **E-mail Sent** in the **Notes/History** tab. You can send the message from the ACT! E-mail window, from the ACT! Contact window, and from Outlook. Let's look at the first two now and we'll look at the Outlook option starting on page 203.

...send an e-mail from the ACT! e-mail window

HOW TO...

1. In the ACT! E-mail window, click the **New** icon on the toolbar or press **[Ctrl+N]** .

☞ *If you selected more than one e-mail in the E-mail System Setup (e.g. Outlook and Outlook Express), then you can change the e-mail package that will send the e-mail by choosing it in the From: drop-down list.*

2. **To...** Type the name (first or last based on the Type Ahead preference you selected earlier) of the person you wish to send the e-mail to in the **To...** area.

   Click the **To...** button to view the Address book to select additional recipients from **All Contacts**, **Current Lookup** or **Groups**

   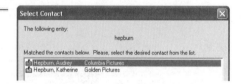

   Click the **To...** to enter a name in the **bcc** area.

   Or, just enter a valid e-mail address.

   If the contact is in your ACT! database, their e-mail address will be used and a history will be recorded.

   If there is more than one person with the same name, a dialog box will display allowing you to select the correct contact.

   If you enter an e-mail address belonging to one of your contacts, a history will still be created. Cool!

3. **[Tab]** to or click in the **Subject:** and fill in the text for the subject line.

4. **[Tab]** to or click in the text area of the e-mail to type your message.

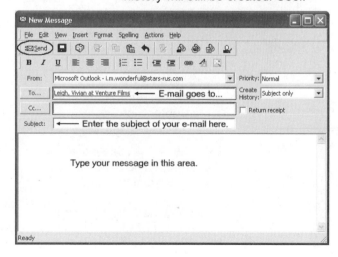

5. Format your message as desired.

You can change the font face, size, color … add bullets … hyperlinks … even pictures.

6. **Spelling, Check Document** or press **[F7]**.

Don't forget to Spell Check.

7. Click an Attachment icon to attach
   a **Contact** record,
   a **Group** of Contacts,
   or a **File**.

8. Change as desired, the
   Priority: option or
   Create History: option or
   Return receipt option.

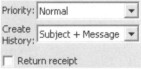

9. Click **Send** or press **[Ctrl+Enter]**.

Depending upon the **Create History** option you selected, a history of **E-mail Sent** is placed in the Contact's **Notes/History** tab.

☞ *If you selected more than one e-mail in the E-mail System Setup (e.g. Outlook and Outlook Express), then you can change the e-mail package that will send the e-mail by choosing it in the From: drop-down list.*

Practice:	Using the ACT! E-mail Window	
Step	**What to do**	**How to do it/Comments**
1.	Open ACT!'s E-mail window, if you haven't already.	**View, E-mail** or click on the **E-mail** button
2.	Send an e-mail to your personal e-mail address with a **Subject:** of : New Action Flick Enter a quick message about a new movie deal with your favorite action star. Select the history option of **Subject only**	Click the **New** icon on the toolbar. (If you entered your signature in the last Practice, it should display in the message pane.) Type your e-mail address in the **To...** area. Change the **Create History:** option to record history (whichever method you like). Fill out the rest of the e-mail and click **Send**.

Try it...

Step	What to do	How to do it/Comments
3.	Where was the history created?	In the first Review exercise, we asked you to create a record with your information in it. If you filled in an ACT! contact record including your e-mail address, this e-mail will be recorded to your Contact's **Notes/History** tab. If you didn't, the history was recorded on the "My Record" (I.M. Wonderful) contact. **[Alt+Tab]** back to ACT! or click the ACT! button on the Windows Task Bar and locate the history.

You can also send an e-mail message starting from the Contact record in ACT!

... send an e-mail from an ACT! contact record

1.	Lookup the Contact to whom you want to send the message	Verify that an e-mail address has been entered for the contact.
2.	Click the **Write E-mail** icon, or click on the **E-mail Address** field to start the process, or choose **Write, E-Mail Message** from the menu.	The ACT! E-mail window opens in the background and then the **New Message** window displays. The message is addressed to the current contact. To change to, or add, another recipient, click the **To...** (or **Cc...**) button and select from your contact list.
3.	Continue addressing, selecting options, and entering the message.	
4.	At the end of your message, enter your signature. You can type it manually, or press **Insert, Signature** to insert the signature you identified to ACT! (page 182).	Your signature text is not automatically inserted in the message when you start from the ACT! Contact unless you modify the emailbody.gmt template to include it.
5.	When you are finished click the **Send** button.	

Practice: *Sending an E-mail from the Contact*

Try It...

Step	What to do	How to do it/Comments
1.	There are no valid e-mails in the sample database. Lookup your real name if you entered it in the first Review exercise.	If your name is not in the Stars R Us database, input it now along with your real e-mail address. For this exercise, the name and address you entered is another premier movie agent.
2.	Start an e-mail with a subject of: **Interested in a Sequel?** Message of: **I understand you represent Arnold. Could we talk?** Insert your signature. Change the history to Subject + Message Now send it.	Click the **Write E-mail** icon or click on the **E-mail Address** field to start the process. The **New Message** window displays. Enter the subject and message as described. At the bottom of the message click **Insert, Signature**. Change the history option as indicated. When finished, click **Send**
3.	Display the **Notes/History** tab if necessary and notice how the e-mail was recorded.	The subject followed by the complete text of the message was recorded in the **Notes/History** tab.

 *If you select the History option of **Attach to Contact(s)** and later want to read the e-mail, you can view the **Notes/History** tab and double-click the graphic to the left of the item you want to read. This will open the message into a message window.*

	Date ▽	Time ▽	Type	Regarding
✉	12/11/2001	9:21 PM	E-mail Message	Subject: Conditions of Movie Deal

Signatures

Don't you hate receiving e-mails from people who forget to include their signature and you have to figure out from their e-mail address who they are (and sometimes that isn't easy either)? It's always a good idea to include your signature on each e-mail that you send out.

E-mail signatures are automatically added to any new message created by clicking the **New** icon in the ACT! e-mail client. However, a signature is not automatically inserted into a message that is started from the Contact's record in ACT!.

When you write an e-mail message from the Contact record, ACT! is using an e-mail template (similar to the way it uses a Letter template when you are writing a letter). You can edit the basic e-mail template to automatically include your signature.

...include a signature on the basic HTML e-mail template

1. In ACT!, click **Write, Edit Graphical (HTML) E-mail Template...**

2. Select **emailbody.gmt** and click **Open**

    Regardless of the Word Processor you selected to use with ACT!, e-mail templates are opened into the ACT! Word Processor window, with the Mail Merge Fields Dialog box displayed.

3. Drag the **Mail Merge Fields** dialog box to the lower right corner of the window if necessary.

    Click on the Mail Merge Fields title bar and drag the dialog box to the lower right side of your screen so you can see the blank e-mail template.

4. From the Formatting bar, select the font you would like to use for your default message text.

    Arial 10 is the standard font used in most e-mail software.

5. Click in the Word Processor window. Press **[Enter]** twice.

    [Enter] twice to place a space between the text and signature.

6. In the **Mail Merge Fields** dialog, click the **My Record field** option and select "Contact" (or First Name) from the **Field:** list.

   Click **Insert**

   Press **[Enter]** and then add other fields as desired (Company, Title, Phone, etc.)

7. Close the window and click **Yes** to save the changes.

If you are the only one using the database, you can just type your signature line. If you will be sharing the database and templates with others, use **Mail Merge Fields** to insert fields into the templates so that your entire team can also use the default e-mail template.

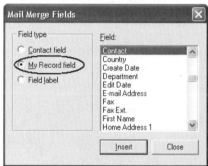

Practice: *Send another e-mail*

Step	What to do	How to do it/Comments
1.	Write another e-mail to this premier movie agent (yourself) and notice how the signature displays.	
2.	Tab to or click in the message body and enter some text to see how the signature is separated from the message.	This is a test.|
3.	Close the e-mail without sending. This message is too boring. Let's dress it up a bit.	I.M. Wonderful President Stars R Us 210-555-1000

 If you reply to an e-mail from the ACT! E-mail window, your signature is not automatically added. After you have completed your reply text, you can insert the signature you entered (in Edit, Preferences, E-mail tab, Composing Options) by clicking on Insert, Signature.

Formatting E-Mail Templates

When you originally set up your e-mail composing options (page 181), you selected whether you wanted to send your e-mails in **Plain text** or **HTML**. Plain text messages include no formatting, but you can change the look of your messages if you selected the HTML option.

You can format your e-mail messages with numbering, bullets, alignment, and different font types, styles, and colors. You can also insert pictures and hyperlinks.

...create an e-mail merge template

How To...

1. **Write, Edit Graphical (HTML) E-mail Template...**

   ☞ *Not all e-mail software will support the HTML formats.*

2. Select **emailbody.gmt**

   or

   double-click the **Other Templates** folder to select a pre-formatted template that comes with ACT!

   Click **Open**

   Regardless of the Word Processor you selected to use with ACT!, the e-mail templates are opened into the ACT! Word Processor window.

3. Before starting changes, click **File, Save As,** enter a filename, **Save**

4. Edit the template as desired, adding mail merge fields, graphics, formatted text, hyperlinks.

   To review how to insert mail merge fields, see page 167.

5. Save your changes and close the document.

Insert Hyperlink

Just typing the web address in a template will not make it clickable when the template is merged.

...attach hyperlinks to an e-mail message

How To...

1. While editing the Graphical E-mail Template, position the insertion point.

2. **Insert, Hyperlink...**

    Click at the end of the http:// text in the **URL:** field and type the web site you want to include in the template.

    You must include "http://" in the URL.

3. **OK**

☞   *Now if you don't want the http:// to display, you can backspace over it in the template.*

Practice: *Formatting Our Signature Line*

Step	What to do	How to do it/Comments
1.	Modify the signature on the default e-mail template. Change the default font for your name to Monotype Corsiva, 18 point, Blue Insert your Title if necessary and make it Arial Italic 10. Insert your Company's web address as a Hypertext link. ☞ *Since we are working on your live system, perhaps you should enter your real web address here instead of the Stars R Us address.*	*<My:Contact:26>* <My:Title:46> <My:Company:25> www.cornerstonesolutions.com <My:Phone:35> *When you want to see your star on the Walk of Fame...* Select your name and click **Format, Font...** Make the Font, Style, Size and Color changes. Do the same for your title. To insert your web address, click **Insert, Hyperlink...**, click at the end of the http:// and type your web address, click **OK**. Now you can backspace over the http:// if you like.
2.	Save and close the template.	
3.	Write another e-mail template to see how it works.	The web address will not be clickable until you actually send the e-mail. You will probably want to send the e-mail and test it before you start to use it in real life.

Try It...

Send/Receive Button

Your system is already set up to automatically send any e-mail that is waiting in the Outbox and to check for any incoming e-mail at specified time intervals. If you are using Internet Mail or Outlook Express, the Send/Receive button on the top of the **ACT! E-mail** window performs an immediate Send/Receive when you are connected (instead of waiting for the next timed Send/Receive.)

If you are using Microsoft Outlook or Lotus Notes, clicking the **Send/Receive** button refreshes the display of message headers in the ACT E-mail Inbox, making sure that the same E-mails display in both the ACT! E-mail Inbox and the Outlook or Notes Inbox.

Creating a Contact from an E-mail

When you receive an e-mail message from a new prospect inquiring about your services, ACT! makes it easy to quickly create an ACT! contact in your database starting from the current e-mail.

...create a contact from an e-mail message

How To...

1. In the **ACT! E-mail Window**, double-click the e-mail to open it into its own window. Then, drag it off to the side.

   This step is not really necessary...you can actually start with step 2. However you may find it helpful in step 4.

2. In the **ACT! E-mail Window**, click on the e-mail that contains the new contact for ACT!

   Only the **Name** and the **E-Mail:** will be automatically selected from the currently selected e-mail.

3. **Actions, Create Contact from Sender...**

    *You can also right-click the e-mail and select **Create Contact from Sender...***

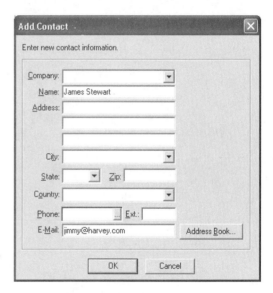

4. The name listed in From will be placed in the **Name:** field.

    *If the name is **jimmy@harvey.org**, then "jimmy" will be placed in the field. If the sender's complete name is listed, then it will be placed in the field.*

   Enter any additional information you have.

   If you opened the e-mail into a separate window, you can copy and paste the pieces of address information into the Add Contact dialog.

5. **OK**

   The contact information is added to the currently open ACT! database.

Practice: *Adding a Contact from an E-mail*

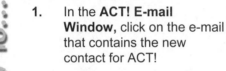

Step	What to do	How to do it/Comments
1.	Locate a contact in your Inbox and add the contact to the Stars R Us database.	You can only accomplish this from the ACT! E-mail window. Follow the procedure outlined above to add a contact to the database.
2.	Look up the contact in ACT! to verify that the contact was entered into the Stars R Us database.	Cool…there it is.

Creating an Activity from an E-Mail

When you receive an e-mail message from a client that requires a follow-up, you can quickly create an activity from within the e-mail window.

…create an activity from an e-mail message

1. In the **ACT! E-mail Window,** click on the e-mail that contains the new contact for ACT!

2. **Actions, Create Activity from Message…**

   *You can also right-click the e-mail and select **Create Activity from Message…***

   A Schedule Activity dialog box will display. If ACT! could locate the contact in your database, their name will display in the **With:** area. Otherwise the activity will be scheduled with you're my Record.

3. Schedule the activity as desired.

4. **OK**   The activity is scheduled.

☞ *If you do not see this option, be sure that you have updated to the most recent version of ACT!. This feature was included with 6.0.3 You can update your version by clicking on **Help, Check for Updates**,*

Attach an E-mail to a Contact

When you receive an e-mail from one of your contacts that contains information that might be important to save, ACT! makes it easy to attach the contents of that e-mail to the Contact's record.

...attach an e-mail to a contact from the ACT! E-mail window

HOW TO...

1. In the **ACT! E-mail Window,** right-click on the e-mail and select **Attach to Contact...**

   You can also click **Actions, Attach to Contact...**

2. Type the...

   last name, first name

   of the contact to quickly locate the contact in the list.

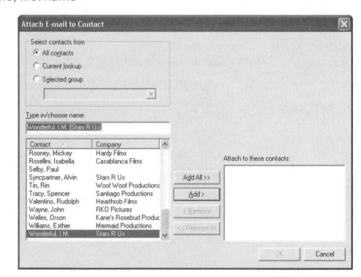

3. Select the contact and click **Add>**

4. Click **OK**.

5. If there was an attachment included with the e-mail, you will be prompted to save the attachment as well.

   If you want to be prompted each time you attach an e-mail,

   uncheck **Don't ask me again**

   and then click

   Yes to save the attachment or   **No** to skip saving the attachment

*You can view the attached e-mail in the **Notes/History** tab. Double-click the graphic to the left of the item you want to read. This will open the message into a message window.*

	Date ▽	Time ▽	Type	Regarding
✉	12/11/2001	9:21 PM	E-mail Message	Subject: Conditions of Movie Deal

Attachments are saved separately from the message text in the **\Email\Local ACT! Folders** folder. If you left the check mark in the **Don't ask me again** option the first time you attach an e-mail, attachments will always be saved (or not) depending upon whether you checked Yes or No. If you want to prompted again, click **Edit, Preferences**, click the **E-mail** tab. Change the default option in the **Attaching messages to contacts** section.

Practice: *Attaching an E-mail to a Contact*

Step	What to do	How to do it/Comments
1.	Attach the same e-mail that you just used to create a new contact in ACT! to the contact you created.	In the ACT! E-mail window, right-click the e-mail you used to create your new contact, **Attach to Contact...**, select the contact name, click **Add>**, click **OK**.
2.	Back in ACT!, locate the attached e-mail and open it.	Open the **Notes/History** tab and locate the attached e-mail message and double-click the graphic to the left of the message.

Try It...

E-Mail Merge

Whether you have a specific message you want to communicate to one or more contacts at a time, ACT! makes that process a snap. We've already seen how easy it is to perform a Mail Merge to Word. The process is nearly identical for E-mail Merges.

In sending out preformatted templates to your ACT! contacts you can send an e-mail to one Contact, a lookup, or a group. You can also choose to include attachments with your e-mail merges. If you send an e-mail using the Mail Merge feature, an individual e-mail will be sent to everyone in the current lookup. If you want to send a single e-mail with everyone's name in the bcc area of the e-mail, it is sent straight from the e-mail window. Let's start with the Mail Merge.

We already created a custom e-mail template (page 191) and we talked about inserting ACT! fields into a template when we were designing Word templates (page 167). Let's take a brief look at some of the templates that came with ACT!

...modify a graphical merge template

How To...

1. **Write, Edit Graphical (HTML) E-mail Template...**

   ☞ *Not all e-mail software will support the HTML formats.*

2. Double-click the **Other Templates** folder to select a pre-formatted template that comes with ACT!

   Click **Open**

   Regardless of the Word Processor you selected to use with ACT!, the e-mail templates are opened into the ACT! Word Processor window.

3. Before starting changes, click **File, Save As,** enter a filename, **Save**

4. Edit the template as desired, adding mail merge fields, graphics, formatted text, hyperlinks.

   It is best to only try to edit the text in these pre-formatted templates. Editing the graphics in the ACT! Word Processor window is difficult at best.

5. Save your changes and close the document.

The templates that came with ACT! are actually HTML files. If you were to open the **bday.gmt** template in an HTML editor like FrontPage or DreamWeaver, it would look like this. If you are familiar with creating HTML documents in one of these editors, you can create your own custom templates to use with the ACT! Mail Merge files. You need only save the file with a .gmt extension.

```
<!DOCTYPE HTML PUBLIC "-//W3C//DTD HTML 4.0 Transitional//EN">
<HTML><HEAD><TITLE>Untitled Document</TITLE>
<META http-equiv=Content-Type content="text/html; charset=iso-8855
<META content="MSHTML 5.50.4207.2601" name=GENERATOR></HEAD>
<BODY text=#000000 bgColor=#ffffff>
<TABLE cellSpacing=0 cellPadding=0 width=600 border=0>
  <TBODY>
  <TR vAlign=top>
    <TD width=125 rowSpan=4><IMG style="WIDTH: 125px; HEIGHT: 673p
      height=673 alt="" hspace=0
      src="
C:\Program Files\ACT\Template\Other Templates\ind_bday_1_left.jpg
    " width=125 border=0></TD>
    <TD width=15> </TD>
    <TD width=425>
```

 You can also copy and paste html code into the Signature line of the Composing Options in Edit, Preferences. This would allow you to reference pictures from a website instead of inserting them in the signature line. (Only an HTML junkie would understand the previous sentence ;-)

... send individually addressed e-mail to each contact in lookup

1.   Perform a lookup that displays the contacts you wish to receive your e-mail.

2.   Choose **Write, Mail Merge....**

     The **Mail Merge Wizard** starts.

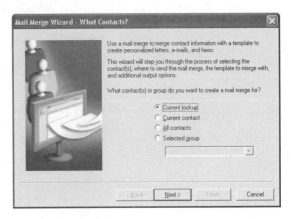

3. Select **What Contacts** you want to create the e-mail merge for and click **Next >**.

You can merge the **Current lookup**, the **Current contact, All contacts** or a **Selected group**. Use the **Current contact** if you are testing the template.

4. Select the method of delivery in the **Send How?** option.

   Click **E-mail** option *(each contact must have a valid e-mail address and you must have e-mail setup to work with ACT! for this to work)*.

   Click **Next >**.

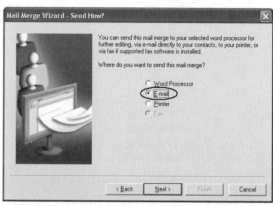

5. Click **Browse...** to locate the template to use in the E-Mail Merge. Select a template and click **Open**.

    Even if your e-mail will send **Text only**, *the graphical templates will be converted.*

   Click **Next >**.

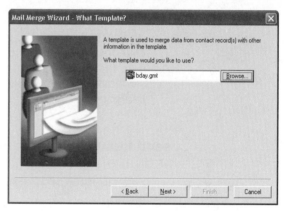

6. Select how you would
    like to **Create History:**
    for the mail merge
    (None, Subject only,
    Subject + Message, or
    Attach to Contact(s)),

    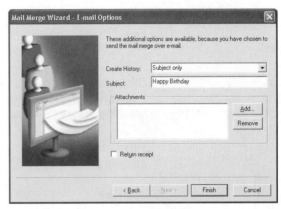

    Enter a **Subject:** for the
    e-mails,

    Add... Attachments as
    desired,

    Check the **Return receipt** if desired.

    Finish

7. **OK** to the confirmation message.

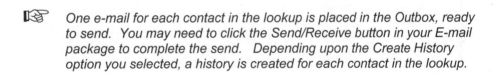 *One e-mail for each contact in the lookup is placed in the Outbox, ready
to send. You may need to click the Send/Receive button in your E-mail
package to complete the send.   Depending upon the Create History
option you selected, a history is created for each contact in the lookup.*

...send only one e-mail with everyone's address in the bcc area

1. In the ACT! E-mail window, click
    New to start a new message.

    You can't create a single e-mail
    containing multiple e-mails
    addresses in the Outlook window
    using your ACT! database.

2. Click the **To...** button to access the
    Address Book.

3. In the **Select from:** drop-down box,
    select from **All Contacts, Current
    Lookup**, or **Groups**.

    Whichever option you choose, the
    associated names are displayed
    in the pane below.

4. Select the Contacts (click on the first name and **[Shift+click]** on the last name) or Group and

Click either the **To->**, **Cc->**, or **Bcc->** button, to copy the names to the selected Message Recipients area.

Be sure to include at least one name in the **To->** area.

Unless you want the others in your list to see each other's e-mail addresses, you should use the **bcc** area.

5. Fill out the rest of the e-mail as desired and click **Send**

Since the Stars R Us database doesn't really have any valid e-mail addresses, we won't do any practice sessions on either of these two procedures.

ACT! Can Make You Glad You Use Outlook

If you use Microsoft Outlook as your e-mail software, you can accomplish most of the same features within the Outlook window that you can from ACT!'s E-mail window.

✔ You cannot send to a lookup/group from Outlook,

✔ You cannot send a Contact or Group as an attachment, and

✔ You cannot create a Contact or an Activity from an e-mail.

However, for either of these functions, you can use the ACT! E-mail window and then go back to using Outlook for your daily e-mail tasks. If you are using Outlook, let's set it up to take advantage of all the productivity features that ACT! offers.

Adding ACT! Address Book to Outlook

If you are using Outlook as your E-mail, you can add your ACT! contacts as an Address Book. The ACT! Address Book will display the Contact name, company name, and e-mail address. Contacts without an e-mail address in ACT! will not show up in the Outlook Address Book. As new contact's (with e-mail addresses) are added to your ACT! database, they will also appear in the Outlook Address Book.

...add your ACT! contacts' e-mail addresses to Outlook

	Outlook 2002	Outlook 2000*
1.	**Tools, E-mail Accounts...**	**Tools, Services... (or Accounts)**
2.	Select **Add a new directory or address book** and click **Next>**	Click the **Services** tab, if necessary.
3.	Select **Additional Address Books** and click **Next>**	Click **Add...**
	☞ *To edit the address book later, select View or change option.*	☞ *To edit the address book later, select Properties.*
4.	Select **ACT! Address Book** and click **Next>**	Select **ACT! Address Book** and click **OK**

How To...

Then...

5. Use the **Browse...** button to select an ACT! database whose e-mail addresses will be included in the Outlook Address book. (You can add up to 3 ACT! databases.)

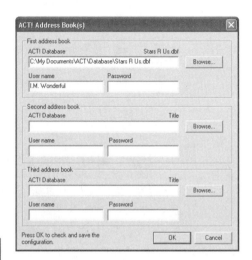

6. Enter your User Name and any associated Password.

7. Enter up to two other databases as desired.

8. Click **OK** until you are finished.

9. Restart Outlook to complete the process. The **Attach to ACT! Contact(s)** icon will be added to the Outlook toolbar.

You must be using Outlook 2000 Corporate or Workgroup mode (not Internet Mail Only) to make these changes (See Help, About Microsoft Outlook to verify your setup options). Go to the support.act.com to find out how to switch from Internet Mail Only to Corporate or Workgroup mode in Microsoft Outlook.

...make your ACT! database the Outlook default

1. In Outlook, click on the Address Book icon. You can also click **Tools, Address Book...** to open the list.

2. In the Address Book, click **Tools, Options...**.

3. Change the **Show this address list first:** option to you preferred **ACT! Address Book**   If you identified more than one ACT! database to Outlook (page 203), select the preferred one.

4. **OK**

Setting Up the Default History Option for Outlook

In an earlier practice, we set up the default **Create History** option in ACT!'s Composing Options dialog (page 181). The Outlook Create History option must be set up separately and will be used only

✔ When you start the e-mail from within the Outlook window, and

✔ Where the e-mail address is found in your ACT! database.

By default, Outlook will instruct ACT! to record the date, time, and subject of each e-mail that you send meeting the previous two conditions. However you can change the default history option.

...set up a default history option for Outlook e-mail

1. In Outlook, **Tools, Options...**

2. Click on the **Mail Format** tab, and verify that the **Use Microsoft Word to edit e-mail messages** is not checked.

   ☞ *In order to record history in ACT!, you cannot use Microsoft Word as your e-mail editor in Outlook.*

3. While still in the **Options** dialog box, click the **ACT!** tab.

4. Select a default history.

   Date, time, and subject records to the Contact's **Notes/History** tab (the default).

   Date, time, subject, and message text records the text of the message in addition to the info captured by the first option. This option syncs messages to remote users. (Your signature is also included.)

   Entire e-mail as an attachment saves a copy of the e-mail to the folder specified in Edit, Preferences, E-mail tab, Folder location and places a shortcut to the e-mail in the Contact's **Notes/History** tab. Attachments do not sync. To review the message, double-click the icon to the left of the message in the Contact's **Notes/History** tab.

Do not save e-mail to history (you can probably figure out this option).

5.   **OK**

Sending an E-mail from Outlook

To send an e-mail from Outlook, click the **New** icon in Outlook. In the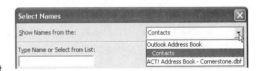
To... text area, you can …

✔   manually enter an e-mail address,

✔   type a person's name exactly as it appears in your ACT! database (if you set up an ACT! Address Book as discussed on page 203), or

✔   click the **To....** button to access the ACT! database to look up the names. If the correct ACT! Address Book is not displayed in the upper-right corner, click on the drop-down arrow to switch to that address book. In the **Type Name or Select from List:** box, type the contact's first and last name as it appears in your database. As you type their name, the list will scroll to that spot in the database. Double-click a name to select it and place it in the **To->** box. Repeat as necessary for other contacts, then click **OK**.

Continue with the e-mail as you normally would. Before sending it, change the ACT! History option (on the toolbar) as desired.   This ACT! History toolbar allows you to change (from the default) how Outlook records the e-mail history to the ACT! database. Click on the drop-down arrow to the right of the history option and select the type of history that will be recorded for the current e-mail.

☞   *If you do not see the ACT! History toolbar, right-click on the current Outlook toolbar and click ACT! History (you can also make this change from the menu by clicking **View, Toolbars**).*

☞   *Outlook has an AutoComplete feature. If you have sent an e-mail to someone before (using Outlook), it will use the e-mail address that Outlook associates with that name, before it goes to the ACT! database to find the correct e-mail address. If it uses it's own address (instead of ACT!'s), no history will be recorded to the contact's record. As you start* *to send e-mail from Outlook (after you have defined the ACT! 6 Address Book), you will want to delete the AutoComplete suggestions until you are relatively sure that it is searching the ACT! database instead of it's own. (To delete the suggestion when it displays, use the arrow key to scroll to the name and press the **[Delete]** key on the keyboard...then complete the entry of the name.) This process will force Outlook to look in the ACT! address book to find the e-mail address that matches the name you just entered. Otherwise, no history will be recorded.*

Attaching Outlook E-Mail to ACT! contacts

Once you have added the ACT! Address Book to Outlook, you can attach an Outlook e-mail message to a Contact's **Notes/History** tab. (You can do this from either the ACT! E-mail window or from Outlook.)

...attach an Outlook e-mail to an ACT! contact

1. In Outlook, click on the message you want to attach to the contact.

2. Click on the **Attach to ACT! Contact(s)** icon.

3. Select the database that contains the Contact.

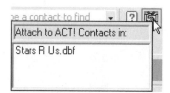

4. In the **Type in /choose name** area, begin to type the last name of the contact.

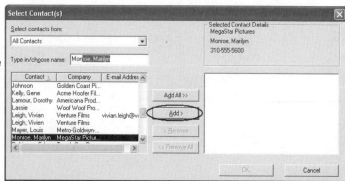

5. When the correct contact is highlighted, click **Add>**

6. **OK**   The e-mail message will display in the
                                              contact's **Notes/History** tab as an
                                              attachment.

When you attach an e-mail to a contact (or group), the message text is stored as a file in the default e-mail folder (C:\My Documents\ACT\Email). You can change the default by clicking **Edit, Preferences**, click on the **E-mail** tab, change the default folder location, **OK**. When storing messages which include an attachment, the attachment is always saved with the message.

Internet Services

To see how we can more completely integrate our ACT! and Internet environments, we will…

- ☑ Familiarize ourselves with ACT!'s Internet Services Browser Window.

- ☑ Use the **Online** menu option to interface with the Internet.

- ☑ Quickly and easily attach web pages to contacts in our database.

Internet Services

ACT!'s Internet services window provides you with access to the web. Because the browser window is incorporated into ACT!, it is tightly integrated with your ACT! data so that you can instantly display web sites stored in the ACT! **Web Site** field, as well as attach relevant web pages to contact records without ever leaving ACT!

There are two primary ways of displaying the **Internet Services** Web browser window

...access the Internet Services Web browser

1. Click the **Internet Services** button on the navigation bar. A browser window will be displayed with the ACT! website as the starting page.

Internet
Services

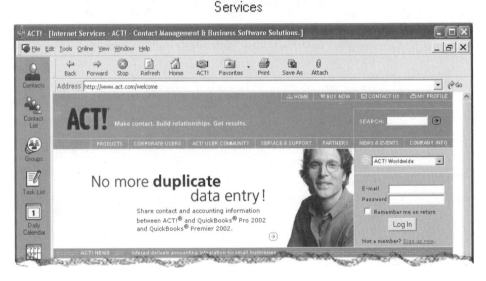

Reviewing the Internet Services Window

The Internet Services window has much in common with the Microsoft Internet Explorer web browser.

You will see many of the same buttons in both programs. You are probably already used to using the **Back** and **Forward** buttons to move through your web searches. The **Stop**, **Refresh**, and **Print** buttons also work the same in both the ACT! Internet Services view and Internet Explorer. But the "sharing" does not end there...

The **Home** button will take you to your currently defined Internet Explorer Home page.

A button that is not shared by Internet Explorer is the **ACT!** button. Clicking this button will take you to the ACT! website. This way you can have both easy access to the valuable information on the ACT! web site, and still access your normal home page.

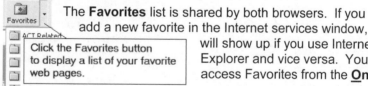 The **Favorites** list is shared by both browsers. If you add a new favorite in the Internet services window, it will show up if you use Internet Explorer and vice versa. You can also access Favorites from the **Online** menu.

Back in the Contact view, if the contact has a URL entered in their **Web Site** field, when your mouse pointer moves over the field, it displays as a hand. If you click on the address, the web site opens into the ACT! Internet Services window.

| Web Site | www.stars-rus.com |
| E-mail Address | johnwayne@rko.com |

You can also type an e-mail address in the Address bar to access any web site.

Address | http://www.cnn.com/

 We love this feature of ACT!. The only hard thing about using the Internet Services Web Browser is remembering to close the window, not the program. ;-)

Adding to Your Favorites

Any time you find yourself browsing the web, you may find a web page that you want to add to your favorites. If you happen to be using the Internet Services browser window (and why wouldn't you?) you can add the current page to favorites quite easily...

... add a web page to Favorites

How To...

1. Display the web page in the ACT! Internet Services browser.

   Click on the Web site link or type the site in the **Address** bar.

2. On a blank part of the web page, right-click and select **Add to Favorites...**

   ☞ *If you click on a graphic, it will add the graphic instead of the web page.*

3. If the suggested name is not to your liking, change it.

   ☞ *You can click the **Create in>>** button to display a list of the folders in your Favorites list and place this new favorite in one of them*

4. Click **OK**.

   The site appears in the Favorites list of both ACT! *and* Internet Explorer (in case you ever go back there again).

☞ *Although you can add Favorites from the ACT! Web browser, you can only edit or delete them in Microsoft Internet Explorer.*

Practice: *Playing on the Web*

Try It...

Step	What to do	How to do it/Comments
1.	Display the ACT! Internet Services browser window.	Click the **Internet Services** button on the Navigation bar. Internet Services
2.	Note the web page that was displayed.	It is the ACT! website home page. A great place to get help, updates, information and add-ins for ACT!

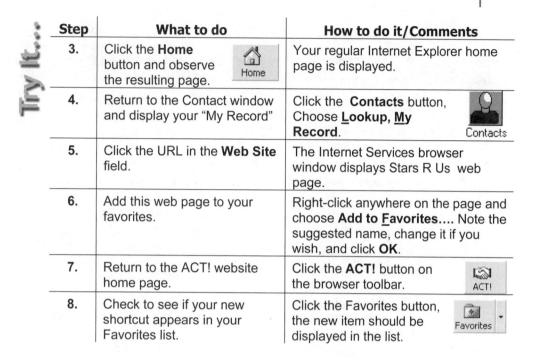

Step	What to do	How to do it/Comments
3.	Click the **Home** button and observe the resulting page.	Your regular Internet Explorer home page is displayed.
4.	Return to the Contact window and display your "My Record"	Click the **Contacts** button, Choose **Lookup, My Record**.
5.	Click the URL in the **Web Site** field.	The Internet Services browser window displays Stars R Us web page.
6.	Add this web page to your favorites.	Right-click anywhere on the page and choose **Add to Favorites…**. Note the suggested name, change it if you wish, and click **OK**.
7.	Return to the ACT! website home page.	Click the **ACT!** button on the browser toolbar.
8.	Check to see if your new shortcut appears in your Favorites list.	Click the Favorites button, the new item should be displayed in the list.

The Online Menu

The **Online** menu provides access to several useful internet related features. When you display the **Online** menu three submenus are available to you.

✔ **ACT!** - This submenu displays several ACT! related links.

✔ **Favorites** – this is the same list you will find in both Internet Explorer and ACT!'s Internet Services browser.

✔ **Internet Links** – These are links to websites, but unlike simple favorites, they can interact with the data on the current contact record. The **OneLook Dictionary** net link, for example can lookup a word from any editable field.

Online, ACT!

The **ACT!** submenu provides many valuable links to ACT! related websites (including a link you can use to buy this book… but if you're reading this you already know how to do that don't you?) If you need help or information about ACT! and it's features this can be a good place to start.

You must have access to the Internet to complete the next exercise.

Try It...

	Step	What to do	How to do it/Comments
	Practice: *Check out the ACT! Community*		

Step	What to do	How to do it/Comments
1.	Select the **ACT! User Community** from the ACT! submenu	Choose **O**nline, AC**T**!, ACT! **U**ser **Community**
2.	Can you locate a certified consultant in your area?	Click the **ACT! Certified Consultants** link to display an introductory page. Now use the drop down lists on the page to locate consultants where you live.
3.	Try some of the other **ACT!** links	A wealth of help and information is but a mouse click away!

 Right below ACT! Certified Consultants was User groups. Why not see if there is an ACT! User group in your area. Local ACT! User groups hold regular meetings and can be a great place to go to improve your skills, expand your knowledge, and get ideas from other ACT! users on how to make ACT! work even better for you.

Online, Internet **L**inks

A few **Internet Links** ship with ACT!. An example of an "Internet Link" is the **OneLook Dictionary**. This link can take any highlighted word from an editable field, and link you to a number of online dictionaries to get the word defined.

... Use the OneLook Dictionary Internet Link

How To...

1.	Display the Contact window if necessary.	Click the Contact button on the navigation bar. Contacts
2.	Select the word you wish to define.	You can use any word in an editable field but If the field contains more than one word, be sure to highlight the one you wish to define. *You cannot lookup words in Note or history entries.*

3.   Choose **O**nline, Internet **L**inks, **O**neLook Dictionary

Shortly a page with links to several different web based dictionaries is displayed.

4.   Click one of the links to the word to display it's definition.

OneLook doesn't define the word, it links you to sources for the definition.

Practice: *Define Your Terms!*

Step	What to do	How to do it/Comments
1.	Display the Contact window if necessary and lookup Humphrey Bogart.	Click the Contact button on the navigation bar, then use the Lookup menu to locate Last name, **Bogart**. Contacts
2.	Highlight the word **prodigal** in the **Last Results** field.	Double click on the word itself to select it, or drag your mouse across it. We want to be sure of the meaning here.
3.	Choose **O**nline, Internet **L**inks, **O**neLook Dictionary	The Internet Services web should shortly display several web based sources for the selected word.
4.	Click on one of the links to the word *prodigal* to display that dictionary's definition of the word.	OneLook dictionary gives you access to a number of online dictionary services.

You may have more internet links in your menu. Often they are designed to read specific fields in the current ACT! Contact record and pass that information on to the linked website. If you have other items in the Internet Links submenu, give them a try... something wonderful might happen!

Attaching Web Pages

It is likely that one day you will come across a web page, whose content has a great deal of relevance to one of your contacts. Perhaps it's a news article about one of your clients or their organization. Perhaps you want to maintain quick contact with a competitors web page.

While you could add such a page to your Favorites and then you could find it again when you need it, this has several disadvantages.

✔ As you find more and more of this type of web page, your Favorites list will quickly grow to the point where it is unmanageable.

✔ Adding a page to Favorites does not associate it with a specific contact.

✔ Favorites are links to the web pages and unless you choose to make them available offline, they may no longer exist when want to see them.

☞ *By attaching a copy of the web page to the contact record itself, you solve all three issues. It does not clutter the Favorites list, it is attached to the contact record and it is an offline copy of the web page, so it will always be available.*

... attach a Web page to a contact record

1. In the ACT! Internet Services browser, display the web page you wish to attach.

    Click on the Web site link field or type the site in the **Address** bar in the Internet Services view.

2. Click the **Attach** button on the **Internet Services** browser toolbar.

    The **Attach Web Page to Contact(s)** dialog box will be displayed

You can choose from **All contacts**, the **current lookup** or select an existing **group**. The contacts will display in the list at the bottom left corner of the dialog.

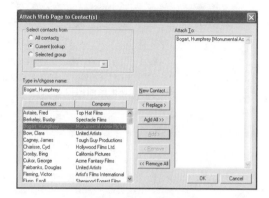

3. Locate and select the contact to which you wish to attach the page. You may specify multiple contacts if you want to attach the page to all of them.

To select a range of contacts, click to select the first one, then hold **[Shift]** and click the last one. All contacts in between will be selected. To select random contacts, click to select the first contact, then hold the **[Ctrl]** button as you click each additional one.

4. Click **Add>**

All selected contacts are added to the **Attach To:** list.

5   Repeat as necessary and click **OK**.

A copy of the web page is saved to disk and attached to the specified contact record(s).

☞   *When you attach a Web page to a contact. It is saved using the Multipurpose Internet Mail Extension format (with a .mht file extension). This file is self contained and does not require a link to the web to view. The .mht file type can be viewed in either in the Internet Services browser or in Internet Explorer.*

Practice: *Attach Bogie's Page*

Step	What to do	How to do it/Comments
1.	Display the Contact window if necessary and lookup Humphrey Bogart.	Click the Contact button on the navigation bar, then use the Lookup menu to locate Last name, **Bogart**. (if you're having a déjà vu right now, don't worry, you *have* done this before.) Contacts
2.	With Bogie still displayed in the contact window, display the Internet Services browser window.	Click the **Internet Services** button on the navigation bar. Internet Services
3.	In the address bar, type the web address below and press **[Enter]**. You should display a web page on Bogart himself.	Web addresses are case sensitive so make sure you include the capital letters exactly as they appear below.
	http://www.reelclassics.com/Actors/Bogie/bogie.htm	
4.	Attach this page to Bogie's contact record.	Click the **Attach** button on the Internet Services browser toolbar, select the **Current Lookup** option to display only Mr. Bogart's record in the list on the left, and click **Add All>>** to place his name in the **Attach To:** list. Click **OK**.
5.	Return to the Contact window and display the **Notes/History** tab on Bogart's record.	Click the Contacts button on the navigation bar, click the **Notes/History** tab if it is not displayed. You should see the newly attached web page at the top of the list. Contacts
6.	Double click the icon for the attached page.	The same page you had previously displayed is still displayed, or is it?

Filter	☑ Notes	☑ Histories	☑ Attachments	☑ E-mail	Insert Note	Detai
Date /	Time /	Type	Regarding	Record Manage
7/25/2002	4:30 PM	Attachment	Web Page Attachment	I.M. Wonderful

Double click the icon to open the attachment.

Step	What to do	How to do it/Comments
7.	Observe the Address bar on the browser.	This page is not on the web. It is stored on your hard drive so it will always be accessible to you.
8.	Return to the Contacts window.	

Try It...

Review: *Using Internet Services*

1.	Use ACT!'s Internet Services window to view today's headlines using a major news source such as www.cnn.com or www.nytimes.com
2.	Attach one of the sites to your own record so that you can click it every morning to review the news on line.
3.	Use the Online menu to access ACT!'s Technical Support page. Click the Knowledge Base option to look up information on troubleshooting your Palm Pilot link with ACT!

Try It...

Sales Opportunities

It's important to keep track of the opportunities available to your company. To understand this valuable tool, you will:

- ☑ Create new and track existing sales opportunities.

- ☑ Edit and update opportunities as the deal progresses.

- ☑ Use reports to display the status of opportunities.

Sales Opportunities

It's great to know the pertinent details about your clients. You've already seen how ACT! keeps track of names and numbers, and even Notes and History to keep you in the know. But what if you want to know about pending deals? Or deals you clinched in the past, including wonderful details like when the deal closed or (better yet) how much the deal was worth?

This is what the **Sales Opportunities** feature is all about. Not only can you track everything we've already mentioned, but you can also estimate the probability of success, note your competition, and generate reports and graphs that put it all on paper.

Sales Opportunities appear on the **Sales/Opportunities** tab in the Contact window (fancy that!). You can tell if the opportunity is open or closed, and if closed, if it was won or lost, by the icon.

✓ - Open Opportunity
♣ - Closed Opportunity/Won
✗ - Closed Opportunity/Lost

...open an existing Sales Opportunity

1. Lookup the contact whom the opportunity involves.

See the procedure on page 39.

2. Click the **Sales/Opportunities** tab, if necessary.

3. Double-click the gray row header to the left of the desired opportunity.

The **Sales Opportunity** dialog box appears for the selected opportunity.

Practice: Checking Out Sales Opportunities

Try It...

Step	What to do	How to do it/Comments
1.	Lookup **Esther Williams**.	<u>L</u>ookup, <u>L</u>ast Name, type **will**, **OK**.
2.	Click the **S<u>a</u>les/Opportunities** tab.	There are 3 opportunities listed.
3.	Open the **Bathing Suits: Commercial** item.	Double-click the gray row header to the left of the item. Notice that the deal includes 4 commercials for bathing suits at $20,000 per spot.
4.	Close the dialog box.	Click **Cancel**.
5.	Notice the different icon for **Mermaid in a Million**. Open it. Can you see why it failed?	This is a closed opportunity and the sale was lost. Double-click the gray row header to the left to open it. According to the **R<u>e</u>ason:**, the script wasn't very good.
6.	Close the dialog box.	Click **Close**.
7.	Open the item for **Water Beauties**. Why is its icon different from the others?	Double-click the row header to its left. This deal worked.
8.	Close the dialog box.	Click **Close**.

...create a new Sales Opportunity

How To...

1.	Lookup the contact whom the opportunity involves.	See the procedure on page 39.
2.	**Sales, New Sales Opportunity** or click the **New Opportunity...** button on the **Sales/Opportunities** tab or press **[Ctrl+F11]**.	The **Sales Opportunity** dialog box appears.

3.	Type a **Product:**.	If you've created a sales opportunity before for this product, click the drop-down arrow and choose from the list. (You can also type the first few letters, and ACT! fills in the product name for you.) If you type in a product that you have never sold before, it will be added to the list.
4.	Type a **Type:**.	Again, there is a drop-down list if you've entered this Type before.
5.	Fill in the number of **Units:** and the **Unit price:**.	ACT! does the math and fills in the **Amount:** for you.

6. Enter a **Forecasted close date:**.   Type a date, or click the drop-down arrow to choose from a mini-calendar. Today's date appears at first by default.

7. Enter a **Probability:**.   This is the likely chance (as a percentage) that the deal has of closing.

8. Enter or select a **Sales stage**.   Type or click the drop-down arrow to choose the phrase that describes the current point in the sales process.

9. If necessary, click the **Additional Information** tab and enter a **Main competitor:** and/or **Details**.

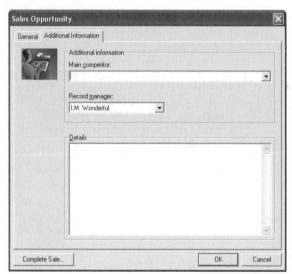

10. Click **OK**.

☞ *You can modify the entries in the Sales stage list at any time (13 sales stages seem a bit excessive for our business). While in the Contact window, choose **Sales, Modify Sales Stages....** Click **Add...** to add new stages, or select an existing stage and click **Modify....** And of course there is always **Delete**. Click **OK** when you're done. Why not start with about 4 or 5 stages and see how you like it. (1. Some interest shown in the offer, 2. Participant meeting scheduled, 3. Preparing/reviewing proposal, 4. Under review by legal, 5. Handling final details...see what works for you.)*

Practice: A New Movie for Rin Tin Tin

Try It...

Step	What to do	How to do it/Comments
1.	Lookup Rin Tin Tin.	**Lookup, First Name**, type **rin**, **OK**.
2.	Create a new Sales Opportunity.	**Sales**, **New Sales Opportunity**
3.	Type **Wonder Dog** in the **Product:** field and **Movie** in the **Type:** field.	Press **[Tab]** to move from field to field.
4.	Enter the following information: **Units:** 2 **Unit price:** 50,000	Notice that the price is formatted as currency for you, and that the Amount: field is calculated for you. (This is a two picture deal).
5.	Enter a closing date that's 2 months away.	Click the drop-down arrow for **Forecasted close date** and choose the date that is 2 months from today.
6.	Enter **50** for **Probability:**, and click the drop-down arrow for **Sales stage** and choose **Some Interest Shown**.	
7.	Add the detail that the picture has a sequel planned called Son of Wonder Dog.	Click the **Additional Information** tab, click in the **Details** field, and type: **2 picture deal; Son of Wonder Dog sequel**
8.	Finish the opportunity.	Click **OK**. The opportunity appears on the **Sales/Opportunities** tab for Rin Tin Tin.

Updating Sales Opportunities

As you work on Sales Opportunities, you can open them at any time to make changes such as selecting a different **Sales stage** or an altered **Pr‌obability:**.

How To...

...edit a Sales Opportunity

1. Open the opportunity.

   See the procedure on page 222.

2. Enter changes as necessary.

   Don't forget that you can click the **Additional Information** tab to enter competition and details.

3. Click **OK**.

☞ *If you can see the information that you want to correct on the Sales/Opportunities tab, you can also modify the opportunity simply by clicking on the field and changing the information...without opening the opportunity.*

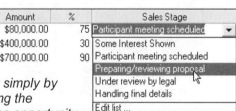

Closing the Deal

The day will come when the deal closes successfully or (gulp!) bites the dust. You can close a deal from the **Sales Opportunity** dialog box or from the **Sales/O‌pportunities** tab.

How To...

...close a Sales Opportunity

1. Lookup the contact for whom you want to close the deal and click the **Sales/O‌pportunities** tab.

   See the lookup procedure on page 39.

2. Click in the ✔ column next to the opportunity you are closing

   or

   double-click the gray row header to the left of the opportunity to open the **Sales Opportunity** dialog box. Once there, click **Complete Sale....**

   The **Complete Sale** dialog box appears.

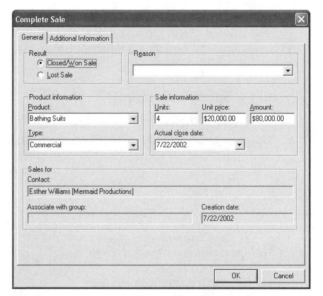

3.	Choose a **Result**.	Click **Closed/Won Sale** or **Lost Sale**.
4.	Enter a **Reason**.	This is a brief phrase about why the deal was won or lost.
5.	If necessary, click the **Additional Information** tab and enter **Details**.	
6.	**OK**	

Practice: *Closing the Bathing Suit Deal*

Try It...

Step	What to do	How to do it/Comments
1.	Lookup Esther Williams again.	**Lookup, Last Name**, type **will**, **OK**.
2.	Close the **Bathing Suits** deal. It's a winner because Esther likes the suits.	Click the **Sales/Opportunities** tab, if necessary. Click in the ✔ column next to the Bathing Suits item. Be sure that **Closed/Won Sale** is selected and type **She loves the suits** for the **Reason**. Click **OK**.
3.	Does the icon for the Bathing Suits deal change on the **Sales/Opportunities** tab?	Yes! It displays the icon for a Closed/Won deal.

Lookup Sales Stage

If you are actively using the sales stages to categorize your opportunities, then you can also lookup your opportunities by sales stage. Since one of our stages (stage 4) is "Under review by legal", you may want to do a lookup to see how many are in that stage so that you can crack the whip on the lawyers to move the deals closer to closing.

...lookup a Sales Opportunity by stage

1. **L**ookup, Sales Sta**g**e...

2. Select the sales stage from the drop-down list.

☞ *Putting an * in the Sales Stage will lookup all contacts with opportunities (open or closed).*

3. Click **OK**.

Contacts with opportunities at the specified stage are displayed.

Unless you are selling a very complicated product, 12 stages may be too many stages to keep track of in categorizing your opportunities.

...modify the Sales Stages

1. **S**ales, **M**odify Sales Stages...

2. **A**dd... or **M**odify... as necessary.

3. **OK**

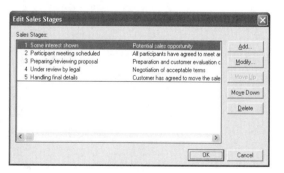

If you want to select and display all your open opportunities, let's look at reports.

Sales Reports

Sometimes you need to see sales information on paper. ACT! has 8 different sales reports and graphs available on the **Reports** menu. Just choose the report you want, make a few decisions about the data and how you want to see it and presto! All your good work appears in a neat, concise report.

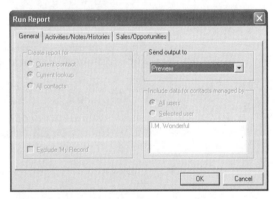

...run a Sales report

1. **Reports, Sales Reports**

2. Choose the report you want to run.

   The **Run Report** dialog box appears.

3. Choose a **Send output to** option, if necessary.

   Printer sends the report directly to your printer.

   Preview displays the report in print preview.

   Fax or **E-mail** transmits the report via either method, if your computer has those capabilities.

   File - ACT! Report saves the completed report to a file that can be printed by anyone who also has ACT!.

   File - Editable Text creates a Rich Text Format file that can be edited by most word processors.

4. Click the **Sales/Opportunities** tab.

   The **Sales/Opportunities** tab of the **Run Report** dialog box appears.

5. Click the desired check boxes to include/exclude **Sales Opportunities**, **Closed/won sales** and **Lost sales** options.

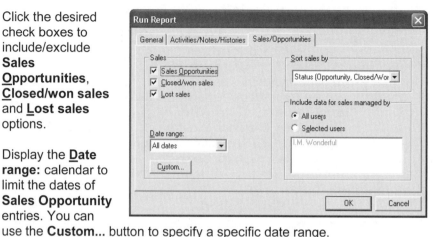

6. Display the **Date range:** calendar to limit the dates of **Sales Opportunity** entries. You can use the **Custom...** button to specify a specific date range.

7. If desired, change the report sort settings by clicking the drop-down arrow for **Sort sales by** and choose an option.

8. To specify information related to specific users of your network database, choose **Selected users:** and click the necessary name(s).

    ☞   *Only those users who have logon privileges to the current database will display in the **Selected users** list. Even if they are a user and you can see their calendar, unless the **Enable logon** box has been checked for this user (under **File, Administration, Define Users...**), you cannot run a report for that person.*

9. Click **OK**.   ACT! generates the report to your specifications.

Practice: *Playing with Sales Reports*

Step	What to do	How to do it/Comments
1.	Generate a Sales List report that's sorted by Closing date for all dates. Preview it on the screen.	Choose **Reports, Sales Reports, Sales List**. Click the drop-down arrow for **Send output to** and choose **Preview**. Click the **Sales/Opportunities** tab and be sure that **Sort sales by** is set to **Close date**. Click **OK**.
2.	Zoom in to see the data in the report.	Click with the mouse or click the **Zoom In** button on the toolbar.
3.	Close the report.	Click **Close**.
4.	Preview a Sales Totals by Status report.	Choose **Reports, Sales Reports, Sales Totals by Status**. Click the drop-down arrow for **Send output to** and choose **Preview**. Click the **Sales/ Opportunities** tab and be sure that all 3 check boxes under **Sales** are checked. Click **OK**.
5.	Zoom in to see the data and then close the report.	Click with the mouse or click the **Zoom In** button on the toolbar. **Close**

Try It...

Sales Pipeline

Sometimes we focus so closely on closing the deal that we forget about prospecting…or filling the pipeline. The idea is that we won't win every deal that we open (we wish). Over time you start to develop your own ratio (e.g. you have to have at least 5 potential deals for every deal that you close.) To verify that you are on track and not focusing too much on one stage of the deal, you can display the Sales Pipeline to see how many opportunities you have at each stage of the deal. Be sure you have enough numbers in the top of the funnel to help you meet the results you need at the bottom.

…display the Sales Pipeline report

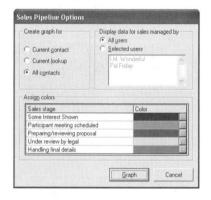

1. **Sales, Sales Pipeline…**

2. Select any options:

    (You may want to start with a lookup of all contacts in a specific state and then run reports based on the **Current lookup** to display opportunities in that state.)

    You could also display only opportunities managed by a **Selected user**

3. Click **Graph**

    Notice that the Sales Stages listed here match the Sales Stage on page 230

The size of each section is fixed and not based on the number of opportunities at each stage.

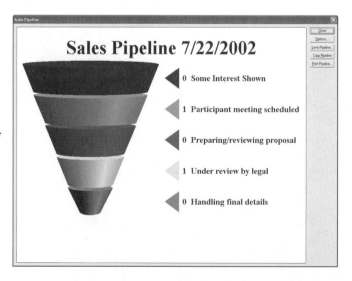

Sales Graph

Sometimes you may want a longer range view of potential deals. ACT! can display your sales opportunities in a graph.

...display the Sales Forecast Graph

How To...

1. **Sales, Sales Graph...**

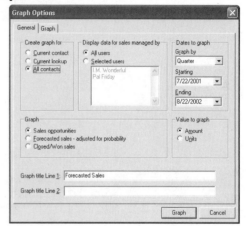

2. Select any options (they are all pretty self-explanatory.)

   The **Graph** tab allows you to change from a line to a bar graph, colors, etc.

3. Click **Graph**.

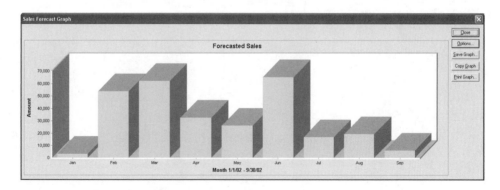

Better start planning for September!

Review: *Sales Opportunities*

Try It...

1. Create a new opportunity for Clark Gable.

Clark wants to produce a movie he has been thinking about: Gone With The Seasons. Stars R Us would cast the movie and get a fee of $7,000/major actor signed. He estimates the film will require 6 leading actors.

He will make a decision by the end of the month whether he will use us or not.

He is reviewing our proposal. We have a pretty good shot since we represent Vivian Leigh (his favorite leading lady.)

However, they are also considering Willy Morris Agency.

2. Close the deal we have pending for Cyd Charisse. We won the deal, but the client had to pay her $25,000 for the appearance. So we get to increase our 10% of the representation from 2,000 to 2,500. Don't you just love negotiating deals!

Groups

Groups are a great way to categorize your contacts. To learn to effectively utilize this feature, you will:

- ☑ Learn how to create and add members to a group.

- ☑ Understand how subgroups are created and used.

- ☑ Practice creating and running group rules.

- ☑ Create notes for different groups.

- ☑ Associate activities with groups.

- ☑ Customize group User fields.

Groups

Groups are a powerful feature of ACT! that allows you to organize, catalog, classify, subdivide, pigeonhole, and otherwise make sense out of groups of contacts and the information that is stored with them. The **Groups** button will sift through and display only the contacts that belong to the selected group.

By this time, we hope you are comfortable performing basic lookups. ACT!'s lookup capabilities are flexible enough for you to display almost any combination of contact records. But lookups have their limitations.

Lookups are *temporary*. You could spend several minutes creating a complex and useful lookup, but as soon as you perform another lookup, wham! Your carefully constructed list is gone.

Lookups need a common bit of information to "look up." What, for example, if you want to create a lookup on a group of contacts who have nothing in common but their love of Basset Hounds? Unless your database has a custom field named **Dog Preference**, you may find this a little more than challenging.

Situations like this are why ACT! has the **Group** feature.

✔ You can create a group at any time for any reason.

✔ A group is a like a saved lookup of contact records and can contain any number of contacts.

✔ When you create a group, you define which Contacts belong to that group. It is possible to add people to a group who have nothing in common (except in your own mind).

✔ When you activate a group, only the records in that group are displayed. This is much the same as a lookup, but a group can be displayed almost instantly whenever you need it.

✔ And the best thing is that any contact can be a member of any number of groups.

☞ *Don't think of groups as permanent things. You can create and delete groups without any fear of actually affecting the Contact records.*

Viewing a Group

Once any group is created, you can display the members in **Contacts** or **Contacts List** view. This has the same effect as performing a lookup (only the Contacts that are members of the group will be displayed).

The Group list button at the bottom of the window, displays the name of the current group. If no group is displayed, the button says **<No Group>.**

✔ Click this button to display a list of groups and subgroups, and choose a group from the list to lookup its Contact records.

✔ You can choose **<No Group>** from the top of this list to display all contacts, but choosing **Lookup, All Contacts** from the menu will accomplish the same thing.

☞ *When a group is displayed, and you add a new contact to your ACT! database, the new contact is **automatically** added to that group. If this is what you want, great! But we are sure you can see the possible downside. It is probably a good idea to choose **Lookup, All Contacts** before you do any data entry, unless you **want** to add new contacts to the group.*

Practice: *Viewing a Group*

Try It...

Step	What to do	How to do it/Comments
1.	In Contact view, display the **Hoofers** group using the Group list button.	Click the Contact view icon if necessary. Click the Group button to pop-up a list, select **Hoofers** from the list.
2.	How many records are displayed?	4, only the members of the Hoofers group.
3.	View the list in Contact List view.	Click the Contact List view icon.
4.	Display the **Prospects** group in this view.	Click the Group button to pop-up a list, select **Prospects** from the list.
5.	Display all contacts.	Choose **Lookup, All Contacts**. All records are displayed.

Changing Group Membership for a Contact

You can see how easy it is to display the contacts that belong to a specific group. However, contacts are not limited to only one group. They can belong to as many groups as you like.

To see which groups a contact belongs to, click on the **Groups** tab in the **Contact** view. From the **Groups** tab, you can add a new contact to several groups, or perhaps *remove* the contact from membership in a particular group.

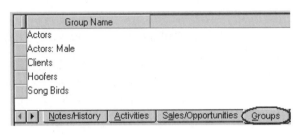

...edit group membership in Contact view

1. Display the contact record.

   Lookup the contact whose group membership you wish to edit.

2. Display the **Groups** tab.

   Click the tab at the bottom of the contacts record to display a list of groups in which this contact is a member.

3. Choose **Contact, Group Membership...** from the menu,

   or

   *right-click in the list area of the **Groups** tab and choose **Group Membership....***

4. Click the group to which you want to add the contact, or from which to remove the contact.

A **Group Membership** dialog box displays a list of available groups, and a list of groups to which the contact currently belongs. Current groups have check-marks next to them. Click a group without a check to add the contact to that group. Click a group with a check to remove him or her from the group (the check-mark disappears).

5. Click **OK** when you are done.

Practice: Changing Membership

Step	What to do	How to do it/Comments
1.	Display the Contacts window.	Click the Contacts button on the View Bar.
2.	Lookup **Orson Welles** and display his **Groups** layout tab. Is he a member of any groups?	Yes, he belongs to the **Actors, Actors:Male,** and the **Prospects** group.
3.	Edit Orson's Group membership.	Right-click in the list area of the **Groups** tab and choose **Group Membership....**
4.	Remove Orson from the **Prospects** group and add him to the **Clients** group.	Click **Prospects** and then click **Clients**. Close the **Group Membership** dialog. Click **OK**.

Try It...

Creating a Group

Now that we have looked at groups, let's create a new group. ACT! makes it very easy (isn't everything easy in ACT!).

...create a group

1. If possible, perform a lookup that displays the contact records you want included in the group.

   You can add individual contacts to a group "on the fly" but if you can do a lookup, defining the group members can be quicker.

2. Choose **View, Groups** from the menu
   or
   click the **Groups** button on the View Bar.

   The Groups window appears. This window displays a list of the groups themselves (if any have been defined).

3. Choose **Group, New Group**
   or
   press **[Insert]**
   or
   click the New Group icon

   The word **Untitled** appears in the **Group Name** field. The word is highlighted.

4.   Type a **Group Name** and an optional **Description**.

Keep the name brief. Elaborate as to the nature of the group in the **Description** box.

5.   If necessary, fill in any remaining fields.

These fields are optional, and may not relate to the group.

Practice: *Creating a Group (Or two)*

Step	What to do	How to do it/Comments
1.	Display the Groups window. Observe the existing groups.	Choose <u>V</u>iew, <u>G</u>roups or click the **Groups** button on the View Bar. Several groups have already been defined. Groups
2.	Create a new group named **Directors**. The description should read **People who direct**.	Press **[Insert]**, type the group name, press **[Tab]** or click in the **Description** box, type the description.
3.	Create another group named **Tough Guys**. The description should read **Actors who can play tough guy parts.**	Press **[Insert]**, type the group name, press **[Tab]** or click in the **Description** box, type the description.

Adding Multiple Contacts to a Group

When you first create it, the Group is just a name. Think of the Group as an empty container and now you have to fill it. You can store several things in groups, but the most common thing is contacts.

...add contacts to a group

1.   Choose <u>V</u>iew, <u>G</u>roups
or
click the **Groups** button.
   Groups

The Groups window appears.

2.   Select the group from the **Group Name** list.

This is the list on the left side of the window. Click the name of the Group to which you want to add contact(s).

3. Choose **Group, Group Membership, Add/Remove Contacts...** from the menu

    or

    click the **Add/Remove Contacts** button on the toolbar.

    or

    click the [Add/Remove Contacts...]
    Contacts tab and click the **Add/Remove Contacts...** button.

The **Add/Remove Contacts** dialog box appears.

The current members of the group are listed on the right side of the box.

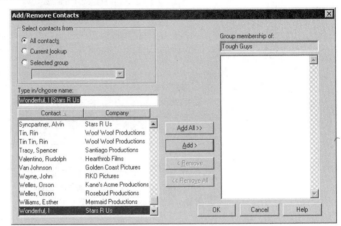

4. Choose the appropriate **Select contacts from** option.

Leave **All contacts** selected if you want to pick individual contact names from the entire contact list.

Choose **Current lookup** to display contacts in the current lookup.

Choose **Selected group** if you wish to select contacts from an existing group. The drop-down list below **Selected group** displays a list of groups from which you may select.

5.   Click a specific Contact name
and click **Add>**

          or

click **Add All>>** to add the entire
lookup,

          or

select a name on the right-side
of the window under **Group
membership of** and click
<Remove

          or

click **<<Remove All** to start all
over with assigning group
membership.

6.   Repeat until all desired contacts
have been added to the group
and click **OK**.

To add one Contact at a time, you
can type their name in the **Type
in/choose name:** box to quickly
search the list (last name first) and
the click **Add>**.

Your group is now populated with
contacts.

Some tips on finding and selecting items in the Group Membership dialog box:

✔   If you want to search for a company name, click the **Company**
column header and type the company name in the **Type in/choose
name:** box. This is helpful when you want to add all contacts that
belong to the same company.

✔   To select a range of Contacts from the list, click the first Contact, hold
down **[Shift]** and click the last desired Contact. All Contacts between
the two will be selected.

✔   To select random Contacts, click the first Contact, hold **[Ctrl]** and
click on each additional Contact. As long as the **[Ctrl]** key is held
down, you will add each record to the selection. When finished
selecting, click **Add>**.

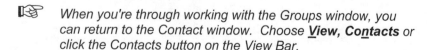

☞   *When you're through working with the Groups window, you
can return to the Contact window. Choose **View, Contacts** or
click the Contacts button on the View Bar.*

Contacts

Try It...

Step	What to do	How to do it/Comments
1.	In Contact view, lookup all contacts with the ID/Status of "Director"	Click the Contacts view icon. **Lookup**, **ID/Status**, type "director", **OK**.
2.	Return to **Groups** view and add the current lookup to the **Directors** group you created in the last practice session.	Click the **Groups** icon. Click on the **Directors** group name to select it. Click the Add/Remove Contacts icon. Select the **Current lookup** option. Click **Add All>>**, click **OK**.
3.	Wait, remove **Orson Welles** from the group. *(After all those wine commercials, he wants to take a rest.)*	With the **Directors** group still selected, click the **Add/Remove Contacts** button again. Select Orson's name from the list on the right and click **<Remove**.
4.	Display the **Contacts** tab for the **Directors** group (at the bottom of **Group** view) to verify that the 3 director's names are displayed.	All of the names you added are listed there. Add/Remove Contacts... | Contact	Company △	Phone | | Gene Kelly | Acme Hoofer Films | 213-555-6099 | | Ginger Rogers | Beautymark Films | 213-555-3845 | | Cyd Charisse | Hollywood Films Ltd. | 213-555-3092 | | Fred Astaire | Top Hat Films | 310-555-3003 | ◄ ► Notes/History | Activities | Sales/Opportunities | Contacts | Library
5.	Add the following contacts to the **Tough Guys** group: **Humphrey Bogart** **James Cagney** **Edward Robinson**	Click on the **Tough Guys** group to select it. Click the Add/Remove Contacts button. In the **Type in/choose name:** box, type "Bo" to select Humphrey Bogart. Click **Add>**. Do the same for Cagney and Robinson.
6.	Change from the **Groups** window back to the **Contacts** window.	Click the **Contacts** button on the View Bar.

| 7. | Lookup **Orson** and add him back into the **Directors** group. After **Citizen Kane**, who could doubt that Orson is a director! | Click on the **Groups** tab. Right-click in the list area of the **Groups** tab and choose **Group Membership....** Click **Directors** to add him to the group. Click **OK**. |

Subgroups

Sometimes one group classification just isn't enough. When you are trying to fill potential parts from your pool of contacts, you may want to subdivide the list of Actors into Male and Female so that you can quickly lookup who might be available. All of your actors would be part of the Actors group, then each actor would also be part of one of the subgroups.

...create a subgroup

1. Click the **Groups** icon on the View Bar.

Groups

2. Select the group for which you want to create a subgroup.

3. **Group, New Subgroup**   Click the group to select it.

4. Type a **Group Name** and any other necessary information.

5. Add contacts to the subgroup as necessary.   See the procedure on page 243.

☞   *Subgroups, like contacts and groups, are automatically saved.*

☞   *Just because a Contact is a member of a subgroup does not automatically make him or her a member of the "parent group." Each group (sub or otherwise) is independent of all other groups as far as their membership is concerned. If you want Contacts in a subgroup to be members of their parent group as well, you must add them.*

Practice: *Making a Subgroup*

Try It...

Step	What to do	How to do it/Comments
1.	Create an additional subgroup for the **Actors** group called **Los Angeles** (always a good list for a quick party invite).	Click the **Groups** icon on the View Bar. Click the **Actors** group and choose **Group, New Subgroup**. Type **Los Angeles** in the **Group Name** box and **Actors in the LA** area in the **Description** box.
2.	Switch to the Contacts window and display the **Actors** group.	Click the **Contacts** button on the View Bar. Click the Group button at the bottom right of the Contact window (it probably says **<No Group>** at this point) and choose **Actors**.
3.	Narrow the lookup to only those actors in Los Angeles.	**Lookup, City**, type **L** (the rest of the name appears for you), choose **Narrow lookup, OK**. There should be 22 records in the lookup.
4.	Add the contacts in the lookup to the **Los Angeles** subgroup.	Click the **Groups** icon on the View Bar. Click the **Los Angeles** subgroup (if necessary) and click the Add/Remove Contacts button. Choose **Current lookup, Add All>>, OK**.
5.	Switch to the Contacts window. Can you easily find your Los Angeles subgroup?	Click the **Contacts** icon on the View Bar. Yes! Click the Group button on the lower right corner and there's **Actors: Los Angeles**.
6.	Lookup all contacts.	**Lookup, All Contacts**

Associating Activities with Groups

An activity will always be associated with a Contact record. But you can use groups to easily schedule activities for all members of a group. .

...schedule an activity with a group

How To...

1. In the Contact window, display the group or subgroup for which you wish to create the activity.

Click on the **<No Group>** button and change to the desired Group.

2. Begin creating the activity. (It doesn't matter whose record you are on.)

Notice that if you had pre-selected the group before scheduling the activity, the **Associate with group:** is filled with the current group name.

Use your usual method to create a Call, Meeting, or To Do. The **Schedule Activity** dialog box displays.

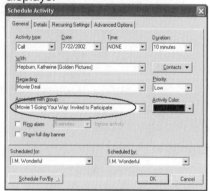

3. Click the **Contacts▼** button to the right of the **With** box and choose **Select Contacts....**

The **Select Contacts** dialog box is displayed. The current Contact is already displayed in the **Scheduled with:** column.

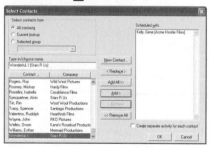

4. Choose the **Selected group** option, then choose the desired group from the drop-down list below. *(This is actually the same as selecting **Current lookup** since you looked up the Group first. Either way you want to do it is fine.)*

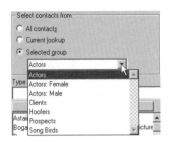

5. If you wish to add all members of the group, click the **Select All** button. If you wish to select individuals, click **Add>>** to add the selected names to the list.

In fact, you can use this dialog box to schedule activities for any collection of Contacts, whether they are part of the same group or not.

6. When the **Scheduled with:** list contains the desired Contacts, choose whether to create a separate activity for each Contact in the list, or one activity for all members.

This is a check-box below the **Scheduled with:** list.

☑ Create separate activity for each contact

If you do not check the box, you are creating *one* activity for *many* Contacts. If you alter a group activity, you alter it for all members of the group. The same is true when you clear the activity.

If you check the box, separate activities will be created for each member of the group.

7. Click **OK** when you are done.

The activity is scheduled for each member of the group, either as a group or as individuals. It is also displayed on the **Activities** tab of the Groups window.

Practice: *Scheduling with the Group*

Try It...

Step	What to do	How to do it/Comments
1.	Lookup the Female Actors (a subgroup in our database.)	In Contacts view, click on the Group list button to display the **Actors: Female** group.
2.	Create a To-do for Pal Friday to send an invitation to this group for a spa day at the Red Door.	Schedule the To-do as you normally would. Click the **Contacts ▼** button and choose **Select Contacts...**, select **Current lookup**, **Add all>>** verify that **Create separate...** is not checked **OK** Don't forget to change the scheduled with to Pal Friday.

Group Rules

Groups are easy to create and valuable assets to any ACT! user, but they are a pain in the neck to maintain manually (your staff keeps forgetting to add new contacts to the appropriate groups.) Keeping groups up to date is important especially if you base reports, or mail merges on group membership. Fortunately, ACT! lets you create rules that can keep your group membership current.

... create a rule for group membership using field entries

1. In the Group window, click the group or subgroup for which you want to create a rule.

Groups

2. **Group, Group Membership, Define Rules...**

   You can also right click the desired group icon and choose Group Membership, Define rules....

The first of the **Group Membership Rules Wizard** dialog boxes appears.

3. Choose **Field values** and click **Next>**.

   If you are familiar with advanced queries, you can apply one to this process as well.

4. Click **The Contact field:** drop-down arrow and choose the field on which to base the first condition of the rule.

 You can also type the first few letters of the field name to select it and then press [Tab] to jump to the next box.

5. Click **Add Value...**. Type or choose a value from the drop-down list and click **OK**.

   Repeat for each value that applies to the selected field.

   Click **Next>**.

The **Add Value** dialog box appears. Here you will set the condition that must be met.

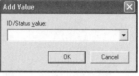

In order to meet the criteria, (and become a member of the group) a Contact record must match one of the values you specify (e.g. all contacts who live in California, Oregon **or** Washington make up our West Coast group. You can keep adding until you have entered all the **OR** criteria.

6. If desired, click the **Use second condition...** check-box and repeat steps 4-5 to establish a second field and value.

When you specify a second condition, a Contact record must match one of the values in the first condition **AND** one of the values in the second condition to qualify for membership in the group. (e.g. a contact whose ID/Status = Client **and** whose City = Los Angeles.

7. Check the group name, the field(s), and value(s) specified.

   Click **Finish** when you are satisfied.

If something is not correct, click **Back** to go back to the appropriate box and make the necessary change(s).

☞ *You can also create rules that apply group membership based on the results of a query. Queries allow much more complex criteria to be specified, but can be a bit harder to master. We will talk about creating queries later in this Guide.*

ACT!

Running the Rules

Once you have created your Group Membership rules, they will just sit there and do nothing until you "run" them.

...run group membership rules

1. Display the Group window and select the group or subgroup for which you want to run the defined rules.

You don't *have* to select the group, but it helps.

2. **Group, Group Membership, Run Rules...**

or

click the Run Rules icon.

The **Run Group Membership Rules** dialog box appears.

Run Group Membership Rules

Note: The entire contact database is searched when group membership rules are run.

Run group membership rules for

✓ Directors

Select All   Unselect All

Run Membership Rules   Close

3. If necessary, click the group(s) for which you want to run the assigned rules.

A check-mark appears next to selected groups. Click a group with the mark, and the group is de-selected.

You can click **Select All** to select all groups, or click **Unselect All** to start over.

4.   **Run Group Membership**

A warning box displays, telling you that the process(es) may take a while. Click **Yes** to continue.

When the process is complete, the **Group Membership Rules Log** appears.

5.   If necessary, click **Save As...** to save the log as a file which can be printed. Otherwise, click **Close**.

Practice: *The Rule(ing) Class*

Try It...

Step	What to do	How to do it/Comments
1.	**Lookup, ID/Status** of Prospect...how many? Now display the **Prospects** Group...how many? We haven't been good about adding contacts to the **Prospects** group. Let's define a rule for the **Prospects** group. All records with **Prospect** entered in the **ID/Status** field should be added to the group.	Click the **Groups** icon on the View Bar. Select the **Prospects** group and choose **Group, Group Membership, Define Rules...**. Choose **Field values** (if necessary), **Next>**, click the drop-down arrow and choose **ID/Status**, and click **Add Value...**. Type **pr** (notice that ACT! completes the word from the defined list), click **OK**, and click **Next>**. Click **Next>** again and then click **Finish**.
2.	Run the rule.	Make sure the Prospects group is selected and click the Run Rules icon. Click **Run Group Membership**.
3.	Read the log and close it.	Several records should have been added to the group. **Close**

ACT!

Try It...

Step	What to do	How to do it/Comments
4.	View the group membership for the **Prospects** group.	Click the **Contacts** tab in the Groups view.
5.	Switch to the Contacts view.	Click the **Contacts** icon on the View Bar. (There are a few Prospects that are Directors.)

☞ *Rules work great for Groups that have a consistent value in a field. However, you can't use rules for all groups. Groups like Male or Female are difficult to automate. Groups like Golf Buddies are also difficult to create rules for. For these types of groups, you have to manually add the contact to the group (page 240).*

Review: *Working With Groups*

Try It...

1.	Create a group called **Silents**.
2.	Add **Rudolph Valentino** and **Clara Bow** to the group.
3.	Create a meeting for next Monday at 4:00 for an hour of voice lessons. Schedule this meeting for the **Silents** group.
4.	Check to see if the meeting appears on the **Activities** tab for both **Clara Bow** and **Rudolph Valentino**.
5.	Clear the activities (erase them). Be sure that the meeting is gone from both records (you should only have to clear it once).

Library Tab

To understand how you can gain quick access to view and edit files that have been created for your contacts using the Library tab feature, we will:

- ☑ Add different types of files to our contacts.

- ☑ Edit the documents within the Library tab.

- ☑ Map ACT! fields to an embedded Excel spreadsheet.

The Library Tab

The Library tab extends ACT!'s ability to attach document files to a contact record by allowing you to view and edit attached documents directly on a tab in ACT!.

Example: If you are tracking sales data for a contact using a Microsoft Excel workbook, you can use the Library tab to view the spreadsheet (without having to open it in Excel) when you need to. You can even edit the spreadsheet data directly on the tab.

The Library tab can display and edit a finite set of file types, and only if the program used to create that file type is installed on your computer. These file types are...

✔   Microsoft Word documents (.doc)

✔   Microsoft Excel spreadsheets (.xls)

✔   Microsoft PowerPoint presentations (.ppt)

✔   Microsoft MapPoint documents

✔   JPEG image files (.jpg) and Bitmap images (.bmp)

✔   Adobe Acrobat files (.pdf)

With Microsoft Excel documents, you also have the option to "Map" fields in ACT! to existing cells on the worksheet. In this way, changes to mapped fields in ACT! can be automatically updated in the Excel spreadsheet.

The Library toolbar provides all of the functionality needed to work with Library documents. If you point to a toolbar button a "tooltip" will display telling you what the button does.

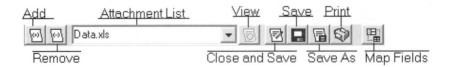

Adding Documents to the Library

You can already attach files to your contact records on the **Notes/History** tab, but many times the attachments get lost among your many other notes and histories. Another advantage of using the **Library** tab to "do the attaching," you will be able to view and edit the documents within the ACT! window.

The first thing you need to know is how to add a file to the library.

...add files to the Library tab

How To...

1. Lookup the contact to whom you wish to attach a file. If necessary display the **Library** tab in the ACT! window

   All documents are attached to the currently displayed contact.

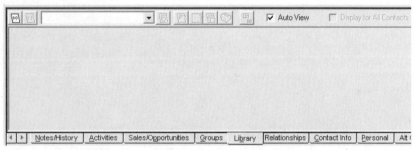

2. Click the **Add Document** button on the **Library** tab toolbar.

   It is the first button on the toolbar. A "**Select a Document**" dialog box will be displayed.

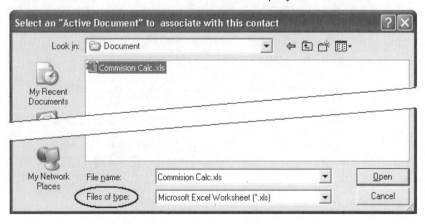

3.	Change the **Files of type:** list box at the bottom of the dialog box to the appropriate file type, if necessary.	The dialog box will only display one type of eligible file at a time.
4.	Use the **Look in:** drop-down to browse to locate the file you wish to attach to the tab.	Sorry, we can't help you here. You have to know where the file is stored and how to get there.
5.	Select the file and click **Open**.	If the **Auto View** check box is checked the last file selected will be displayed on the library tab. If **Auto View** is not checked, the name of the document will appear in the Attachment list on the Library Tab but the document will not be displayed.
6.	Repeat the process for each document you wish to add.	You may attach up to **20** documents to a contact in the **Library** tab..

☑ Auto View

 You can also add a document by dragging a compatible document from the Windows Explorer or browser window directly onto the library tab.

When you attach a document to the **Library** tab, it will also appear as an attachment item in the **Notes/History** tab. The **Regarding** text for the attachment will contain the file name and the word "**[Library]**". It is this identifier that the **Library** tab uses to identify it's specific attachments. You should not edit or delete the **[Library]** identifier.

Filter	>	☑ Notes	☑ Histories	☑ Attachments	☑ E-mail	Insert Note	Details...
	Date ∇	Time ∇	Type	Regarding			Record Mar
	7/27/2002	11:36 AM	Attachment	Commision Calc.xls[Library][Active]			I.M. Wonderful
	7/27/2002	11:35 AM	Attac	Library Identifier m.doc[Library]			I.M. Wonderful
	11/24/1998	11:24 AM	Field Changed	ID/Status - Client			Pal Friday

Document currently displayed on Library tab.

Files attached through the Library tab may be available to others if they are stored on a shared folder (on a server), however the files will not sync to remote users.

Practice: *Adding Document Files to the Library*

Try It...

Step	What to do	How to do it/Comments
1.	Locate Audrey Hepburn's record in the **Stars R Us** database.	Choose **Lookup, First Name...** type **Audrey** and click **OK**
2.	Display the **Library** tab and attach the Word Document named **Audrey Hepburn.doc**. This file should be located in the ACT! **Document** folder. *The standard location for the folder is **My Documents\ACT\Document**.*	Click the **Add Document** button on the Library tab toolbar. If necessary, change the **Files of type** list box at the bottom of the dialog box to **Microsoft Word Document (*.doc)**. Browse to the Document folder, locate and select **Audrey Hepburn.doc**. Click **Open**.
3.	Add the document named **HepburnA-Charcoal.bmp** to Audrey. (in the... c:\Program Files\Act\Layout folder)	Click the **Add Document** button on the Library tab toolbar. If necessary, change the **Files of type** list box at the bottom of the dialog box to the program associated with **Bitmap Image (*.bmp)**. Select **HepburnA-Charcoal.bmp**. Click **Open**.
4.	Are you able to view the contents of either of the documents?	If not, don't be concerned, read on.

Viewing Library Files

A Library file will only display in the **Library** tab when you tell it to. Even if the **Attachment List** contains a list of attached files, the **Library** tab will display as blank unless …

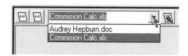

1. You click the **View** button on the **Library** toolbar. This will display the file whose name is currently displayed in the **Attachment List** box. It will remain displayed until you move to another record.

2. You click the **Auto View** check box on the **Library** toolbar. This will automatically display the last file viewed and whose name is displayed in the **Attachment List** box. As you move from record to record, the most recently viewed file (assuming the record has one) will automatically be loaded and displayed.

☑ Auto View

… view a document

 How To…

1. Display the **Library** tab if necessary. If the name of the desired file is not displayed in the **Attachment List** click the drop-down list button and select the file.

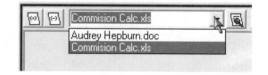

2. If the file is still not displayed on the tab, click the **View Document** button.

This will cause the selected file to display in the tab. This is just a view and cannot be edited at this point.

3. If you wish the currently selected file to display automatically as you move from record to record, put a check in the **Auto View** check box.

When this box is checked, the file listed in the **Attachment List** will automatically be loaded to view when you display a record with a Library file attached.

 *Large documents can take a while to display. If you are moving from record to record with the Library tab displayed this may slow you down a bit, especially if each of the files were created by different software packages. Turning off **Auto View** will restore performance.*

Practice: *Viewing Files*

Try It...

Step	What to do	How to do it/Comments
1.	If you are not viewing Audrey Hepburn's Contact record, display it now. Display the **Library** tab.	Choose **Lookup, First Name...** type **Audrey** click **OK**.
2.	If the **Auto View** check box is checked, uncheck it.	The check box is located on the right of the Library tab toolbar. ☑ Auto View
3.	Use the **Attachment List** to display the library file that is *not* currently displayed	Display the **Attachment List** and select either **Audrey Hepburn.doc** or **HepburnA-Charcoal.bmp**, whichever is not currently selected.
4.	Is the file displayed?	Nope!
5.	Click the **View Document** button	Now you see it...
6.	Now display the other file	Select the file name from the Attachment List.
7.	Did the file display?	...now you don't!
8.	Check the **Auto View** check box.	The document now displays.
9	Switch back to the other document again.	This time the file displays automatically

☞ *If you view or edit a file on the library tab when the program that created the file is running, the **Library** tab warns you that you should close that program. While the file will still display in the tab, it is recommended that you close the program in question (Word, Excel, PowerPoint, etc.)*

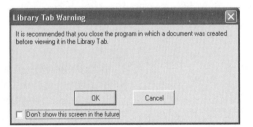

Editing Library Documents

Up to now, all you have done is *view* your Library files. These files are located on your hard drive and can be opened and edited in the programs that created them, but you may find it more convenient to edit them directly on the **Library** tab.

... edit a document in the Library tab

How To...

1. Select the file from the **Attachment List** and, if necessary, click the **View Document** button on the toolbar.

   You must view the file before you can edit it.

2. To edit the file *in* the Library tab, click the **Edit Document** button

   The file will be displayed in editing mode. Toolbars specific to the application in which the file was created will be displayed above the Library toolbar.

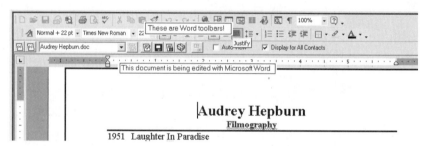

3. Edit the file as necessary.

   The extra toolbars are the same as in the original application and work as they normally would.

4. When you are done editing, click the **Close Document and Save Changes** button on the **Library** toolbar (you will notice, it is the same button as **Edit Document**) You will be asked if you wish to save, say **Yes** if you wish to save your changes.

   The document will remain displayed in view mode after you close the editing mode.

☞ *Editing a document "in place" has its appeals, but it also has its limitations. You will notice that several buttons on the document application toolbars are "grayed out". These commands are not available when editing on a tab. There is also the question of space. Editing a large document on the tab severely limits how much of the document you can see at any time. If you wish to edit the document in a separate window, display the __Notes/History__ tab, locate the document and double-click the icon to the left of the item. This will open the document into its associated application. Be sure to save and close the file before you return to ACT!.*

Practice: *Editing*

Try It...

Step	What to do	How to do it/Comments
1.	If you are not viewing Audrey Hepburn's Contact record, display it now. Display the **Library** tab.	Choose **Lookup, First Name...** type **Audrey** click **OK.**
2.	We spelled Audrey's last name incorrectly in the **Audrey Hepburn.doc**. It should be **Hepburn** (not Hepbern).	If necessary, select the **Audrey Hepburn.doc** from the **Attachment List**. If **Auto View** is turned off, click the **View** button.
3.	Correct the misspelling.	Click the **Edit** button and make the change.
4.	Save and close the document.	After you correct the spelling click the **Close Document and Save Changes** button. Click **Yes**, if you are prompted to save your changes.

Display for All

The **Display for All Contacts** checkbox allows you to move between contact records and continue to display the currently open file on the Library tab. The document will maintain its present mode (view or edit).

✔ Using **Display for All Contacts** allows you to view or edit a file regardless of which contact is displayed.

✔ If you choose to activate this feature you should be aware that the file is always linked to the *original contact*. It is not multiple versions of a file; it is a single file.

✔ You can use the **Save Document As** button to create a copy of the file (with a different name) for the currently displayed contact. **However…** when you do this, the new file is not automatically linked to the contact record. You must add the newly saved file to the **Attachment List**.

When **Display for All Contacts** has been checked, the current file displays in view (or edit) mode as you move from Contact to Contact in your ACT! database. If you were on the My Record, displaying the file when you checked the **Display for All Contacts**, then only those files available from the **Attachment List** of the My Record are available for viewing as you scroll through the database.

This feature could be quite handy if you attached Price Sheets, Product Spec Sheets, Telemarketing scripts, etc. to the My Record and then clicked **Display for All Contacts**. As you worked in your database throughout the day, all important Company documents could immediately be displayed with the click of a drop-down button. (However, remember a maximum of only 20 files can be maintained in one Contact's **Attachment List**.)

☞ *Files associated with other Contacts are not available to view from the **Attachment List** drop-down until you uncheck **Display for All Contacts**.*

Mapping ACT! Fields into Excel

The **Library** tab's field mapping utility allows you to "connect" fields in your ACT! database to cells in an Excel worksheet. Once these fields are mapped, editing the Excel workbook on the **Library** tab will automatically update the worksheet to reflect the values from the mapped fields in ACT!.

Example: You record the amount of your client's last film salary in a field in ACT!. You will get a commission based on that amount. You can set up field mapping so that the data in the ACT! field merges into an appropriate cell in an Excel spreadsheet that calculates your commission. When you change the value in ACT! and then edit the worksheet on the Library tab, the new value is placed in the mapped field in Excel and your commission is recalculated.

Preparing the Excel File

If you wish to map ACT! fields to Excel, you first need to create and save the basic Excel spreadsheet. As you design the spreadsheet, keep in mind that if you enter something into the cells where you plan to insert the ACT! data, then it will be easier for you to complete the mapping process. For example, in the cells where you plan to map ACT! data, enter some descriptive text or a number merely as placeholders. At a minimum, you must have something entered in the lower right corner of the area you will map to (if your spreadsheet will go to column F and down to row 23, then place a period in F23). This should make all cells through F23 available for mapping.

In the example to the right, we will replace cell A3 (which currently is the text "Contact Name" and is formatted as Bold) with the actual Contact name from the ACT! database. When we insert the Contact's Name, it will take on the same formatting attributes of the cell that displays the data.

	A	B
1	**Stars R Us**	
2	**Commission Calculation Worksheet**	
3	**Contact Name**	
4	Last Film Salary	-
5	Commission Rate	15%
6	Commission	-

In cell B4, we entered a 0 as a placeholder and in cell B6 we entered the formula =B5*B4. Once you map the values, the ACT! data will replace our "dummy" data in cells A3 and B4 and then update cell B6.

 We highly recommend that you make a backup copy of the Excel "template" file before you map the ACT! fields to it, in case you want to make modifications later.

...map fields to an Excel spreadsheet

1. Add, View, *and* Edit the Excel workbook you wish to use.

   Add the Excel file to the **Attachment List**, if necessary. Click the **View Document** icon, then click the **Edit Document** icon. You must be in *edit* mode to map fields.

2. Click the **Map Fields** button on the **Library** tab toolbar.

   The **Field Mapping** dialog box is displayed.

   On the left is a list of all the contact fields in your ACT! database.

   On the right is a list of all cells in the Excel worksheet that have something entered in them (non empty cells).

    If you didn't enter some text, a number, or a "space" in the cell when you created the original Excel file, the cell will not be available for mapping.

3. Select the field you wish to map from the **ACT! Fields available** list at the left.

   Select the cell you wish to map the ACT! field to, from the **Excel Data available** list on the right.

   You are defining the link from the ACT! field to the Excel cell. But don't click OK just yet!

4. Click the **Add** button. (*this is an easy step to forget, and nothing happens if you don't click **Add**).*

   The mapped relationship(s) will be displayed in the **Currently Mapped Fields:** list.

5. Repeat steps 3 and 4 until you have mapped all the desired fields.

    Don't forget to click the **Add** button for each one.

6. If you want the data to automatically update whenever you edit the

    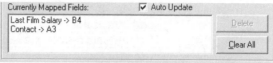

    document on the tab, make sure the **Auto Update** check box is checked.

7. Click **OK**.

    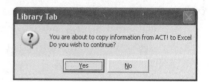

    *You will be asked if you want to copy the information from ACT! to Excel. Respond **Yes** to bring the Excel document up to date.*

8. Save and close the Excel document.

    Do not move off the current record until you have saved the document and returned to view mode.

9. Answer **Yes** to save the changes.

    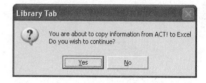

☞ *The following practice assumes that you have Excel on your PC. If you do not, continue with the next chapter.*

Practice: *Mapping Fields*

Step	What to do	How to do it/Comments
1.	Lookup the "My Record" and attach the **Commission Calc.xls.**	You can find this file in the **\My Documents\ACT\Database** folder.
2.	View and then Edit **Commission Calc.xls** on the Library tab.	Display the Library tab if necessary. If it is not already displayed, select **Commission Calc.xls** from the Attachment List. If the document does not *automatically* display, click the View Document button then click the Edit Document button.
3.	Display the Map Fields dialog box.	Click the **Map Fields** button on the Library toolbar.
4.	Map the **Contact** field to cell **A3**. Map the **Last Film Salary** field to cell **B4**. *Don't forget to click Add for each mapped field.* *We are about to map the **Contact** field in ACT! to cell A3 in Excel. Cell A3 currently contains the words **Contact Name**.*	Locate and select **Contact** in the **ACT! Fields available** list, Locate and select **A3** from the **Excel Data available** column, click the **Add** button to add this definition to the **Currently Mapped Fields:** list. Repeat, mapping the **Last Film Salary** field to cell **B4**. Click **OK** and respond **Yes** when asked if you want to copy the information.
5.	Save and close the Excel Document.	Click the **Close Document and Save Changes** button on the Library Toolbar.

(Try It...)

If you have the **Auto Update** option checked for your Excel links, and then check the **Display For All Contacts** check box at the top of the Library tab, the Library tab will update the worksheet with the current contact information as you move from record to record. **You must be in Edit mode for this update to occur**. Keep in mind however, it is still one document and linked to the original contact only

☞ *If you save and close while you are viewing a different contact, it is that contact's data that will be saved, not the data the document is linked to. However, when you view the file again in Edit mode, the data for the current contact will once again be displayed.*

If you keep an Excel Commission or Invoice template attached to the My Record, it is easy to then view the calculated results for other records in your database.

...display an Excel "template" with a lookup

1. Lookup the contact that contains the sample template.

   Templates like Invoices are good examples for this feature.

2. Select, View, and Edit the Excel file.

3. Click **Display for all Contacts**.

4. Lookup contacts to view.

   You could lookup a specific contact or ID/Status of Client

5. Scroll through the contacts to see the calculated results of each record.

6. Update any ACT! field data, click the Save icon on the ACT! toolbar (not the Library tab toolbar), and the spreadsheet will be updated with the new information.

If you want to save a displayed template with the current data, break the connection with the ACT! fields so that it no longer updates by following the next two steps.

7. To save the specific data to a file with a new name, click the **Save Document As** icon on the Library tab toolbar.

This would be valuable for saving an Invoice as

Inv-Hepburn-2002-09-29

8. Click the **Add Document** icon to attach the newly saved file to the current contact.

Practice: *Calculating Other Commissions*

Try It...

Step	What to do	How to do it/Comments
1.	You should still be viewing the Commission Calculation worksheet in edit mode on I.M.'s record. Click the **Display for all Contacts** on the **Library** tab	
2.	Lookup all Clients.	**Lookup, ID/Status...**, type Client, click **OK**.
3.	Move from Contact to Contact and view the changes in the Commission Calc worksheet.	
4.	Update the **Last Film Salary** for Judy Garland to $45,000	**Lookup, Last Name,** type gar, **OK,** click on the **Status** tab and change the Last Film Salary to $45,000. Click on the Library tab again and then click the **Save** icon on the ACT! toolbar. Updated!
5.	Lookup Kate's record and display her picture again.	You cannot display her specific files until you remove the check from the **Display for All Contacts.**

Removing Library Documents

At some point you may wish to remove a document from the library tab. Removing a Library document will not actually delete the file, it will only remove the reference to it in ACT!

... remove documents from the Library tab

1. Display the contact to whom you have attached the document, display the Library tab.

    If you have attached more than one document, the document you wish to remove may not be displayed in the attachment list.

2. If the file name is not already displayed, use the drop-down arrow to display the **Attachment List** and select the desired document.

    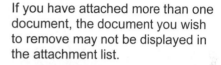
    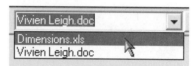

3. Click the **Remove Document** button on the **Library** toolbar

    This will remove the item from the list *and* from the **Notes/History** tab. However, *the file will not be deleted.* The file will still exist in its original folder until you delete it.

☞ *If you do not want the Library tab to display, you can hide it by clicking* **Edit, Preferences...,** *remove the check from* **Enable Library Tab, OK.**

Review: Library Tab

1.	Attach the **StarsRUs Invoice.xls** (found in the \My Documents\ACT\Database folder) to the My Record and then create an invoice for Cyd Charisse. Save the invoice and attach it to her record.
2.	Try attaching other documents to contacts in this database.

Database Administration

If you find yourself administering an ACT! database, there are a few skills you might wish to cultivate. In this section we will,

☑ Learn the basics of database maintenance.

☑ Familiarize yourself with ACT!'s built in backup and restore utilities.

☑ Begin to clean up our database, dealing with duplicates and replacing old data.

☑ Create new logon users.

Database Maintenance

As your database becomes larger and larger, there are a few things you can do to reduce the size of the file and speed up your queries. These fall under the category of Database Maintenance. Compress and Reindex operations are primary to the general health of your database, and they should be done on a regular basis.

Records are not truly deleted until you compress the database. Compressing "rebuilds" the data, removing the records marked for deletion and filling in the holes they leave behind.

While you are compressing your database, it is a good idea to reindex as well. Reindexing rebuilds the index files which the database uses to organize your ACT! data.

...maintain your database

1. **File, Administration, Database Maintenance...**

   The **Periodic Maintenance** tab of the dialog box is the most often used.

   The **Compress Database** option removes the blank space left behind when you have deleted Contact records, notes, histories, opportunities, etc..

   It is a good idea to enable the **Remind me again in** option to set a reminder to perform this important task.

The **Database Maintenance** dialog box displays.

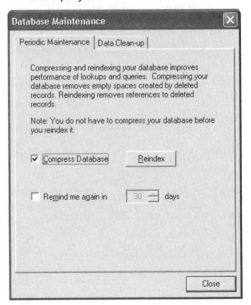

2. If you wish to remove old notes, histories and activities among other things. You can display the **Data Clean-up** tab.

    On the **Data Clean-up** tab, place a check in the appropriate check-boxes, specify how far back to keep the items

While it may seem desirable to keep this information forever, in a mature database these items can take up more space than the Contact information. (Do you really need a record of a phone call you made to a Contact *3 years ago?*)

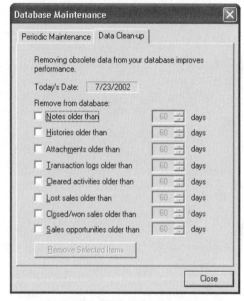

3. Click either

    Remove Selected Items
    or
    Reindex

    (depending upon which tab you are viewing). They both Reindex the database.

When you click **Reindex,** a **Working...** dialog apprizes you of the progress. Depending on the size of the database, this can take a while. *Be patient.*

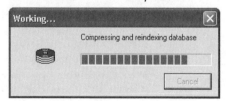

☞ *DO NOT, under any circumstances, reboot your machine during this process. Even if you see a message that ACT! is not responding. Don't believe the message. ACT! will eventually complete the process. Rebooting at this time may irreparably damage your ACT! database.*

Setting a Password for Yourself

You may add a password to your database anytime you decide that you want to password protect your data.

...add a password to your database

How To...

1. **File, Administration, Set Password...**

   The **Set Password** dialog box displays.

2. If you do not currently have a password, start by entering your **New password:** and then **Retype new password:** As you type, your password will display as ***

    Passwords are not case-sensitive. They may contain spaces and numbers.

3. Click **OK**.

 *If you want to remove your password, use the same procedure except type your current password in the **Old password:** area and leave the **New password:** and **Retype new password:** areas blank. Click **OK** and your password will be replaced with a blank password.*

There is an option that allows ACT! to **Remember password** as you log in. Then what is the point of a password! Either remove the password or uncheck this option.

 Actually in multi-user environments, some users leave it checked to make it easier to log in from their own PC, while others on the network would have to know their password in order to log on as them.

Deleting A Database

As you work with ACT! you may find yourself with a useless database. Perhaps you merged two smaller databases into one, and the smaller one is now redundant. The problem with deleting the database from the Windows Explorer is the number of files that actually make up an ACT! database. If you don't delete all of the supporting files, they end up wasting disk space. And then there is the possibility of inadvertently deleting a file from a database that you want to keep! Also, we have heard of people (not you of course) that delete a database by clicking **File, Open** and then clicking on the database they wish to delete and then pressing the **[Delete]** key. This method will not delete all of the associated files and leaves a mess behind.

Instead of using these other methods to clean up old databases, use ACT!'s built-in delete database feature.

...delete a database

How To...

1. **File, Administration, Delete Database...**

   A **Delete Database** dialog box is displayed.

2. Select the file you wish to delete.

   Be careful. You cannot undo this action.

3. Click **Delete**.

4. Click **Yes** to confirm the deletion.

   The database and all related files are deleted.

☞ *You are not permitted to delete a database that is currently open. (But that's a good thing!) Also if a database is password protected, you must know the password before you can delete it.*

Backup

In the 1967 movie "The Graduate," a friend of Benjamin Braddock's family pulled young Ben aside and offered him, "One word, just one word...plastics!" Back then, watching the movie, we remember giggling at the idea that plastics would be worth investing in. We did **not** invest in plastics back then. Considering the growth of the plastics industry since '67, we **do** regret not listening to what in retrospect was sound advice.

We learned our lesson back then. Now we have one word for you... just one word...**backup**!

If you put ACT! to good use, your contact data will be critical to the operation of your business.

- ✔ As your data matures, the loss of all those contacts and the Notes, Histories, and Activities associated with them could be devastating.

- ✔ If you backup your data regularly, however, you will never be in a position where you have to reconstruct your entire database. (A task that may well be impossible.)

- ✔ Unfortunately, regular backups are easy to forget, given all the other important things we have to do each day. But what is more important than protecting your data? So how do you remember this most important of tasks? We are glad you asked....

ACT! comes with a built-in backup utility that not only can backup all of your database information, but can remind you when it is time to backup again.

You need to decide two things:

- ✔ Where your backup will be stored (this should not be on the same disk drive as the database files for what we hope are obvious reasons-hard drive crash...PC stolen).

- ✔ How often you want to be reminded (a lesser-used database might be backed up with less frequency than one that is constantly being changed).

...backup your ACT! database

How To...

1. Choose **File, Backup...** .

    The **Backup** dialog specifies the name of the **Current database:**, and suggests a location and name for the backup file.

    👉 *The backup utility compresses the data in your database into a ".zip" file. This allows a great deal of data to be stored in a minimum of disk space.*

The **Backup** dialog box is displayed:

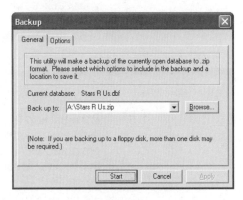

2. Use the **Browse...** button to change the suggested location and file name for the backup as desired.

Any location other than the drive where the actual database is located is acceptable. Backup suggests A:\ (your diskette drive). The backup can span multiple diskettes, but if you have a high capacity alternative (like an Iomega Zip© drive or a network drive), you will probably prefer using it instead.

3. Click the **Options** tab.

    Use **Options** to specify what to backup. If you customize any of the items in the **Include** list, you probably want to back them up. If you use only ACT! standard reports, labels, etc. there is no need to back them up.

    It's a good idea to enable the **Remind me to backup up every** option, to specify how

The **Options** tab displays:

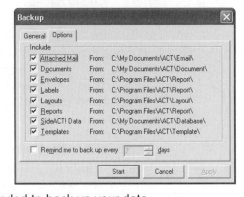

often you would like to be reminded to back up your data.

4.   When you are done specifying the location and options for your backup, click **Start**.

ACT! proceeds to back up your data. Backup progress is displayed:

5.   If the backup requires more than one diskette, you are prompted as necessary. When the backup is complete, you will be notified.

☞   *If you tell ACT! to remind you to backup at a set interval, the next time you start ACT! (after that interval has passed) you will be reminded it is time to backup. You can refuse to backup (Cancel), you can even tell this reminder to shut up, but we don't recommend it.*

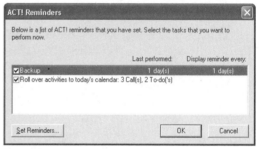

Restoring a Backup

It's not much good to backup if you can't get the backup "back up." Restoring a backup is an easy task. In fact you did it at the beginning of this study guide if you restored the database from the CD.

...restore a backup

1.   If your backup was done to removable media, place the media in the appropriate drive.

Examples of removable media are 3 ½" diskettes, Zip© disks, etc.

2.   Choose **File, Restore…** from the menu.

The **Restore** dialog box is displayed.

The name and location of the last backup is already displayed. The default database folder is also set for you.

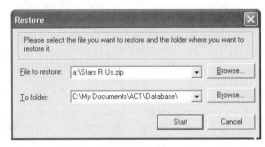

3. If the file you wish to restore is not specified, or if the **To folder:** location is incorrect, use one of the **Browse...** buttons to change them, and click **Start**.

The database will be restored to the specified folder. ACT! will apprize you of its progress.

☞ *ACT! includes some additional templates in sub-folders under the main \Report, \Template folders. When using ACT!'s Restore feature, the files that were originally maintained in the subfolders will be placed in the their respective main folders.*

Practice: *Backup Your New Database*

Step	What to do	How to do it/Comments
1.	Even though your study guide database is just for practice, let's back it up.	You should have the **Stars R Us** database open.
2.	Backup the database to a diskette in the A:\ drive. Do not back up **Envelopes**, **Labels**, **Layouts**, or **Reports**.	Place a diskette in your disk drive, if necessary. Choose **File, Backup...**, in the **Backup** box, type **A:\STARS**, display the **Options** dialog tab, remove the checks from the first four check boxes, and click **Start**. When the backup is complete, click **OK**.

☞ *In real life, that process takes a great deal longer. We are aware of how boring performing back ups can be, but consistent backups are the best deterrent to crippling data loss. Don't forget them!*

Reminders

"Remember to take your briefcase." "Don't forget your lunch." "Wash behind your ears." These are all reminders. Sometimes they're necessary in order to get the job done, but sometimes they are just plain annoying.

You just saw an example of an ACT! reminder, when you chose to remind yourself to backup your database. ACT! has reminders for everything from rolling over activities to today's calendar to running group membership rules. With the exception of roll over reminders (which display whenever you open your database), you can set reminders to run at any interval you wish. Reminders prompt you to backup your database, perform database maintenance, run group membership rules, update your Outlook calendar, etc. If this works for you, great! If it makes you nuts, there is a way to silence those task masters permanently.

...set reminders

1.   **F**ile, Set **R**eminders...

2.   As necessary, click the drop-down arrow and choose a type of **Reminder:**.

Options are: Backup, Database maintenance, Roll over activities to today's calendar, Run group membership rules, Synchronize, Update Outlook and ACT! calendars.

3.   Choose a **Display Reminder** option.

Click **Every** and then type or click one of the arrows to specify the number of days between reminders.

Click **Don't remind me again** to disable the selected feature.

4.   Repeat steps 2 and 3 as necessary until all options are set to your liking.

Each option can have a different time interval.

5.   Click **OK**.

Practice: *Silencing Reminders*

Step	What to do	How to do it/Comments
1.	Display the **Set Reminders** dialog box.	**File, Set Reminders...**
2.	What is the current setting for **Roll over activities to today's calendar**?	Choose the option from the **Reminder** list.
3.	Turn off the Rollover options.	Remove the check-marks for all three boxes, click **OK**.

Try It...

Cleaning up the Data

Over time your database will need a little spring cleaning. You will find duplicate names in the database. There will be companies whose name or address information needs to be changed (on 25 records…Yikes).

Duplicates

Who knows how they get there, but almost every database will eventually contain duplicate names. Sometimes you forget that you already input the name. If you are working in a multi-user environment, someone might not have used the Lookup command to see if the name was already in the database before they input the name again. If you input names from another database or another source, you can bring in duplicates.

ACT! does have a tool that can help you locate some of these duplicates, but there will still be some you will have to find on your own.

…lookup duplicates

How To…

1. **Tools, Scan for Duplicates**

   ACT! determines duplicate contact records based on 3 fields. If the "Company", "Contact", and "Phone" fields match *exactly* (down to the period after Inc.), then the record would be considered a duplicate. If all three fields do not match, ACT! will not tag the records as duplicates.

2. Duplicates will be displayed in a lookup for you to deal with. If no duplicates were found, you will see the message to the right.

Actually it is usually pretty rare for ACT! to find duplicates this way (they occur usually only in multi-user sync environments). If you are entering data and you input a new record that matches the Company, Contact and Phone of another entry, then ACT! will display a warning letting you know that you are trying to create a duplicate record.

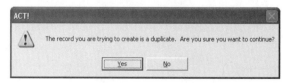

Tips for Dealing with Duplicates

However, sometimes you just know that there are duplicates in the database and you need to find and deal with them. While not very sophisticated, the way we have found to be the easiest is to display the database in Contact List view. Add the First Name and Last Name columns to the list (see page 63 to refresh your memory) to the right of the Contact name. Click on the Last Name column to sort alphabetically by Last Name. Start scrolling to eyeball the database and find the duplicates.

Contact List

As you locate duplicates, you could add them to a Duplicate group to deal with them later or you could deal with them now. The simplest way to deal with them now is to look at each record in Contact view to determine which record to keep (or cut and paste any data from the record you plan to delete into the record you plan to keep). Then you can select and cut the notes and histories from one contact record and paste them into the record you plan to keep. You can do the same for activities and opportunities.

☞ *If the activity, history, etc. was performed by someone else, cutting and pasting will transfer ownership to the person logged on doing the clean-up work. You may need to re-assign the activities, notes, etc.*

There are several more complicated ways of doing this. For example, you could edit the "duplicates" so that their Company, Contact, and Phone information do match exactly and they can be located with the **Tools, Scan for Duplicates** command. Once you have this list, export the data to a database named **Duplicates**. OK, now this is the scary part. Do we need to tell you to Backup your database before trying this one? Delete all of the duplicate records…Yes all of them. Now import the **Duplicates** database. On import, the fields from the record with the most recent Edit Date will be used, and all notes, histories, activities, opportunities, etc. will be merged into one record. This is a good method for dealing with lots of duplicates with notes and activities entered by several logon users.

Practice: *Dealing with Duplicates*

Try It...

Step	What to do	How to do it/Comments
1.	Use the menu option to find duplicates in our database.	**Tools, Scan for Duplicates** None found.
2.	Display the database in **Contact List** view. Add the **Last Name** and **First Name** columns to the right of the Contact name.	Right-click the column header and select **Add columns to view…** Select the fields and click **Add**. **OK** Drag the fields to the right of the Contact name.
3.	Lookup all records if necessary. Do you see any duplicates? Why didn't ACT! find the duplicates?	Vivian Leigh. Her first name was spelled differently.
4.	Her first name is spelled with an "e" not an "a" Vivien Correct the spelling of her name in the wrong record.	
5.	Now scan for duplicates again.	Now ACT! can find the duplicate since the Company, Contact, and Phone number now all match exactly.
6.	Let's decide to keep the record with the e-mail address and delete the other. However, the "wrong" one has 3 histories we want to keep. So cut and paste the notes into the keeper and then delete the record without the e-mail address.	Move to the record without the e-mail address and click on the **Notes/History** tab.

Click on the first history icons at the far left to select the whole line. Then **[Shift+click]** on the last icon. Click on the menu command, **Edit, Cut** (or press **[Ctrl+X]**).

Move to the record with the e-mail address. Click on the menu command, **Edit, Paste** (or press **[Ctrl+V]**). Voilá, the histories have been transferred. |

Edit Replace

Do you have one company name spelled 25 different ways in the database? Is the city name spelled just as many wrong ways? Do you have a client that has moved and now you have to change the address line on lots of records? All of these changes can be easily handled by ACT!'s Replace command.

...replace field data in multiple records

How To...

1.	Lookup the records that need to be changed.	You may have to work with the contacts in the Contact List view in Tag mode to get to the list that you want.
2.	Return to **Contacts** view if necessary and select **Edit, Replace**	The command is not available in **Contact List** view mode.

Contacts

3.	ACT! displays a blank record screen.	It looks as though you have pressed the **[Insert]** key to insert a new record, but the toolbar only has a few icons on it, instead of the normal long toolbar.
4.	Type the new data in the field(s) that needs to be changed.	If you are correcting the Address for all records in the lookup, enter all of the corrections on the Address fields including City, State and Zip if necessary.
5.	Click the **Apply** button.	

6.	Click **Yes** to apply the changes to the lookup.	You are sure that you did the lookup aren't you? If you didn't perform a lookup first, this change will be applied to the entire database (which would be the 'current' lookup.)
7.	If prompted, click **OK**.	You may receive an message that no records match your lookup criteria. You you just changed them all...of course there are no more records that match that old criteria.

☞ *To replace a field with data and make it blank, click in the field that you want to be blank and press [Ctrl+F5]. It enters <<BLANK>> in the field. You can also use the Replace dialog to copy one field to another or to swap fields.*

Step	What to do	How to do it/Comments
1.	We received a notice that Tough Guy Productions has moved from Los Angeles to… 1400 Smith Street Houston, TX 77002 Phone: 713-661-5095 Fax: 713-661-5096 No suite number	Lookup all contacts that belong to the Company Tough Guy Productions. In **Contacts** view, **Edit**, **Replace** Enter the new address and phone number information. Click in the 2nd address line and press **[Ctrl+F5]** to erase any data in this field. Click the **Apply** button.

Try It…

Setting Up a Multi-User Database

ACT! can be set up on a network so that other users can access the same database at the same time. You will only need to do three things to prepare for this type of setup.

✔ move the database that everyone will share onto a networked drive to which everyone in your team has access. (You might as well move the layout, template, and report folders to the shared drive as well, so that everyone can share everything.)

✔ add logon user names to the database

✔ change the edit preferences on each logon users PC to enable ACT! to find the database to the mapped drive on the network.

Creating New Logon Users

A Contact database located on a network can be shared by many users. This has many advantages, among which are shared access to common information and ease of maintenance. In order for many people to share a single file and still maintain private records, they must be defined as users.

...define a database user

1. Enter the new users as a contact record first.

   You can use the Duplicate command to fill in your company name, address and phone number first. A real time saver.

2. **File, Administration, Define Users...**

   The **Define Users** dialog box is displayed.

   A list of current user ID's is displayed on the left side of the dialog box.

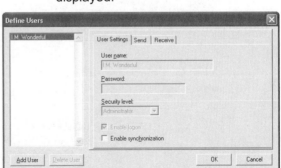

ACT!

3. Click **Add User**

   A new User is created with a default user name of **User1**.

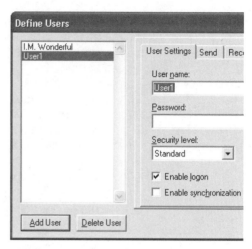

4. Type a new user name.

   This is their ID for this database. You can use their actual name or create an abbreviated ID of some sort.

5. Set the password, if desired.

   If you do not specify a password, none will be required for entry into the database under this ID.

6. Choose **Enable logon** and select a **Security Level**.

   Choose from three security levels:
   Standard - user can see, add, delete, and modify records, and synchronize with another database or user. This user cannot add new users to the database, perform maintenance on the database, or modify the database fields.
   Administrator - user can make any changes they wish to the database.
   Browse - user can look but not touch. No changes can be made to records, nor can new records be added.

7. Repeat for each user you wish to define, and click **OK**.

   A list of your new user names displays. You must assign each a My Record.

8. As each new user is highlighted, click **Assign now...**

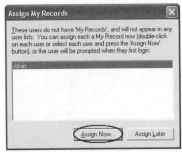

9. Since you have already entered the new user's name and address (Step 1), don't retype it here, click **Select...** to select it from your ACT! database.

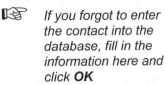

☞ *If you forgot to enter the contact into the database, fill in the information here and click OK*

10. Start typing the last few letters of the user's last name to help quickly scroll to it. When you have clicked on the user's name to select it, click **OK**.

Repeat steps 8-10 as necessary to setup the rest of the users.

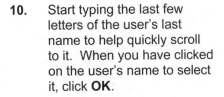

☞ *Once you have defined more than one login user, users are asked to logon when they open this database. They need to know their ID exactly as it appears in the user list and their password (if any). ID's and passwords are not case sensitive.*

File Locations for a Multi-User Database

Once you have set up the user to login to the database, you need to make some minor changes to their ACT! so that they can more easily open the database and share ACT! files. These changes are all made in the **Preferences** dialog.

 The network drive that holds the database should be mapped on each person's PC. For information about mapping network drives, see Microsoft Windows help in how to "map a drive letter."

...change default file locations

How To...

1. **Edit, Preferences**, click on the **General** tab if necessary.

2. In the **Location:** area, browse to the drive and folder on the network where the database has been saved and click **OK**.

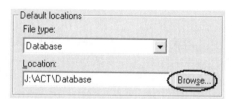

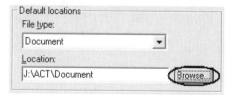 *If you copied the Document, Layout, Macro, Mail, Query, Report, and Template folders to the network drive, then you should also map each PC's **Default locations** to the new locations so that each user can share the files.*

3. Click the drop-down button in the **File type:** area and select **Document**

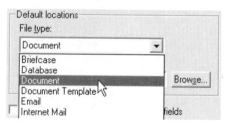

4. After you have selected a new **File type:**, then **Browse...** to the Document folder on the shared network drive.

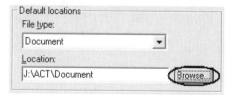

5. Repeat steps 3 and 4 for the remaining **File type(s):**

   Document Template,
   Email,
   Internet Mail
   Layout
   Macro,
   Netlinks
   Query,
   Report, Label, Envelope

6. Click **OK**.

Sharing these folders means that as you update the files, the changes are immediately available to other users of the database.

Some folders like Briefcase and Spelling Dictionary should remain on the local PC (if some user adds an incorrect word to the dictionary, do you really want everyone in the company to use that dictionary?)

After you have changed the preferences for the user, open the database for them. When you click **File**, **Open** the database name should be displayed.

Review:	*Database Administration*	
	1.	Open the Personal database and back it up.
	2.	Then you can Compress and Reindex the Personal database.
	3.	Make Pal a logon user in case she needs to access our private contacts.
	4.	Reopen the Stars R Us database.

Try It...

ACT!

Database Design & Layouts

To be able to view the data you want in the exact way you want it, you will:

- ☑ Create a new customized database

- ☑ View existing layouts.

- ☑ Create a new layout.

- ☑ Add and format fields.

- ☑ Save and test a layout.

- ☑ Create custom tabs.

- ☑ Edit field entry order and set group stops.

Creating a New Database

Creating a new database is not something you do everyday. In fact, most users do it only once. In this Study Guide you have worked with a sample database we created for your use. Now that you are ready to go forth into the world of Contact Management, you need to know how to create your own ACT! database.

When ACT! creates a new database, it creates it with a single record already in it. This is the My Record we talked about earlier. The contents of the My Record are important because ACT! uses them in reports and document templates to enter things about you, like company name, address, phone etc. The My Record also defines you as a user in a multi-user database.

...create a new database

How To...

1. Choose **File, New...** from the menu

    or

    press **[Ctrl+N]**.

The **New** dialog box appears. **ACT! Database** is the default selection.

2. Click **OK**.

    ACT! assumes you want to save your new database in a folder named **Database**. It is recommended you save any new files you create in the folder that ACT! displays.

The **New Database** dialog box appears.

3. In the **File name:** box, type a name for your new database, click **Save**.

When you click **Save**, a new database is created. Once the structure is complete, ACT! displays an **Enter "My Record" Information** dialog box.

4. Enter the information for the "My Record" for your new database.

 It is not uncommon for this dialog box to contain data that is not yours. Don't dwell on where this information came from, just replace it with the name, address, etc. of the person for whom this database is being created (probably you) and click OK.

5. When you click **OK** a confirmation dialog box is displayed. Assuming you have entered the **My Record** information correctly, click **Yes**.

This confirmation step should reinforce the importance of this step.

ACT! can only have one database open at a time. When you create a new database, ACT! closes the open database before it begins creating the new one. Don't confuse database windows with Word Processing windows. You can have several documents open that are related to the same database. However, only one database is open at any time.

You can create a new database for yourself now or later. However for the purposes of this guide, the following customization exercises assume you are still using the Stars R Us database.

Customizing Contact Fields

You may have noticed all of the **User** fields available to you in the Contacts screen. These fields are just begging to be customized to your needs. You may want to customize the field for several reasons.

First you want to give the field a *specific name* so that as you enter data you always put the same kind of information into the same field (Did you put the customer # in User 1 or User 2 on all those other records? Well, let's just name the field so you don't have to remember which one you want to use.)

Secondly, you can *change the size of the field*, so that if you need to type in a lot of information, ACT! will give you enough space. On the other hand, if you want User 3 to be "Mailing List?" and all you want to enter is "Y" or "N", then you could change the field size from 50 characters to 1 character and save some space in your database.

Fields can be customized to hold a variety of specialized data types and can display pop-ups of pre-defined answers to ease data entry. They can be forced to display uppercase characters only, initial capital letters, or web site addresses, to name a few. You also can require that the field contain dates or numbers only.

You can change the customization options for any field in your database. Most often you change the User fields (because you're the user and that's what they are there for). When you run out of those fields to modify, you can start adding new fields.

...customize a field

How To...

1. Display the Contacts screen. If the field you wish to customize is displayed, move the insertion point into the field.

   You do not have to select the field you wish to customize, but it saves you some time.

2. Choose **Edit, Define Fields...** from the menu.

   The **Define Fields** dialog box is displayed:

The field you selected before issuing this command is automatically selected. This is a long list, and pre-selection can make the process easier.

If it is not already selected, scroll to the field and click to select the field you wish to modify.

3. Change the options for the field and click **OK**.

The **Define Fields** dialog box is described on the following pages.

There are three tabs that hold the customization options to customize our fields.

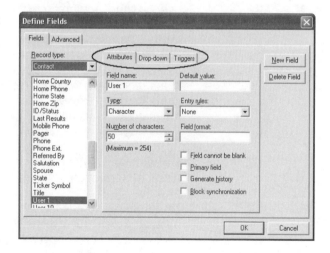

✔ Attributes

✔ Drop-down

✔ Triggers

The Attributes Tab

Let's focus on each of the tabs separately as we modify the database design. Attributes allow you to specify many things about a field:

Fie̲ld name: - What name do you want the field to have (**User 1** is just a bit too generic, don't you think)? Keep it short, but spaces are allowed.

Default ̲value: - Any data specified for this attribute automatically appears in the field when you create a new Contact record. You should specify a default value when most new Contacts should have the same information in this field like the default Account Exec or the default State if all your jobs are in TX.

Typ̲e: - What kind of data is permitted in this field? There are a wide variety of choices available in this drop-down list. Choose the one that is most suitable for your uses.

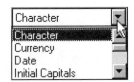

Character allows you to type any combination of characters and numbers that you like. All character-based fields (Character, Initial Capitals, Lowercase, Uppercase or URL) have a maximum of 254 characters. If the user needs to type any more than that, they need to use the Notes feature in ACT!.

Initial Capitals will make the first character of each word a capital letter and each succeeding letter lowercase…regardless of how the user inputs the data. This field type is great for use with simple fields such as those requiring a "Yes" or "No" answer so that all answers maintain the same format. However it can also cause problems. For example if you made the Contact field an "Initial Capitals" field, then "Jane de laVega CPA" would become "Jane De Lavega Cpa".

Lowercase would make any text entered…well…all lowercase. As in all character-based fields, numbers are allowed.

Uppercase is handy for fields that will contain a single character as an answer (like "Y" for Yes or "N" for No) or for customer codes (which may be a combination of characters and numbers, but you want all the characters entered as uppercase).

URL will make any web address entered an active link that when clicked opens the specified web page in ACT!'s Internet Services window.

Currency will *display* a dollar sign and minimum of 2 decimal places, regardless of what lower number you enter in the **A̲fter de̲cimal:** option.

If you enter 0 places after the decimal, then all numbers are rounded down to the lowest integer. If you want to print reports with no $ signs or decimals points, use the **Numeric** field type (which not only uses commas, but it will also allow you to display no numbers after the decimal point). This field can be used in ACT!'s Summary (Total, Average, Minimum and Maximum) calculations.

Numeric allows a maximum of 18 numbers (more than a trillion) Commas and decimal points don't count as part of the number of digits you assign, but will display. Any alpha characters in this field will be ignored. This field can be used in ACT!'s Summary (Total, Average, Minimum and Maximum) calculations.

Phone fields automatically format numbers entered as a phone number (with dashes and parentheses) according to the country selected. The default country for ACT! is selected upon installation of the program. If the user enters the Country in the address area, prior to entering the phone number, the phone will be formatted to that country's standards along with the appropriate country code for dialing internationally.

Date or **Time** Both Date and Time fields are formatted according to the settings in the Windows Regional Settings (found in Control Panel).

Annual Event option only displays if the field **Typ_e:** is Date. Classifying a date field as an Annual Event, makes that field available for searches based on the month and day only (ignoring the designated year). This option is ideal for birthdays, anniversaries, annual contract renewal dates, etc.

☞ *If you have an existing character-based field that you would like to change to an Annual Event field, it is best to create a new date field (with the Annual Event option checked). Next, change all of your existing dates to a numeric format (12/5 instead of December 5). Years are optional. You can then use the **Edit, Replace** feature...click on the **Copy a Field** icon to copy from the character-based field into the new date field. This method insures that as the dates are converted from character to date, that you do not lose any of your original information if you need to correct it in the new field.*

Entry rules: - This option contains up to three choices:

✔ **None** - you may enter data by any method (by typing or from a drop-down list). This is the normal option.

✔ **Protected** - the user may not enter or edit data in this field. You may view the contents only. Data can be imported into this field, but the user cannot edit the data. (You can always unprotect for short periods of time to enter data.) The field will appear with a gray background in the Contacts view indicating that the user cannot edit the field data.

✔ **Only from drop-down** - the user may not type data into the field. Field entry is only permitted from a drop-down list (see page 308 for more on drop-down lists). If you use this option, the field cannot be blank.

Number of characters: - How many characters can be entered into this field? The maximum length of a character field type is 254 characters, but be realistic. Be sure to designate only the number of characters that you need. For example, if you have a field that uses Y for Yes and N for No and those are the only options for the field, then change the number of characters to 1. Numeric and Currency fields can only be 18 characters long (which is more than a trillion). Commas, dollar signs, or decimals are not counted as part of the 18. Other field types have their own restrictions. The user may not exceed the number of characters specified by this attribute.

Field format: - Allows you to specify how the data entered in the field is to be automatically formatted. This attribute is only available for Character, Initial Capitals, Lowercase, and Uppercase data types. You cannot define a format for numeric fields. Field format is used when you need your data to have a very specific layout (like a social security number, for example).

☞ *Changing a field's format in an existing database can result in the loss of existing data. Any data that does not fit in the specified field format will be lost once you click **OK**.*

Entry format is defined using special symbols that control what type of data can be used and where:

This Code:	Represents this type of character:
#	Numeric (no letters or symbols)
@	Alphabetic (no numbers)
%	Alphanumeric (data entry anarchy!)

*If you right-click on the **Field format:** label in the **Define Fields** dialog box, it will display the codes and what they represent in a pop-up help box.*

When you specify a field format, you may only enter the types of characters specified by the field format. If you type more characters than the format specifies, they do not appear (e.g. the Number of characters is set to 50, but your field format is %%%%, then only 4 characters can be entered.). You may also specify default characters like parentheses or dashes.

Example:	Code:	Meaning:
LL-123	@@-####	Two alpha characters and three numeric characters. The dash would be entered for you.
A34-(ABC)	%%%-(@@@)	Three alpha or numeric characters and three alpha only characters. The dash and the parentheses are entered for you.

To enter any of the three placeholder symbols as actual symbols in the field, enter them preceded by a backslash (\) character. For example, \#### would display the # symbol once and then allow the entry of three numeric characters.

There are four other attributes we should discuss before we move on. These attributes are represented by four check boxes. Not all of these affect how data is *entered* into the field, but they can have a profound effect on your database in general.

Field cannot be blank - Need we say more? While this is a great option to remind you to fill in the really important fields, it can also be very irritating when used in practice…so use it sparingly.

Primary field - The contents of primary fields are duplicated when you choose **Contact, Duplicate Contact...** from the Contacts screen menu, or **Group, Duplicate Group** from the Groups screen menu. Use this option for any field you wish to be carried over to a new Contact.

 The default primary Contact fields are Address 1, Address 2, Address 3, City, State, Zip, Company, Country, Fax, and Phone. The default primary group fields are Address 1, Address 2, Address 3, City, Country, Description, Parent ID, Group Level, Division, State, and Zip. You might want to change Web Site, Ticker, and ID/Status to Primary fields.

Generate history - Generate history fields cause a history entry to be created when the field is modified. If you apply this attribute to a field, and then make a change to the field, an entry is created on the **Notes/History** tab. The entry records which field was changed, the date on which it was changed, and the data that was changed in the field. We have already seen two fields like this...do you remember? Last Results and ID/Status.

Block synchronization - When database synchronization with other users or database files takes place, changes can be made to the fields in your database. If you have defined a field for your own personal use, the block synchronization attribute prevents the field from being changed when you apply a synchronization message (more on this later). The attribute also prevents the field data from being sent when you send a synchronization message.

Once you have set all of the desired attributes and clicked **OK**, be patient. On larger databases, processing changes can take some time. Whenever possible we recommend setting up the fields before entering data into your database.

Practice: *Field Attributes*

Try It...

Step	What to do	How to do it/Comments
1.	While still in the Stars R Us database, display the **Define Fields** dialog box for the **User 1** field.	Click the **User 1** field and choose **E̲dit, D̲efine Fields...**.
2.	Change **User 1** to Social Security # with a maximum of 11 characters. Format the field to display like this: 123-45-6789	Make sure **User 1** is the selected field. In the **Fie̲ld name:** text box, type the new field name. Change the **Nu̲mber of characters:** from 50 to 11. Click **Y̲es** if a message displays warning about a potential data loss. In the **Field f̲ormat:** text box, enter: ###-##-####
3.	Change **User 2** to "Min Film Salary". Change the **Typ̲e:** to Numeric with 8 characters before the decimal and 0 characters after the decimal (surely we will never go over $99,000,000/film.) Make it a history field so we can tell when the minimums changed.	Click on the **User 2** field and change the name. Click the drop-down for **Typ̲e:** and select **Numeric**. Answer **Yes** to verify that you understand there may be a loss of data. Enter 8 before and 0 after. Place a check in the **Generate h̲istory** field.
4.	Save your new settings.	Click **OK**.
5.	Lookup these stars and enter their SS# and minimum film salaries: Clark Gable...................... 345-78-6789 .... 55,000 Humphrey Bogart .... 025-67-0987 .... 48,000 Clara Bow .... 934-45-2345 .... 27,000 ☞ *SS#s will seem difficult to enter, since you will have to click at the beginning of the field (or press the [Home] key) to enter the date. Don't worry...we'll fix this.*	
6.	View the **Notes/History** tab for Gable, Bogart, and Bow to see how the salaries were recorded.	Changes are saved to a contact record as soon as you change to another record. Clara's "Min Film Salary" will not display in Notes/History until you move off her record and then back to it.

The Drop-down Tab

Using drop-down lists can speed the process of entering data, especially in those fields where a limited number of choices are possible. ACT! provides preset lists for several fields, but even they can't know everything. You may find yourself wishing you could add entries of your own, or perhaps remove unneeded entries from a particular list. Well, guess what....

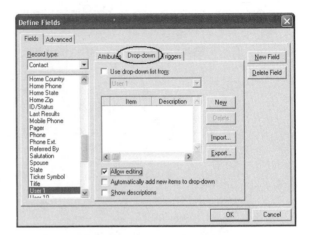

The **Drop-down** tab allows you to create or modify a drop-down list for a database field. You can also use this tab to remove the drop-down arrow from fields that will never have drop-down values.

You can identify a field with a drop-down by the drop-down button that appears to the right of the field when it is active.

✔ All of the character-based User fields may contain drop-down lists.

✔ If you have several fields that need the same information in their drop-downs, you can share one list among several fields. This feature cuts down on data entry and helps in upkeep.

✔ Once you use a drop-down from another field, you may edit the list from any of the fields that share the list. Changes made to the drop-down list in one field are reflected in all sharing fields.

✔ If you wish to create a new list or add to an existing one, it is simple to add individual items to a field (empty or otherwise).

...create a field with a drop-down arrow

1. Click in the field to add a drop-down list. **Edit, Define Fields**....

2. Click the **Drop-down** tab.

3. To use an existing drop-down list, click the **Use drop-down list from:** check box and select the desired field from the list box. (e.g. Home City uses the City drop-down list…no need to retype all those cities!)

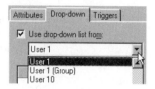

4. To create your own list…

   To add an item, click **New**. Type the Item and **[Tab]** to (or click in) Description to type one if desired.

   To delete an item, select it and click **Delete**.

5. To allow the users to make changes to the drop-down list, put a check in **Allow editing**.

   To update the list as the user types in new entries, put a check in **Automatically add new items to drop-down**

   To **Show descriptions**, put a check in this feature.

6. To Import a drop-down list, click **Import**...

   ☞ *A Browse button, displayed at the right of the text box, can help you find your text file if you don't know the path.*

   Append imported items: option will add to any existing list items.

   Import item descriptions: imports the descriptions (if any) to the second column of the list.

7. Click **OK** to apply the changes.

Descriptions are useful for helping the user understand the code (e.g. Is MS Mississippi or Missouri?) If **Show descriptions** is checked then the descriptions will display, but they will not affect what is stored in the field.

If you want to remove the drop-down arrow from a field, remove the check from the **Allow editing** option.

Automatically add… can be handy for adding new cities to the drop-down as you work new territories, but it can also record misspelled cities in the drop-down.

An **Import** dialog box displays:

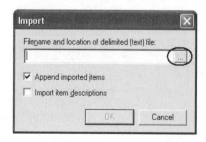

Practice: *More Fields with Drop-downs*

Try It...

Step	What to do	How to do it/Comments
1.	Edit the field definition for the **Social Security #** field and remove the drop-down option. This field should not be a drop-down field.	Click the **Social Security #** field, choose **Edit**, **Define Fields....** click the **Drop-down** tab. Remove the check from the **Allow editing** option.
2.	Change **User 3** to "Mailing List", with an Uppercase type, using only 1 character. The Default value is Y. Change it to be only from drop-down and don't allow any editing. The drop-down should display the following list and associated descriptions: N No Y Yes Be sure to show descriptions in case someone doesn't know what N means.	Change the field name in the appropriate box. Change the **Type:** to Uppercase. Change **Number of characters:** to 1. Enter a **Default value:** of Y Change **Entry rules:** to be **Only from drop-down.** Click on the **Drop-down** tab and click **New**. Enter "N" in the Item area. **[Tab]** to the Description and enter "No" Repeat for Yes. Uncheck **Allow editing**. Check **Show descriptions.**
3.	Change **User 4** to "Contract Renewal". Change the type to an annual event date.	Change the field name in the appropriate box. Change the **Type:** to Date. Click **Annual Event**
4.	Click **OK** to apply the changes.	
5.	Enter a Social Security # for My Record. Notice that the drop-down arrow no longer displays.	Click in the Social Security # field and enter whatever you like for the Social.
6.	Indicate that you want to be on the Mailing list.	Click in the Mailing List field and click the drop-down arrow to select Y.
7.	Enter the end of this month for your own contract renewal date.	

Creating Drop-down Lists for Importing

When you need to create a new list and the list is long, you will find the process faster if you create a text file containing the list information and import it into your ACT! field.

In order to be "importable," the data in your text file must be in a delimited state. If "delimited" sounds like one of those computer nerd terms....it is. But don't let it bother you. Delimited simply means a text file with dividers (delimiters) between each part of the record. There are only two parts possible in a drop-down list, the **item** and the **description**. The delimiter is a simple comma (,) between an item and its description and a hard return (meaning you press **[Enter]**) between lines.

You can create a text file in most any word processor, but the easiest place to do it is in the Windows Notepad. (Every Windows computer has this simple text editor usually found in Start, Programs, Accessories, Notepad)

...create a delimited text file for a drop-down

1. Run your text editor.

    You can use your favorite word processor, but we recommend the Windows Notepad. **Start, Programs, Accessories, Notepad**

2. In a text document, type the first entry, type a comma (,), then type the description. Press **[Enter]**.

    Susan,South
    Ted,West
    Coni,Central

    Each line becomes another entry. (*If you do not wish to type a description, you may omit the comma as well.*)

    ☞ *If the list contains words with spaces in them, you should put quote marks around the entries.*

    "Theodore Cooper","West Region"

3. When the list is complete, save the file as a text file. Text files have a **.TXT** file extension.

    If you are using Notepad, it saves as a text file by default. If you are using your word processor, you must tell it to save the document as a text file.

4. Close the file.

    Remember where you saved it. You will need this information later.

Most things that have to do with drop-downs (editing, adding, and deleting items) can be performed without displaying the **Define Fields** dialog box. There are, however, a couple of attributes you can control only from there.

All<u>o</u>w editing - Remove the check from this check-box and the field will not allow any user to add or change entries to the available list.

<u>S</u>how descriptions - If you wish the drop-down to display the description (if you entered one) for the items in the list, place a check in this box.

...import a delimited text file

1. Click the field.
    Edit, <u>D</u>efine Fields....

2. Click the **Drop-down** tab (if necessary), and click **Import....**

    ☞ *A Browse button is displayed at the right of the text box. You can click this button to find your text file if you don't know the path.*

An **Import** dialog box displays:

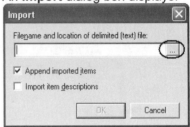

3. Specify the location and name of the delimited text file in the box provided.

    Type the path and filename, or use the Browse button to locate the file.

4. Choose the appropriate import options.

    If you leave **Append imported items:** checked, the file is added to any existing list items. If you check **Import item descriptions:**, the descriptions (if any) are placed in the second column of the list.

5. Click **OK**.

    The text file is imported for the selected field.

Practice: *Do You Have an Import License?*

Step	What to do	How to do it/Comments
1.	So many movie companies are opting to shoot in Canada now. We need to add the Canadian province abbreviations to our database. We've created a text file of Canadian province abbreviations and descriptions and placed it in the… \My Documents\ACT\Document folder. Double-click it to open the list to see what it looks like.	Review the list to see how it was created.
2.	Click on the **State** field and import the Canadian Provinces (Canada.txt).	Click on the **State** field. Click on the **Drop-down** tab if necessary. Click on the **Import…** button. In the **File_name…** box enter \My Documents\Act\ Document\Canada.txt Be sure to check **Import item descriptions**. **OK**
3.	Notice that the Home State field uses the same drop-downs as State, so now the Home State field also will display the Canadian province abbreviations.	Click on Home State and verify that the **Use drop down list from** is checked and that the shared list is **City**.
4.	Click **OK** to apply the changes.	
5.	Click in the My Record Home State field and enter the abbreviation for Manitoba.	Scroll to Manitoba and select the MB abbreviation.

Try It…

Minor Changes to the Drop-down List

If you need to make minor additions or changes to your drop-downs, there is an easier way. (You don't mind if we show you the easier way, do you?)

...modify a drop-down list

1. Click in the field that contains the list you wish to modify and press **[F2]**.

    A pop-up list displays containing the items in that field's list, plus several command buttons.

2. If you wish to modify an existing item, click the item in the list and click the **Modify...** button. Change the item as desired and click **OK**.

    When you click the **Modify...** button, a box with the item and (if present) description displays:

3. If you wish to add a new item, click the **Add...** button. Enter a new item and (if you wish) a description, and click **OK**.

    When you click the **Add...** button, an empty box with **Item:** and **Description:** fields is displayed:

☞   *If **Allow Editing** was not checked for a specific field, then you cannot edit the list this way (it's not allowed!). So you will have to edit a drop-down list by displaying the **Define Fields** dialog box and editing the list on the **Drop-down** page.*

Practice: *Modifying Drop-Downs*

Try It...

Step	What to do	How to do it/Comments
1.	Can you believe that Hollywood is not one of the cities listed in ACT!'s list of major cities?! What were they thinking? Add Hollywood to the drop-down list for cities with a description of "Home to the Stars"	Click in the City field and press **[F2]** (or you could scroll all the way to the bottom of the list and click **Edit list....**) Click **Add...** and enter "Hollywood" in the **Item:** box. In **Description:**, enter Home to the Stars.
2.	Lookup Alvin (one of our employees). Stars R Us offices are in Hollywood. Update his record by typing the city.	Notice that as you type H, Hollywood is filled in for you.
3.	Use the drop-down to display the list of cities. Where is the description of "Home to the Stars"?	When we defined the fields, we opted not to **Show descriptions**. After all what can you say about cities? The description will display only if you press **[F2]**...not in the drop-down list.

Editing the Database Structure

If "Allow Editing" is not checked, you have to make changes to your drop-downs using **Edit, Define Fields** command. However, if you are in a multi-user database, everyone in the company has to exit the database before you can make changes to the structure. When you try to access the Define Fields dialog box, and other users are logged into the database, will see the Lock Database dialog box indicating which users are currently logged into the database.

The polite thing to do would be to call them to ask if they could exit ACT! for a few minutes while you make a few necessary changes to the database. However, sometimes they are not at their desk. In fact, they left the building two hours ago...they must have left ACT! open at their desk. Instead of trotting over to their work area, you can issue the command here to close the ACT! database on their PC.

Clicking on the **Lock** button will display a message that the Administrator (you) is preparing to close the database and they have 5 minutes to complete whatever it is they are doing before ACT! shuts down (unless you changed the minutes to 1 ☺). The users who are logged out by the system will still have ACT! open on their screen, but with no database displayed.

When all users have been logged out, the Define Fields dialog box displays and you can make your changes.

Practice: *Modifying Drop-Downs*

Try It...

Step	What to do	How to do it/Comments
1.	Audrey called and asked to be removed from the mailing list. (She travels so much overseas now and our stuff only gets lost.) Enter R in the drop-down for her record.	Changing her to N doesn't work. Someone else might see Audrey marked with an N and change it back to a Y…after all she is a client and should be receiving our mail. You can't enter an R since we selected an Entry rule of only from drop-down, AND since we removed the check from **Allow Editing**, we can't change it here.
2.	Edit the database structure to add: R Remove to the drop-down list for Mailing List.	Click in the Mailing List field, **Edit, Define fields…**, click on the **Drop-down** tab. Click **New**. Enter "R," **[Tab]** to Description and enter "Remove." Click **OK**.
3.	While we are defining fields, let's say we used up all the **User #** fields and now we need to add another field named **Coffee** (Character 80, no drop-down)	Click **New Field**. Type the new field name of Coffee. Change the **Number of characters:** to 80. Click on the **Drop-down** tab and remove the check from **Allow editing**. **OK**
4.	Back in the Contacts view, put an R on Audrey's record.	It works now.
5.	Find the Coffee field.	You can't find it. New fields must be manually added to all existing layouts. We'll get to it in a few pages.

The Triggers Tab

The **Triggers** tab lets ACT! run a macro script or other commands when the field is entered or exited.

Example: The contents of a particular field are determined by a rate sheet stored in an Excel workbook. When you enter the field, you would like to display the rate sheet automatically. Or perhaps you would like to enter the data you just placed in an ACT! field into a worksheet.

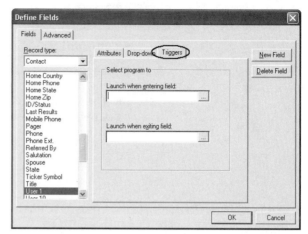

...create a trigger for a field

1.	Display the **Define Fields** dialog box for the desired field.	See page 300.
2.	Click the **Triggers** tab.	
3.	Click either the **Launch when entering field:**, or the **Launch when exiting field:** option.	Depending on whether you want the event to occur before or after you enter your ACT! data.
4.	Enter the path and name of the program's executable file, or specify the macro or script you wish to run.	You may use the Browse button to locate the executable file or macro. Script filenames must be entered manually. We will discuss macros beginning on page 404
5.	If you wish to run a program and then open a specific file, follow the path and name of the program with a space and the path and name of the file.	You must type this path and name. It is probably a good idea to have it written down before you start this process.
6.	Click **OK**.	The database is updated and your program now runs when you enter (or exit) the field.

Say you wish to launch Excel and open a worksheet file called **Your Invoices.xls**. Your command might look like this:

C:\Microsoft Office\office\Excel.exe c:\My Documents\Invoices.xls

You could use the Browse button to locate **Excel.exe**, but you would have to type the path to the **Invoices.xls** workbook file. Of course, your file locations may vary.

Practice: *Adding a Trigger*

Step	What to do	How to do it/Comments
1.	Remember how awkward it was adding the Social Security # which had been created with a Field format? Let's add a trigger that automatically moves the insertion point to the beginning of the field. Let's edit the Social Security # field.	Click in the Social Security # field that you created and then click **Edit, Define Fields**
2.	Add the macro "Home.mpr" as an entry trigger to the Social Security # field. The macro has already been created for you and placed in the \Macro folder (we'll learn how to create our own macros later).	Verify that the "Social Security #" field is selected. Click on the **Triggers** tab. Click on the Browse button in the **Launch when entering field:**. Change the **Look in:** folder to the \Macro folder if necessary. Change the **Files of type:** to **Macro Files (*.mpr)**, then click on "Home.mpr" and click **Open**.
3.	Save your definition changes.	**OK**
4.	Now try entering a few Social Security #s	Cool!

Try It...

Defining and Modifying Layouts

ACT! comes with several pre-defined Contact and Group layouts. Layouts allow you to display the information stored in your Contact database in many different ways.

Simply put, a **layout** controls which bits of contact information are displayed, and where and how they are displayed on your screen (the same data, just arranged differently). As we add *new* fields to the database, you will not be able to see or enter data into the fields until you add them to your layout.

Each Contact Layout consists of static information that displays in the top portion of the screen and the tabs at the bottom.

✔ All layouts have **Notes/History, Activities, Sales/Opportunities, Groups** tabs (and **Library** if it is enabled), but the rest of the tabs are a part of each individual layout.

✔ You can create new or modify existing layouts.

✔ Layout changes are not confined to the current database. When you change or create a new layout in ACT!, the new or changed layout can be used by any ACT! database. This can be good or bad. If another database does not have the same fields as the one the layout was created for, some fields may be missing or displayed in strange places.

Creating Design Layouts

To modify an existing or create a new layout, display the Design Layouts screen.

...display the Design Layouts screen

How To...

1. If you wish to modify an existing layout, display the layout that most closely matches what you want.

    While you can open and modify any layout, displaying the layout you want to modify is more efficient.

2. Choose **Tools, Design Layouts**.

    The current layout is displayed in Design view.

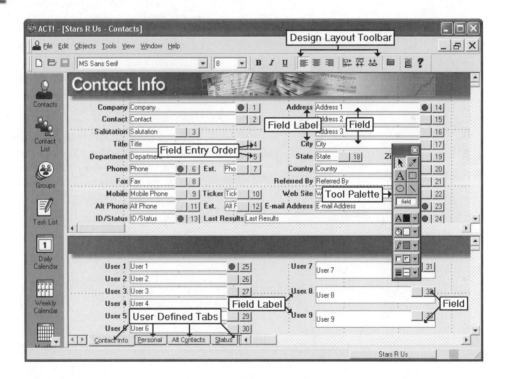

Notice the difference in the Design Layout between Fields Labels and Fields. The numbers that display on the fields indicate the sequence of moving from field to field when the user presses **[Tab]** or **[Enter]**. Notice that Design Layout has its own toolbar.

☞ *If you don't see the Field Entry Order numbers, in design layout, click* ***Edit, Field Entry Order, Show***

Since you can't edit **Notes/History, Activities, Sales/Opportunities, Groups** or **Library** tabs…you can't see them here. The Tool Palette is used for making changes to the layout.

Practice: *Design Layouts*

Try It…

Step	What to do	How to do it/Comments
1.	Display the Contacts screen. Make sure **Contact Layout 800x600** is the current layout.	If necessary, click the Contacts button. The name of the current layout is displayed on the Layout button at the bottom of the screen. If it does not say **Contact Layout 800x600**, click the button and select the appropriate option.
2.	Switch to Design view.	**Tools, Design Layouts**
3.	Observe the Design screen.	Everything is there, but instead of displaying Contacts, this screen displays the names of the Contact fields. Note the lack of **Notes/History, Activities, Sales/Opportunities, Groups** or **Library** tabs. You cannot modify these tabs, so they do not display in the Design screen.
4.	Leave the Design screen displayed.	

Once you are in the Design screen, you can modify the existing layout, open and modify another layout, or create a new layout.

Saving Layouts

Whether you are starting from scratch or modifying an existing design, it is always a good idea to save the design with a new name.

...save a layout

1. With the layout Design screen displayed, choose **File, Save As...** from the menu.

The **Save As** dialog box is displayed:

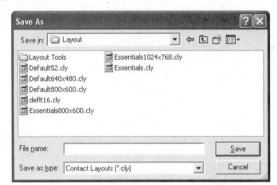

☞ *ACT! assumes you wish to save your layouts to the **Layout** folder.*

2. Type a file name for your Layout file.

This is the name that will be listed on the Layout button, so type a short, descriptive name.

3. **Save** Click the **Close** icon to return to the **Contacts** view.

The layout as it is currently defined is saved to the Layout folder.

✔ Contact layouts are stored in layout files. These files have a .CLY file extension.

✔ These layout files are stored in a folder specified in the **Preferences** dialog box. You can display this dialog box by choosing **Edit, Preferences...** from the menu and displaying the **General** dialog page. In the **Default locations** section, click the **File type** drop-down arrow to display **Layout**. The **Location** of the folder that stores the layout files is displayed in the text box. If you are creating a layout that you want others to be able to use, you will need to give them a copy of the file or copy it to the network drive for everyone to use.

☞ *In case you get a little crazy and design a dozen new layouts, you can delete those you don't need. Open the Windows Explorer and delete the necessary .CLY file from the **Layout** folder. The default folder location is C:\Program Files\ACT\Layout.*

Practice: *A New Layout*

 Try It...

Step	What to do	How to do it/Comments
1.	You should still be displaying **Contact Layout 800x600** in Design view. Save the Layout as "Stars R Us"	**File, Save As...** Stars R Us, click **Save**. The Contact Layout button displays with the new layout name.
2.	Leave the Design screen displayed.	

The Tool Palette

The Design screen has its own toolbar at the top of the screen and a floating Tool Palette toolbar. The Tool Palette contains many of the tools necessary to add and format objects on the layout.

☞ *If you do not see the Tool Palette, choose **View, Show Tool Palette** from the menu. You can hide the Tool Palette by choosing **View, Hide Tool Palette** or clicking on the Close button on the palette.*

If you point to a button on the Tool Palette, you may expect to see a tool tip "pop up" to tell you what the button does. Life is full of disappointments, since the expected tips are not to be found. Don't be concerned, we have provided documentation right here. (No applause, please....okay, maybe a little.)

The Tool Palette is divided into two sections. The top seven buttons are used to select objects and attributes and create the various objects you use in your layouts.

The bottom five buttons are used to format objects. These buttons are divided into two parts: a large button that displays the currently selected format and a smaller drop-down button that can be used to display a palette of choices.

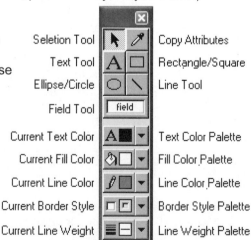

Once you make a choice from the palette, it becomes the new current setting and displays on the larger portion of the button.

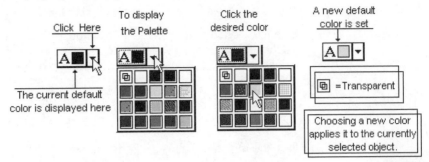

☞ *If the Tool Palette is in the way on the screen, point to the dark bar across the top (the Title bar) and drag it to another area of your screen.*

Modifying Layouts

While you can start from scratch to create a new layout design, it is usually easier to modify an existing one. You may want to reposition the fields or change their size. You must select the fields or their labels in order to size or move them on the Layout screen. These fields and labels are called **objects**. You can select one or many objects at a time. If you select many objects, any modifications you make are made to all of the selected objects.

...select one or more objects

1. To select a single item, make sure the Selection tool is active. Click the item you wish to select.

Click the Selection tool. A selected object displays square handles around its perimeter.

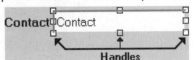

2. To select additional objects, press and hold down the **[Shift]** key and click the next, and the next, and the next....

As long as you hold **[Shift]**, you add each object you click. (If you click an object that has already been selected, you de-select it.)

☞ *To select multiple objects at once, you can click on the background and drag around all the fields and labels that you want to select. This selects all objects that the rectangle (that you just drew) either encloses or touches.*

How To...

...size a layout object

1.	Select the desired object(s).	If you select multiple objects, you may size them all at once.
2.	Place the mouse pointer on a selection handle.	The mouse pointer becomes a double-headed arrow when positioned properly.

3.	When the mouse pointer displays as a double-headed arrow, drag ↔ the handle to change the size of the object.	If you selected multiple objects, they size proportionately.

Try It...

Practice: *Making the fields smaller*

Step	What to do	How to do it/Comments
1.	We need to shorten the length of the three fields that we created earlier.	If you did not change the field names for User 1, 2 and 3...just use those fields in this practice session.
2.	Drag over the 3 fields that we created to select them all. Don't select the labels to the left. ☞ *Start by clicking on the background between User 5 and Contract Renewal.*	Social Security # · Social Security # · ● 25 · Min Film Salary · Min Film Salary · 26 · Mailing List · Mailing List · 27 · Contract Renewal · Contract Renewal · 28 · User 5 · User 5 · 29

Step	What to do	How to do it/Comments
3.	Make them smaller. They should be about 1 inch wide.	
		Position the mouse pointer on the center right handle of any of the selected boxes, and drag to the left until the box is the correct size.
4.	De-select the objects.	Click an open area of the layout Design screen. The handles disappear.
5.	The Mailing List should probably be the smallest since it is only 1 character.	Click on the Mailing List field (not the label). Drag it to a smaller size. Don't forget to leave room for the drop-down arrow to display.
6.	Save your layout.	Choose **File**, **Save** from the menu, or click the Save toolbar button.

Moving Objects

The layout of the screen may not work for you. Perhaps you want to move the address fields to a tab on the bottom and move the Assistant Name to the top half of the view. Maybe you would like to move the State and the Zip fields to the right of the City field to allow room for more fields.

...move an object on the tab

1.	Select the object(s).	If you select multiple objects, you can move them all at once.
2.	To move the selected objects to a different tab (or from the bottom half to the top half) click **Edit, Cut** Click on the new tab (or top half) to make that pane active, click **Edit, Paste**.	When you click **Edit, Paste** the selected objects will be moved to the middle of the current pane. If you are just moving the field within the same pane, go to the next step.
3.	Point to the selected object(s).	If you have selected multiple objects, you may point to any of the selected objects.
4.	When the mouse pointer displays as a four-headed arrow, click and hold the left mouse button and drag the object to a new position.	If you have selected multiple objects, they move as one.

 You can also use the arrow keys on the keyboard to move selected objects with much finer control.

☞ *Remember, the field box and the label text that usually appears to its left are two separate items. If you want to keep them together as you move them, be sure to select them both first.*

Practice: *Moving around*

Step	What to do	How to do it/Comments
1.	Let's move the **Mailing List** field from the **Contact Info** tab to the top half of the screen to the right of **Salutation**.	Drag over the Mailing List field and label. **Edit, Cut** Click in the top half of the screen and select **Edit, Paste**. Point to the object(s). When the pointer displays as a four-headed arrow, drag the objects to the right of **Salutation**. Don't worry if they don't perfectly line up. ACT! has a tool for that.
2.	Move the **Mailing List** label closer to the field.	Click on the label only and use the arrow keys to move the label to the right.
3.	Save your layout.	Choose **File, Save** from the menu, or click the Save toolbar button.

☞ *We know it is tempting to drag the field from the bottom tab to the top half, but it's not advisable. Sometimes in the dragging process you drop in an area that you can never find again. If you do drag an object and then it doesn't display (Lost in Space), then you might as well close the layout without saving your changes. Otherwise, you'll never get it back.*

Try It...

Aligning Objects

If your fields or labels are not lined up with one another, you can have ACT! line them up into neat, straight lines.

...align fields or text objects

How To...

1. Drag over the objects to be aligned.

   Click the Selection tool if it's not activated. The first selected object displays clear, square handles around its perimeter.

2. **[Shift+click]** additional objects that you want aligned. You can also **[Shift+click]** any object to remove it from the selected group.

   The object with the clear handles determines the alignment for the rest of the selected objects.

3. Single-click the object you want to act as the primary object.

   When you select multiple objects, one has clear handles and the rest have black handles. The object with the clear handles is the primary object of the group. If you perform an alignment on the group, for example, the other objects align to the primary object.

4. Click one of the Alignment icons

   or

   choose **Objects, Align...** to display the **Align** dialog box.

5. Select the desired alignment option.

   Remember, all selected objects will align on the primary object (the one with the clear handles).

6. Click **OK**.

   The objects are aligned. They remain selected.

☞ *If you select several objects and then realize that you chose the wrong primary object, single-click the object you want to be the primary (this object should already be selected). The clear handles display on that object and the rest remain selected.*

Practice: *Laying out your Layout*

Step	What to do	How to do it/Comments
1.	Let's line up the **Salutation** and **Mailing List** fields with each other. Align everything to the **Salutation** field.	Individually select each object by clicking the first field, hold **[Shift]**, and clicking the remaining items, or by dragging an imaginary square around the objects. Handles should appear around each selected object. Be sure that the **Salutation** field has the white handles (if not single-click on it) and then click on the **Align Vertically** icon. ☞ *Edit, Undo if you accidentally included a field that wasn't supposed to be in the alignment or the wrong primary field was selected.*
2.	Delete the **Department** field and label and move **Referred By** to its place. Align the fields and labels.	Click on the **Department** field and label and press **[Delete]**. Move the **Referred By** field into its place.
3.	Move the Home Phone number from the **Personal** tab to the top of the screen to the right of Fax. Change the label to just Home (phone is kind of obvious).	Click on the **Personal** tab and select the Home Phone field and label. **Edit, Cut** Click on the top half of the screen and select **Edit, Paste**. Drag the selected fields to the right of Fax.
4.	Lengthen the labels for **Social Security #** and **Contract Renewal** so that all of the text displays.	Since they are already aligned on the right, drag the field labels from the left to lengthen them.
5.	Save your layout.	Choose **File, Save** from the menu, or click the Save toolbar button.

Try It...

Adding Items to Your Layout

As you add additional fields to your database, they will not automatically appear on any of the existing layouts. New fields must be manually added to any layout on which you wish them to appear. For this, you use the **Field** button on the Tool Palette.

...add fields to your layout

How To...

1. Click the **Field** button on the Tool Palette.

   The button appears to be pressed in when it is active.

2. Position your mouse pointer where you want the top left corner of the field to be. Click and *hold* the left mouse button.

   You use the mouse to draw the field box.

3. Drag the mouse pointer down and to the right until the field is the size you want it to be. Release the mouse button.

   The new field is placed at the position and size you specified. The **Fields** dialog box displays.

   The **Fields** dialog box contains a list of all fields in the Contact database that have not yet been placed on the layout. The list is in alphabetical order (numbered items listed first).

   Fields can only be placed once on any layout.

4. Locate and select the field you wish to be displayed in the control you just created (by control we mean the box you just drew). Choose whether to add a label to the box.

   If you leave the **Add label** check box checked, a field name is placed as a label to the left of the field box. When you use the layout, the field box displays the contents of the field, while the label displays the name of the field.

5. Click **Add**.

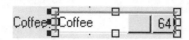

The box you drew now displays the name of the field that it contains. If you chose to add a label, it displays to the left of the box. The **Fields** dialog box remains open.

6. If you wish to add additional fields to your layout, you can select them and click **Add**. Each new field is added below the previously added field. Each new field is the same size as your original.

When you add a field to the layout, it is removed from the list of available fields.

 You cannot add the same field to the layout twice.

7. Click **Close** when you are done.

8. Click the selection tool to turn off the Field button.

If you don't click the selection tool, ACT! assumes you wish to draw another field.

 Once you click a button, it tends to stay clicked. When you are done with a tool on the Tool Palette, be sure to click the Selection tool. Otherwise, you will be creating objects you did not mean to create.

Try It...

Step	What to do	How to do it/Comments
1.	Let's add the Coffee field that we created in the practice on page 317 to our new layout. Place it where the Mailing List field used to be on the **Contact Info** tab. Make it about the same size as **User 5**.	If you didn't create the field in the earlier practice, do it now. Click the Field button. [field] Click and drag to place the field above Contract Renewal. When you release the mouse button, the **Fields** dialog box appears. Click on the **Coffee** field and click **Add**.
2.	Close the **Fields** dialog box and de-select the Fields button on the Tool Palette.	Click **Close** to dismiss the dialog box. Click the Selection tool to turn off the Field button.
3.	Observe the layout. The label is not bold like the rest of the labels and it doesn't line up on the left. The field has a 3-D bevel around it, which also doesn't match the rest of the fields.	We'll do some formatting to make everything match in a few minutes.
4.	That's not going to be enough room for 80 characters. Let's move **Contract Renewal** to the top of the screen below **Country** (where Referred by originally was). Make the **Coffee** field tall enough for 2 rows of text.	Cut and Paste **Contract Renewal** to the top of the layout under **Country**. Click on the **Coffee** field to select it. Size the field to two rows high. Coffee Coffee 71 Click here to drag to 2 rows.
5.	Save and close your layout.	Click the Save icon. Click the Close icon.
6.	Enter my coffee preference as: "Tall, 2 sugar, no fat, no foam latte, with a sprinkle of cinnamon on the top."	How impressed would clients be if you could "remember" that!

Layout Tabs

All layouts have five tabs already defined (**Notes/History, Activities, Sales Opportunities, Groups** and **Library**). If you have a strong feeling of deja vu right now, it's because we said this before. As you add more objects to your layout, you may find you want to rename or add your own tabs to the layout to better organize the data.

...create a new tab or rename an existing tab

How To...

1. From the Design Layout screen (**Tools, Design Layouts**), choose **Edit, Tabs...** from the menu.

    *If no tabs are yet defined, the list of **Tab Layouts:** is empty.*

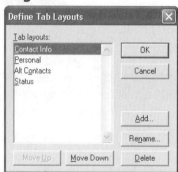

2. Click the **Add...** button to add a new tab.

   or

   Select an existing tab and click **Rename** to give the tab another name.

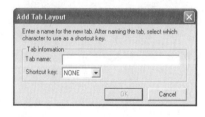

3. Enter a **Tab Name:**
   If you wish to define a shortcut key for the tab, pick a letter from the **Short key:** drop-down list.

   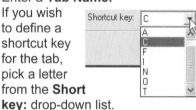

   Click **OK** to return to the Define Tab Layouts.

   The name you type will appear on the tab at the bottom of the screen.

   The letter you choose as the **Shortcut key:** will be underlined on the tab. The user can display this tab by holding the **[Alt]** key and pressing the underlined letter. Take care not to choose a letter already used by another tab, or on the menu.

4. If you want to change the order of the new tab, click the **Move Up** or **Move Down** button.

   Any new tabs are inserted at the bottom of the list (and thus to the far right in the tab display).

5. Click **OK** again to return to the Design screen. The new (empty) tab appears at the bottom of the layout.

You can display the **Define Tab Layouts** dialog box any time to add new tabs, rename or delete existing tabs, or change the tab order.

☞ *Select an existing (and hopefully blank) tab and click **Delete** to remove it from the layout. Any fields that remained on the deleted tab will also be removed from the layout, however you can add them once again to the layout.*

Practice: *A New Tab*

Step	What to do	How to do it/Comments
1.	Create a new tab for your layout named: **Address**. Move it to the top of the list.	**E**dit, Ta**b**s..., **A**dd..., type **Address**, choose **D** from the **Shortcut key:** list and click **OK**.
2.	Select all of the address fields on the top of the tab. Move them to the **Address** tab.	Drag over the address fields and labels. **Edit, Cu**t Click on the **Address** tab and select **E**dit, **P**aste. Drag the selected fields to the upper-left corner of the Address tab.
3.	Move the Home address fields from the **P**ersonal tab to the **A**ddress tab.	
4.	Save and close the layout.	Click the Save icon. Click the Close icon.

Adding Text

You may wish to add *additional* text to your layout. In this case, you are not connecting to anything in the Contact database. Text is just that...static text.

...add text to your layout

1. From the Tool Palette, click the Text button.

2. Point to where you want your text to begin, click and hold the left mouse button, and drag a box the approximate size you want for your text. When you release the mouse button, the text box appears with the insertion point flashing inside.

Don't be too concerned about the size of the box. You can always adjust it later.

3. Type the text.

As you type, extra text wraps and the box grows vertically to contain the text.

4. If you wish to create another text box, create it now. If you are done, click the Selection button to turn the Text Box tool off.

Practice: *Add a Layout Title*		
Step	**What to do**	**How to do it/Comments**
1.	Add our company name to top part of the layout where the address fields were. Enter the text: **Stars R Us**	**Tools, Design Layouts** Click the Text tool, and click and drag a box in the blank area on the top of the layout. When you release the mouse button, type **Stars R Us**.
2.	Turn off the Text tool.	Click the Selection tool (easy to forget, isn't it?).
3.	Observe the new text.	Supremely un-exciting isn't it? Don't worry, we'll dress it up shortly.
4.	Save your changes, but leave the layout displayed.	

How To...

Try It...

Formatting Layouts

You can control the look of your layouts with a variety of options including typeface, type size, text color, and background color. Applying formatting can serve to make your layouts easier to read and use. Formatting also makes your layouts look really, really cool!

...apply a format to a part of the layout

1. Select the object(s) you wish to format.

You may apply the same format(s) to multiple objects.

2. Choose the format option to apply.

Color, line, and fill formats are on the Tool Palette. Font and alignment formats are located on the toolbar at the top of the design window.

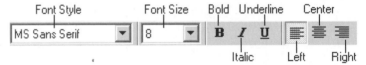

3. Choose any additional formats you wish to apply while the object is still selected.

The format buttons are identified above.

When you click a color or style, the change applies to all selected objects unless it is not a valid option for that object. For example, a simple line does not have a fill color.

You can also right-click any object (field or field label) to display its Font and Style properties.

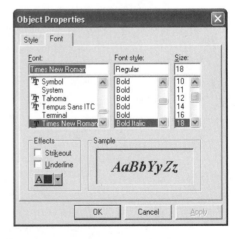

Practice: *Formatting Practice*

Try It...

Step	What to do	How to do it/Comments
1.	While still in the Layout Design view of your new layout, select the text (**Stars R Us**) you created earlier.	Make sure the Selection tool is active and click the text (handles appear around it to indicate that it's selected).
2.	Change the font of the text to **Times New Roman**. Change the size to **18** points, and make it bold and italic.	On the toolbar at the top of the screen, choose the font name from the Font List, choose **18** from the Font Size list, and click the Bold and Italic buttons
3.	If necessary, resize the box so the text all fits on one line.	When you add text to a box, or change the size of the text, the box grows vertically but not horizontally.
4.	Experiment on your text with some of the Tool Palette format buttons. Try changing the text color, the fill color, the line color, etc., and see what effect these options have on the selected object. Find a combination of options that pleases you (after all, you're the one with taste here).	Current Text Color — Text Color Palette Current Fill Color — Fill Color Palette Current Line Color — Line Color Palette Current Border Style — Border Style Palette Current Line Weight — Line Weight Palette *You can also right-click any object to display its Properties box.*
5.	Change the Coffee field and label to match the others. Right-align the labels and left-align the fields.	Click on the field label and make it Bold. Line it up with the other labels. Click on the Coffee field and use the **Border Style Palette** drop-down to change the border to match the other fields (usually the first option.) Drag over the labels and click **Objects, Align, Align right edges, OK** Drag over the fields and use the toolbar icon to align left.
6.	Save and close your layout and admire your work.	Click the Save icon. Click the Close icon.

Testing Your Layouts

Your layouts may display a number at the far right of each field. This number is the sequence in which the user will move through the layout to enter data. When you move fields around in a layout, you may need to renumber the fields to put them back in the proper order.

How the user moves through the layouts (using **[Tab]** or **[Enter]**) depends on the preferences defined on their PC. In the **Edit, Preferences** dialog box, select the method that you want to use to move from field to field. Whichever key you choose, the remaining key will be used to move through the layout in larger jumps called group stops.

Practice: **Testing Entry Order**

Step	What to do	How to do it/Comments
1.	Starting in the Company field, use the keyboard to move from field to field (either by pressing the **[Tab]** key or the **[Enter]** key depending upon how your system is set up). Observe how the focus proceeds from field to field in your layout.	As you continue moving through the layout, you can tell that we need some work. We need to change some of the tab order.
2.	Leave the layout displayed.	

Try It...

Field Entry Order

When you enter data in your ACT! database, you usually use the **[Tab]** key to move from tab stop to tab stop (field to field). If you press the **[Enter]** key, you don't move from field to field, but rather, from group stop to group stop (unless you changed your Preferences and then the reverse is true). What constitutes a group stop to you and to the designer of the layout you are using may be two different things.

Fortunately, you can control the order in which fields are selected when you press **[Tab]** and which fields are group stops when you press **[Enter]**. The order in which you move from field to field is called **field entry order**.

...display current field entry order (if numbers aren't currently displayed)

1.   **Tools, Design Layouts**

2.   **Edit, Field Entry Order, Show**

    You can hide the field entry order indicators by choosing **Edit, Field Entry Order, Hide** *from the menu.*

The field entry order and group stop indicators are displayed to the right of each field. A field entry indicator is a numbered button, a group stop is a button with a red octagon (group *stop*, get it?).

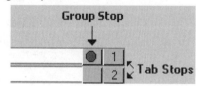

If you wish to change the field entry order, you may find it easier to clear the existing order.

...clear the field entry order

1.   With the desired layout displayed in Design view, choose **Edit, Field Entry Order, Clear**.

All field entry and group stops are cleared.

Once the order is cleared, you can mark the field entry order by just single-clicking with the mouse.

...set field entry order

How To...

1. Click the tab stop section in the field entry order button (the one on the right) for each field in the order in which you want to access them.

   Tab Stop ↓

   ↑ Group Stop

   Each time you click a button, the next number in sequence is added.

There are three things to remember when setting field entry order:

✔ If you have more than one tab defined for your layout, each field on each of the tabs is part of the entry order. You need to keep track of which tab should be accessed first, second, third, etc.

✔ If you have a field that is only occasionally used (like Ticker Symbol), you may eliminate it from the field entry order by simply not clicking its button. If no number appears on the field entry order button, it's not part of the order.

✔ If you click a button that already has a field entry sequence number, you will remove that number. ACT! always uses the next number in sequence whenever you click a blank button.

☞ *You can control the sequence for field entry order on a field-by-field basis. Group stop sequence is also controlled by the associated field entry order sequence. If no tab stop number is entered then the group stop will also be skipped.*

☞ *If you wish to automatically set the field entry order to the "most obvious" sequence, choose* **Edit, Field Entry Order, Reset**. *The field entry order is set starting from top to bottom, left to right. Tabs are included front to back.*

Practice: *Clearing and Setting Field Entry Order*

Step	What to do	How to do it/Comments
1.	Display the field entry order, if necessary.	**Edit, Field Entry Order, Show**
2.	Observe the numbers. Obviously **Mailing List** and **Referred By** are out of sequence.	They are mostly sequential, but you can see where the problems lie.
3.	OK, let's start from scratch. Clear the field entry order.	**Edit, Field Entry Order, Clear**
4.	Experiment with defining a new field entry order manually. Entry order should reflect the most logical order to *enter* data, and not necessarily the order in which they appear (*although the two usually coincide*). ☞ *If a field label is covering up the tab stop, you can't click the label to put a number on the field. You will have to make the label smaller so that you can click the tab stop.*	Click the Tab Stop button for each field. As you click each one, the next number in sequence is displayed. Don't bother with Group Stops yet.
5.	Test your tab order after closing (and saving) your layout.	Click the Close button and then **Yes** (to save). Press **[Tab]** to move from field to field.

Group Stops

Normally, you move from field to field in ACT! by pressing the **[Tab]** key (**[Shift+Tab]** moves you backwards). However, have you ever pressed **[Enter]** just to see what would happen? Instead of moving to the next field, you may jump several fields ahead. This type of stop is known as a **group stop**.

✔ For many users, it's common to skip over several fields when filling out a Contact's information.

✔ By defining strategic group stops, you can use the **[Enter]** key to move quickly between the most common fields and still use **[Tab]** to navigate field to field.

...set group stops

1.	Display the field entry order for the layout.	Of course, you need to be in Design Layout view.
2.	Click the Group Stop button for each field you wish to designate a group stop.	The Group Stop button is the one to the left of the Tab Stop button. An octagon appears for each group stop.
3.	To remove a group stop, click the existing Group Stop button.	The octagon disappears and the group stop is no more (how sad!).

How To...

Practice: *Setting Group Stops*

Try It...

Step	What to do	How to do it/Comments
1.	Make sure you are in Design view for your layout. Make sure the field order buttons are displayed.	**Edit, Field Entry Order, Show**
2.	Set a group stop at **Company, Phone, Address 1**, and **City**.	Click the Group Stop button for each of these fields.
3.	Save and close the layout.	Click the Save button, then click the Close button.

Step	What to do	How to do it/Comments
4.	Test your tab stops and your group stops.	If you press **[Tab]**, you move from field to field, skipping none. If you press **[Enter]**, you skip over the fields that are less likely to be used.

Try It...

Changing from Gray to Beige

If you tabbed all the way through to the end, did you notice that the **Status** tab has a gray background? Whenever you add a tab, the last tab to the right may loose its background color. It's easy to add it back.

...change background color to beige

How To...

1. **Tools, Design Layouts**

2. Click on the tab with the gray background.

   The **Status** tab?

3. Right-click on the background, select **Properties**.

   From the dialog box displayed there, you can choose a pattern, color, or bitmap (.BMP) graphic image for your background.

   ☞ *The bottom tabs use a color graphic named Dflt5bg.BMP. The top half of this tab uses a graphic named DefaultBarBG.bmp. Both files can be found in the C:\Program Files\ACT\Layout folder.*

   You can browse to graphics in the c:\program files\act folder or any other folder.

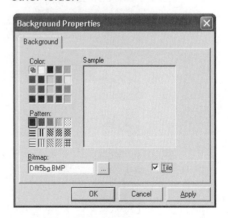

   Click **Tile** if necessary

4. **OK**

Review: *Design Layouts*

Try It...	**1.**	To your layout, move the **Assistant** information to the top where Address info used to be.
	2.	Edit User 9 to be Directions. Then move the field to the Address tab.
	3.	Copy the blue line graphic from the **C**ontact Info tab to the new **A**ddress tab.
	4.	Give the Status tab the same color as the other tabs.
	5.	Test the new layout.

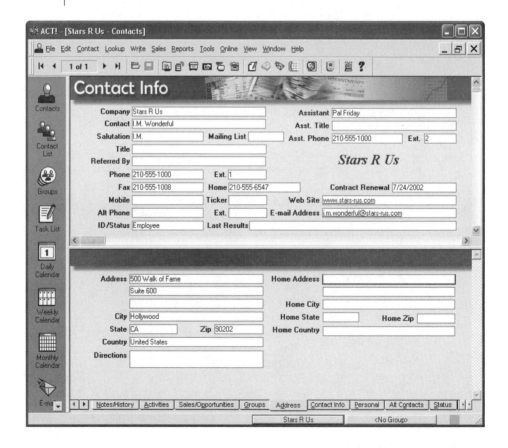

Running and Designing Reports

To be able to design and run your own custom reports, you will:

- ☑ Understand how the ACT! Report writer generates reports from the ACT! database.

- ☑ Review the reports that come with ACT!

- ☑ Examine the Report Designer window.

- ☑ Create a new and modify existing report templates.

- ☑ Place fields on the report, adding and sizing report sections

- ☑ Print Preview and run a custom report.

- ☑ Modify the Reports menu.

ACT! Reports

ACT! does a wonderful job of tracking contact information and helping you keep in contact through letters. ACT! can also produce detailed reports about your activities that can help you get a handle on how you spend your time, who you talk to, and when. You can print a report that lists all you know about a contact or just a list of phone numbers. ACT!'s pre-defined reports are pretty complete and impressive. As with everything in ACT!, you can create your own reports or further customize the existing ones.

Creating a pre-defined report is very simple. You need only tell ACT! which contacts you want to include, which report you want to use, and where to send the report (printer, fax, e-mail, or print preview). You can also filter such items as Notes/Histories and Activities, such that only certain dates or date ranges print.

...generate an ACT! report

1. Choose **Reports**, and click the report you want from the menu.

The **Run Report** dialog box appears.

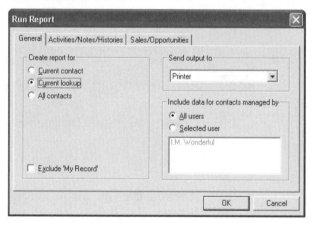

2. Choose a **Create report for** option.

Click <u>C</u>urrent contact to include data only for the person displayed in the Contact screen.

Click C<u>u</u>rrent lookup to include data for the records in the current lookup or group.

Click A<u>l</u>l contacts to include everybody in the database.

☞ *Click the E<u>x</u>clude 'My Record' check box if you don't want to include information about you in the report.*

3. If necessary, click the drop-down arrow for **Send output to** and choose an option.

Printer sends the report directly to your printer.

Preview displays the report in print preview.

Fax or **E-mail** transmits the report via either method, if your computer has those capabilities.

File - ACT! Report saves the completed report to a file that can be printed by anyone who also has ACT!.

File - Editable Text creates a Rich Text Format file that can be edited by most word processors.

4. Click the **Activities/Notes/ Histories** tab and choose filter options if necessary.

The **Activities/Notes/ Histories** tab of the **Run Report** dialog box appears.

5. Click the desired check boxes to include/exclude **Notes/History** and **Activities** options. Display the **Date range:** calendar to limit the dates of **Notes/History** or **Activities** entries. You can use one of the **Custom...** buttons to specify 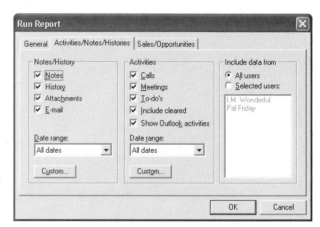 a specific date or drag over a range of dates.

To specify information related to specific users of your network database, choose **Selected users:** and click the necessary name(s). For example, only notes and activities entered by a specific user will display in the report.

 *If the selected report does not include **Notes/History** or **Activities** information, these options will be unavailable. Don't let this bother you. You can't filter something you don't have.*

6. Click **OK**. ACT! generates the report to your specifications.

 When you run a report in ACT!, any filter settings that are changed are remembered by ACT! for use the next time your run the report.

Practice: *Generating a Report*

Step	What to do	How to do it/Comments
1.	Generate a **Notes/History** report for everybody in the database. View the report on the screen.	Choose **Reports, Notes/History**, click **All contacts**, click the drop-down arrow for **Send output to** and choose **Preview**, and click **OK**.
2.	Leave the report preview displayed on the screen.	

Try It...

The Anatomy of an ACT! Report

Each time you run a report, ACT! goes out and gets the data it contains. If you have added contacts, Notes, histories, or other items to your database, the report adds them as necessary the next time it is run.

✔ By default, reports will generate data on the Current contact, the Current lookup, or All contacts. So unless you want to run reports on the entire database all of the time, create a lookup before you run the report.

✔ Every time you run a report it is up to date, because every time you run a report, it gathers new information from the database.

✔ Because of this, you cannot edit a report once it has been generated (like you can with a document in the word processor).

While you can send your report directly to a printer, you may find it useful to preview it before you print. When print preview first displays, the first page of the report displays in full page view.

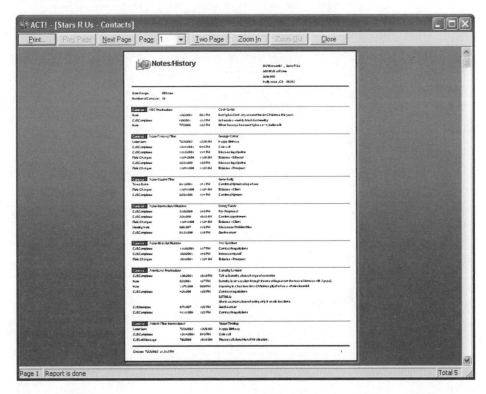

The text in the preview window will be "Greeked". Greeked text cannot be read. ("It's Greek to me!" Get it?)

...increase/decrease magnification

1.   Position the mouse pointer on the preview page where you would like to take a closer look.

2.   The mouse pointer will look like a magnifying glass with a + in it. Click once to zoom in one level.

3.   Click a second time to zoom to the closest view.

4.   When the magnifying glass mouse pointer displays a minus, clicking will zoom back to full page view.

☞   *You can also click the **Zoom In** and **Zoom Out** buttons if you wish, but the mouse click method described here is usually more efficient.*

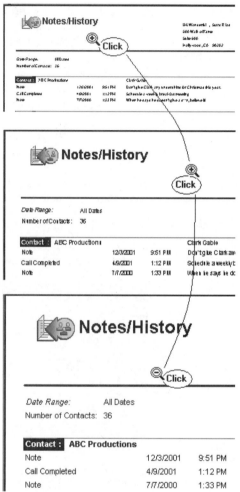

...navigate to different pages

1.   Click the **Next Page** button or press **[PageDn]**.

The next page appears on the screen in whatever magnification you are currently viewing.

2.   Click **Prev Page** or press **[PageUp]**.

The previous page appears.

☞ *You can also jump to a specific page. At the top of the print preview window, the current page number is displayed in a drop-down list. Click the list button to display a list of page numbers. Select a page from the list to display it in print preview.*

If the preview shows what you want, you are ready to print your report. Click the **Print...** button on the print preview toolbar to display the **Print** dialog box. From there you can choose basic print options and send the report on to the printer.

Practice: *Viewing the Notes/History Report*

Try It...

Step	What to do	How to do it/Comments
1.	A **Notes/History** report should be on your screen.	If not, choose **Reports, Notes/History, All contacts, Preview, OK**.
2.	Zoom in as far as you can.	Click the preview page twice. Easier to read isn't it?
3.	Zoom out to a full page.	Click anywhere on the preview page.
4.	How many pages are in the report?	Look at the lower right corner of the status bar. (There are 5 pages.)
5.	View the last page.	Click the **Next Page** button, or press **[PageDn]** until you can't go any farther.
6.	Return to the first page using the **Page:** drop-down list.	Click the list button to the right of the **Page:** box and click the number **1** to return to page 1.
7.	Close the Report window.	Click **Close**.

Which Report Do I Want?

As we mentioned before, there's a whole list of different reports you can create in the Reports menu. The table below explains a little bit about each one.

Report	What's in it
C̲ontact Report	Everything there is to know about a contact, including activities, Notes, and History.
Contact D̲irectory	A listing that includes business and home addresses and phone numbers.
P̲hone List	A simple columnar list of Company name, Contact name, office phone, and mobile phone.
T̲ask List	Calls, meetings, and to-dos.
N̲otes/History	Notes and History items that you've added yourself and those automatically inserted by ACT!.
H̲istory Summary	Total numbers of attempted calls, completed calls, meetings held, letters sent, and fields defined.
H̲istory Summary Classic	A listing of each selected contact with activity totals laid out in columnar format.
A̲ctivities/Time Spent	Activities scheduled (those that you haven't cleared) and time spent. The time value comes from the amount of time blocked off on a calendar for each activity.
Contact S̲tatus	Data from the **ID/Status** and **Last Results** fields, as well as To-do activities.
Source of R̲eferrals	Data from the **Referred By** field.
Gro̲up Reports	A listing of all groups and who's in them, as well as three others that break down information about groups.
Group Membership	Lists the names of all contacts by Group Membership
Group Summary	Displays field information for each group along with associated Notes, Histories and Activities
Group Comprehensive	Adds Contact information to the Group Summary report.
Group List	Displays group names and descriptions, along with associated Sub-groups

Report	What's in it
Sales Reports	Track data entered on the **Sales/Opportunities** tab in the Contact screen.
Sales Totals by Status	Displays information on Sales Opportunities sorted and subtotaled by Status (Open, Closed, Won)
Sales Adjusted for Probability	Displays information on Sales Opportunities sorted and subtotaled by Status with Adjusted Totals
Sales List	Displays information on Sales Opportunities sorted by Status and then by Close Date
Pipeline Report	Displays information on Sales Opportunities sorted and subtotaled by Sales Stage
Sales by Record Manager	Displays information on Sales Opportunities sorted and subtotaled by Record Manager
Sales by Contact	Displays information on Sales Opportunities sorted and by Contact
Sales Graph	Displays Sales Opportunities Total Amounts graphically
Sales Pipeline	Displays Sales Opportunities by Sales Stage Graphically
Other Report	Displays a list of available reports in the default \Report folder. In this view, there is another folder named \Other Reports. Double-click this folder to display 4 additional reports
Calls & Meetings Sum	A simple columnar list of Company, Contact name, # Attempted Calls, Completed Calls, Meetings Held and Messages Left by Contact.
Count Group Membership	Totals number of contacts in each group and subgroup.
E-mail List	A simple columnar list of Company name, Contact name and E-mail address.
Fax List	A simple columnar list of Company name, Contact name and Fax number.

Practice: *Report Practice*

Try It...

Step	What to do	How to do it/Comments
1.	Generate a Contact Report for Clark Gable and preview it.	Perform a lookup for Clark Gable, choose **Reports, Contact Report**, select **Current contact**, click the drop-down arrow for **Send output to** and choose **Preview**, click **OK**.
2.	Zoom in to read his activities.	Click a couple of times on the report to magnify it. Scroll down to the bottom of the page to see his activities.
3.	Close the report.	**Close**
4.	Generate a Phone List for everybody in the database.	Choose **Reports, Phone List**, select **All contacts**, click the drop-down arrow for **Send output to** and choose **Preview**, click **OK**.
5.	Does the My Name record appear in the list?	**Zoom In** and scroll down to see it in the list. (The list is sorted by Company, so look for **Stars R Us** in the first column of the report.)
6.	Close the report, and generate it again. This time, don't include the data from My Record.	Click **Close**, choose **Reports, Phone List**, select **All contacts**, click the drop-down arrow for **Send output to** and choose **Preview**, click the **Exclude 'My Record'** check box, click **OK**.
7.	Is the I.M. Wonderful record in the list now? Close the report.	No, you turned it off.
8.	Generate an Activities/Time Spent report all contacts for next week.	Choose **Reports, Activities/Time Spent**, select **All Contacts**, select **Preview**, click the **Activities/Notes/History** tab, click the list button for **Date range:** (under Activities) and select **Next Week** from the list, click **OK**.

Step	What to do	How to do it/Comments
9.	Observe the information presented by the report.	This report summarizes activities for the specified time period. **Cleared** and **Open** activities are listed for each contact and total time is calculated for each.
10.	Close the Report window.	**C**lose

Report Templates

Templates are used to create documents, labels, and reports. ACT! provides a wide variety of these templates and you may find that they suit all of your needs initially. Eventually, however, you may want to modify an existing template or create one for a purpose not thought of by ACT!'s creators.

Reports can sort, organize, group, and otherwise make sense of large amounts of data. Report templates are easy to create once you understand the Report Design screen.

✔ If ACT! already has a report template that suits your needs, you should use it.

✔ If ACT! has a report template that almost meets you needs, you can modify it.

✔ If none of the report templates provided by ACT! suit your needs, you can create your own.

...create a new blank report template

1.   <u>F</u>ile, <u>N</u>ew...

2.   Select **Report Template** from the list.
                                           This creates a blank template.

3.   **OK**
                                           You are deposited in design view for a new, blank, report template.

☞ *If the Tool Palette is in the way on the screen, point to the dark bar across the top (the Title bar) and drag it to another area of your screen.*

Practice: *A New Report Template*

Step	What to do	How to do it/Comments
1.	Before we start the report template, **Lookup, All Contacts**	You should always do a lookup prior to creating a report so that you have data with which to test the report.
2.	Create a new report template.	**File, New...**, select **Report Template** from the list of objects, **OK**.
3.	Observe the report template Design screen.	Drag the tool palette out of the way if necessary.
4.	Leave the report displayed.	

Try It...

The Report Design Screen

The report template Design screen is initially divided into three sections: the **Header** section, the **Contact** section, and the **Footer** section. A section label at the bottom left of the section identifies each of these sections.

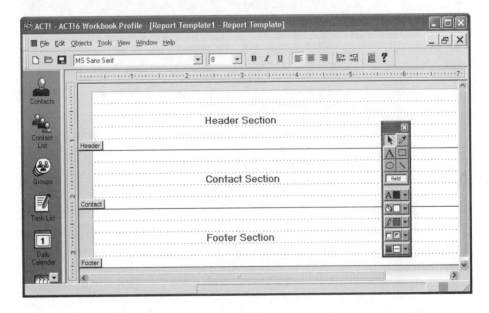

To create a report, place text and fields on the report Design screen. The section in which you place your text or fields determines the position where data appears on the printed page.

The Header Section

Fields and text placed in the Header section appear at the top of each page of the printout. Any data you wish to display at the top of every page in the printout needs to go in the Header section.

Some examples of header information might be:

```
┌──────────────────────────────────────────────────────────────────────┐
│ Stars R Us Telephone List                          ●My:Contact         │
│ Date                                               ●My:Phone           │
│                                                                        │
│ Header                                                                 │
└──────────────────────────────────────────────────────────────────────┘
```

✔   The title of your report

✔   The date the report was generated

✔   Fields from your 'My Record' (your name, department, title, etc.)

The Contact Section

Fields and text placed in the Contact section repeat for each Contact in the current group/lookup. This is the report itself. Any field in the Contact database can be displayed here.

Some examples of Contact information might be:

```
┌──────────────────────────────────────────────────────────────────────┐
│    C:Contact          C:Company            C:Phone                     │
│ Contact                                                                │
└──────────────────────────────────────────────────────────────────────┘
```

✔   Contact name

✔   Contact address information

✔   Phone numbers

The Footer Section

Fields placed in the Footer section appear at the bottom of each page in the printout.

Some examples of Footer information might be:

✔   The date and/or time the report was generated

✔   The page number

Beyond these obvious differences, there are many similarities between the Report Designer and the Design Layout screen (the one where you design the layout of Contact information, remember?).

✔   Fields and text are added to a report in the same way as they are added to a layout (pages 332 and 337).

✔   Fields and text are formatted in a report the same way as they are in a layout (page 338).

In other words, if you know how to add objects and format a layout, you know how to do the same in a report template.

Adding Report Objects

You start designing your reports by placing the fields you want your report to contain in the appropriate section.

...place fields in your report

1. Display the Tool Palette, if necessary.

If the tool palette is not displayed, choose **View, Show Tool Palette**.

2. Click the Field tool to activate it. Use the mouse to draw the field to the approximate size, shape, and position you want.

field

The **Field List** dialog box is displayed. The Report version of this box is a bit more complex than the one in Design Layout.

Each tab of the **Field List** dialog box provides access to fields of different types, and from different areas of ACT!. The **Contact** tab provides a list of fields that relate to Contacts, the **Group** tab provides fields that relate to Groups, and the **System** tab provides system information like page number, date, time, etc.

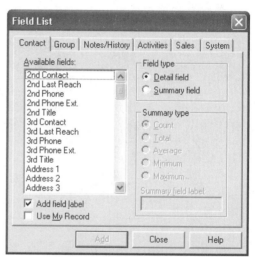

3. Choose the field you wish to display in the control you just created (by control we mean the box you just drew).

In the Contact section of the report, you should add only fields from the **Contact** tab. Other field types like **Group** and **Notes/History** fields, can be placed (and will only work) in their own sections.

4. Choose whether to **Add field label**.

A check box at the bottom left of the dialog box is supplied for this.

5. Click **Add**.

The field is assigned to the box you created with the mouse.

☞ *Another difference between layouts and reports is that in reports you can place a single field multiple times within the same report.*

6. You can click additional fields and click **Add** to place them on the report below your original.

These fields match the original in size and horizontal position.

7. Click **Close** when you're done.

☞ *You may have noticed the **Use My Record** check box below the **Add field label** check box. When this box is checked, the fields you add to the report display the information from your record only. Use this option only in the Header or Footer of the report where you wish your name or pertinent information about you to appear.*

☑ Add field label
☐ Use My Record

Formatting Reports

Formatting reports is done the same way as formatting the layouts. View those procedures starting on page 325 if necessary.

Practice: *Creating a Custom Phone List*

Step	What to do	How to do it/Comments
1.	In the Header section, add a text label that reads **Stars R Us Telephone List**. Make the text **Bold** and **18 points**. Resize the label (if necessary) to display all of the text.	Click the Text tool, drag a box in the top left corner of the Header section, and type **Stars R Us Telephone List**. Click the Selection tool, then click the new text box to select the box as a whole (handles should appear at each end of the box). Click the Bold button and change the type size to **18** using the toolbar. If necessary, point to the right handle (the mouse pointer becomes a two-headed arrow), and drag to the right until all the text is visible.
2.	At the top right of the Header section, add the **Contact** and **Phone** fields from *your* record. Do not add field labels.	If necessary, scroll to the right to see the top right corner of the "page." Click the Field button, and drag the first field at the top right of the report form. Remove the check from the **Add field label** check box, and check the **Use My Record** check box. Select **Contact**, click **Add**, select **Phone** click **Add**, and click **Close**. Click the Selection tool.
3.	Add a date just below the report title and line it up on the left side with the title.	If necessary, scroll back to the left. Click the Field button, drag a box below your report title, click the **System** tab, and choose **Date** from the **Available fields:** list. Click **Add**, **Close**, and click the Selection tool. Drag over the 2 objects to select them and click the left align icon.

Step	What to do	How to do it/Comments
4.	Save the report to the default folder and call it **Stars R Us Phone List**. Leave the report displayed in design mode.	**File**, **Save As...**, type the file name, and click **Save**. Your report should look roughly like the example below.

Stars R Us Telephone List

Date   [My:Contact]
                                                        [My:Phone]

Header

Print Preview

As you design the report, you will want to preview it to see how it looks. Often the most efficient way of doing this is Print Preview.

...Print Preview your report

1. With the report in Design view, choose **File, Print Preview**.

   The report is displayed in the Print Preview window. At the top of the Print Preview window is a specialized toolbar:

2. Forget about the **Zoom In** and **Zoom Out** buttons. Click the preview itself once to zoom in one step, click again to zoom in tighter, and click once more to zoom back to the starting level.

   You also see buttons at the top of the Print Preview window that display the next or previous page(s), and display two pages at a time.

3. When you are done with Print Preview, click the **Close** button on the Print Preview toolbar to return to the design screen.

Practice: *Print Preview and Add More*

Try It...

Step	What to do	How to do it/Comments
1.	Print Preview your **Phone List** report.	**F**ile, Print Pre**v**iew
2.	Try zooming in and out. Only the Header displays right now.	Click the Preview page to zoom in, click again, and click yet again.
3.	Close Print Preview.	Click the Print Preview **Close** button.
4.	To the Contact section of your report, add the following fields. **Contact** **Phone** **Mobile Phone** **Home Phone** Include the field labels for these fields.	Click the Field button and drag the first field in the Contact section. Leave the check in the **Add field label** check box. Locate and select **Contact**, click **Add**, repeat with **Phone, Mobile**, and **Home Phone**. Click **Close** and click the Selection tool.
5.	Drag the field *labels* up to the **Header** section and arrange them as column headings. Arrange the fields below each label and size accordingly.	Click each field or label to select it and drag to the desired location. Try to make your report look like the illustration below. You may need to point to the title bar of the Tool Palette and drag it out of the way.
6.	Save your report.	Click the Save button.

Stars R Us Telephone List

Date | My:Contact | My:Phone

Header	Contact	Phone	Mobile Phone	Home Phone
	C:Contact	C:Phone	C:Mobile Phone	C:Home Phone

Contact

Step	What to do	How to do it/Comments
7.	Print Preview your **Phone List** report.	**File, Print Preview**
8.	Try zooming in and out.	Click the Preview page to zoom in, click again, and click yet again.
9.	Observe the problems with the layout.	The labels at the top of each column do not align with the data in the column. There is waaaaaaay too much space between the Contacts.
10.	Close Print Preview.	Click the Print Preview **Close** button.

Sizing Sections

Placing fields in the Contact section of a report causes the information contained in those fields to be repeated for each Contact in the report. The vertical space taken up by the Contact section in the Design screen is a direct reflection of the space each record will take up on the printed page.

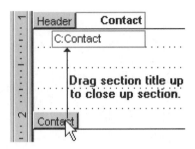

✔ If the Contact section is 1.5 inches high, each Contact record has 1.5 inches of space on the page.

The other sections work the same way.

✔ If the Header section is two inches high, the fields, text, etc. in the header take up the first two inches of every printed page.

✔ The data in the Footer section takes up as much space on each page as displayed in the Design screen.

It is likely, therefore, that you must change the size of sections from time to time (actually, most of the time) to suit your needs. Fortunately, this is easy.

...size a report section

1. Place the mouse pointer on the section title at the *bottom left* of the section.

If the section titles are not displayed, choose **View, Show Section Titles** from the menu and scroll all the way to the left.

2. Click and hold the left mouse button, and drag the section title up or down as needed.

You cannot make a section smaller than its current contents or the lowest field.

☞ *You have probably already noticed the horizontal "grid" lines that run across each report section. Any item you place on a report automatically fits between these lines. When you size a section, it tends to snap to the next grid line. This is a good thing, so don't let it bother you. This is also why you can only size objects horizontally.*

Practice: *Sizing and Dressing Your Report*

Try It...

Step	What to do	How to do it/Comments
1.	While still in your **Phone List** report, size the **Contact** section so it uses as little space as possible.	Drag the gray **Contact** section title up as far as it will go.
2.	Move the column labels in the Header Section up a row. Then use the Tool Palette to create a horizontal line in the Header section below the column labels. ☞ *Holding [Shift] as you drag a line constrains it to perfect vertical, horizontal, or 45 degree angles.*	Drag over the column labels and drag them up one row. Click the Line tool on the Tool Palette. Hold down the **[Shift]** key and drag a line across the Header below the column headings. Don't forget to click the Selection tool when you are done.
3.	The labels you used for column headings are right aligned. The text in the columns is left aligned. As a result, the headings don't line up over the data. Change the alignment of the column headings to left.	Drag over the column labels to select them (don't include the line you just drew). Click the Left align button located on the toolbar at the top of the window. Center / Left / Right
4.	Select each of the column labels and its corresponding fields and left align them.	You cannot drag over these fields because the line is in the way. Click on the Contact column label and the Contact field, click the left-align icon. Repeat for each of the phone numbers.
5.	Add a page number to the **Footer** section with a label of "Page:" and close up any remaining space.	Click the Field tool and drag a control one row below the Contact section. Click the System tab, click Page Number, click **Add** Drag the **Footer** section title up as far as it will go.
6.	Preview the report. Does it look a little better? However it is not sorted by last name.	**File, Print Preview**

Step	What to do	How to do it/Comments
7.	Close **Print Preview** and make any additional adjustments you would like to the report before we move to the next "section." Save your work and close the report.	**File, Close, Yes** The report should look similar to the example below.

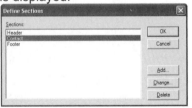

Stars R Us Telephone List — My:Contact / Date / My:Phone / Contact / Phone / Mobile Phone / Home Phone / Header / Contact Contact / C:Phone / C:Mobile Phone / C:Home Phone / Footer umber

Summary Sorted By

Sections are a way that ACT! uses to display information in a report. Many times, one section is not enough. For example, in the report we have been working on, the list is sorted by Company (which is the default). Sometimes that sort just isn't what we need. A **Summary sorted by** subsection can help us rearrange our phone list in a better order.

...create a subsection in a report

1. Open the report template.

   Click in the section that will contain the subsection and choose **Edit, Define Sections**....

   Or right-click and select **Define Sections...**

   The **Define Sections** dialog box is displayed:

2. The section you will work with is selected. If not, select it.

   Subsections are often created for the **Contacts** section.

3. Click the **Add...** button.

The **Add Section** dialog box is displayed:

Only those section types that are valid with the section you chose are available. The rest are grayed-out.

4. Choose the type of subsection you wish to add.

The available options depend on which section you selected before clicking **Add...**. More complete descriptions are on page 376.

5. Set the desired section options at the bottom of the box, **OK**.

The new subsection is added to the list. The relationship between the section and the subsection(s) is displayed by indenting the subsections in the section list.

6. Add additional sections if you wish, and click **OK** when done.

You are returned to your report.

In this next practice we will begin to look at sections. We will start by using the simple **Summary sorted by:** option to sort the report by Last Name. This section can also contain totals. After we have selected the **Summary sorted by:** option, a dialog box displays asking whether the summary should be placed **Above** or **Below** the Contacts section. For sorting, you usually select **Above**.

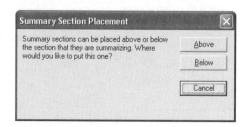

Section Options

Each report section can also have options set for it that control how the section reacts when the report is printed.

<u>P</u>age break before each section places a page break at the beginning of the specified report section.

Allo<u>w</u> section to break across multiple lines allows a section to wrap to another page instead of moving the entire section to the next page.

Collapse blan<u>k</u> lines does not display fields and associated titles if the fields are blank.

Co<u>l</u>lapse blank section does not display a section if it does not contain any information in the associated fields.

Once you master sections, a wide variety of reports are possible. You can create a report that lists your groups, then within each group lists the members of the group, then for each Contact in the group lists the Activities associated with that person.... Mind boggling, isn't it? The point is, with a little practice you can create some amazingly detailed reports.

 We won't pretend that the Report Designer is easy to understand. We had some growing pains ourselves. The best way to understand sections and how they relate to each other is to practice. If you make a mistake, try again. So let's try a simple subsection.

Practice: *Sorting by Last Name*

	Step	What to do	How to do it/Comments
Try It...	1.	Let's sort the Phone Report by Last Name.	Choose **Reports, Edit Report Template...** select **Stars R Us Phone List**, click **Open**.
		☞ *If you sort by Contact, the list will be sorted by first name.*	Click in the Contact section, right-click and select **Define Sections...** With the Contact section highlighted, click **Add...** Click the **Summary sorted by:** option. In the field list, click on **Last Name**. Click the **Collapse blank section** option. **OK** Click **Above**, click **OK** Close up the summary section.
	2.	If you like you can add a second sort for first name	Click in the Contact section, right-click and select **Define Sections...**
			With the Contact section highlighted, click **Add...** Click the **Summary sorted by:** option. In the field list, click on **First Name**. Click the **Collapse blank section** option. **OK** Click **Above**, **OK**
			Close up this summary section, too.
	3.	**Print Preview** to verify that your sorts work. Save your work so far.	**File, Print Preview**, review the list to verify the sort then click **Close**. Save your work.

Stars R Us Telephone List

| Date |

| Contact | Phone | Mobile Phone | Home Phone |

Header

| Summary of Contact | Total Contacts = | Count(C:Last |

#1 Summary of Contact sorted by Last Name field

#2 Summary of Contact sorted by First Name field

| Contact | Contact | C:Phone | C:Mobile Phone | C:Home Phone |

Summary Fields

ACT! provides several ways to summarize the data in your database. You can generate a Count of specific fields (this counts all fields – not unique fields). The Count summary type should only be used to count character types of fields. It may return invalid results on dates and numeric fields. You can also calculate a Total, Average, Minimum, or Maximum for a specific field as long as the field is defined as a numeric or currency.

...place summary fields in your report

How To...

1. Display the Tool Palette, if necessary.

   If the tool palette is not displayed, choose **View, Show Tool Palette**.

2. Click the Field tool to activate it. Use the mouse to draw the field to the approximate size, shape, and position you want.

   The **Field List** dialog box is displayed. The Report version of this box is a bit more complex than the one in Design Layout.

3. In the Field type, click **Summary field**.

   In the Summary type area, select the type of calculation you would like to perform.

   ☞ *You need to select the Summary type first, since the Summary type will limit the Available fields to choose from.*

4. Choose the field you wish to summarize.

5. Enter a **Summary field label:** if desired.

   Summary labels must be manually entered.

6. Click **Add**.

   The field is assigned to the box you created with the mouse.

7. Click **Close** when you're done.

Practice: *Sorting by Last Name*

	Step	What to do	How to do it/Comments
Try It...	1.	Let's add a summary field to see how many contacts are in the list. You have to pick a field for the summary. What is wrong with Last Name as the field to summarize.	Click in the Contact section, right-click and select **Define Sections…** With the Contact section highlighted, click **Add…** Click the **Summary** option (you don't need to select a field, the summary will be for the contact list.) Click **OK** Click **Above** to put the totals at the top of the report, click **OK** Click the Field icon and place in the Summary of Contact section a **Summary field** for **Record Manager** (all records have Record managers; not all records have contacts.) The **Summary type** should be **Count**. Enter a **Summary field label:** of "Total Contacts'" Close up this summary section as well.
	2.	As a bonus, see if you can add several Summary fields of Minimum Film Summary. Show the Minimum, Maximum, Average and Total. Add the summary fields to the end of the report.	We know that these fields are not in the report. They don't have to be in a report to be summarized by the report.

Stars R Us Telephone List

Date

| Contact | Phone | Mobile Phone | Home Phone |

Header

| Summary of Contact | Total Contacts = | Count(C:Last |

#1 Summary of Contact sorted by Last Name field

#2 Summary of Contact sorted by First Name field

| Contact | Contact | C:Phone | C:Mobile Phone | C:Home Phone |

More Sections

You may want to include other information in a report besides simple field information. Sections allow you to add information from the **Activities** tab, the **Notes/History** tab, the **Sales/Opportunities** tab or the **Groups** tab. Any given Contact could have many of these entries associated with it. If you wish to display a list of these items for each Contact in your report, you can do so by creating a subsection of the **Contact** section.

The types of sections and the options affecting them can be a bit bewildering at first. Here is the total list of the section types and their meanings:

Title header - Data placed in the Title header appears at the top of the first page only. No Page header prints on that page. The remaining pages print Page headers normally. Typically this is used as a cover page.

Header -Data placed in the header appears at the top of every page (except the Title header). Use the header for any information that you want on every page, such as the current date, column headings for the subsections, your "My Record" information, or a company logo.

Group - A Group section contains information from fields in Group records. The information in the Group section appears for each group that you include when you run the report.

 *You may not include more than one Group section in a report. You cannot include both a Group and a Contact section in a report. You can, however have a Group section with a Contact **sub**section.*

Contact - The Contact section contains information from fields in your Contact records. The information in this section is repeated for each Contact included in the report.

 *You may not include more than one Contact section in a report. You cannot include both a Contact and a Group section in a report. You can, however have a Contact section with a Group **sub**section.*

Notes/History - A Notes/History section contains information from the Notes/History tab. A Notes/History section can be included below either a Contact section or a Group section.

 You must first have a Contact or a Group section in your report template before you can include a Notes/History section.

Activities - An Activities section contains information from fields in the Activities tab. You can include an Activities section below either a Contact section or a Group section.

☞ *You must first have a Contact or a Group section before you can include an Activities section.*

Sales - A Sales section contains information from fields in the Sales Opportunities tab. You can include a Sales section below either a Contact section or a Group section.

☞ *You must first have a Contact or a Group section before you can include a Sales section.*

Group subsection - A Group subsection contains information from the Groups tab for the Contact (such as to which groups the Contact belongs).

☞ *You may only include a Group subsection if you have a Contact section in the report template.*

Contact subsection - A Contact subsection only applies to Group reports. It contains information from fields in the Contacts tab of a Group record.

Summary sorted by - The Summary sorted by section performs two tasks. It sorts the report by the contents of a field (you specify the field when you add the section to the report), *and* it contains a summary of the values in the Contact or Group section sorted by a specific field. For example, the History Summary report includes a Summary sorted by section that displays total counts of the associated Notes and History sorted by type. You can also use a Summary sorted by section just to sort a section without putting any summary fields in the section.

Summary - Summary sections appear above or below the body of the report. Summaries contain calculations that summarize fields in the report body. Examples of Summary actions are total, average, count, and minimum or maximum value. You can also use a Summary section as a "section header," which places headings at the top of each column in the section being summarized.

Both the **Summary sorted by** and the **Summary** section will prompt you for a location. **Summary sorted by** is usually placed **Above** for effective sorting. **Summary** is placed where you want to display the totals.

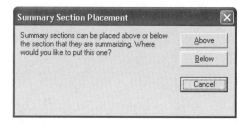

Footer - Data placed in the footer appears at the bottom of every page (unless you use a Title footer). Common uses of the footer are displaying the page number, date, or time.

Title footer - The opposite of the Title header, the Title footer appears only on the *first* page of the report. The Page footer does not print on the first page when a Title footer is used.

Object Source Information

With so many sources from which to choose, it is possible to become confused as to the source of the fields on your reports. You may have already noticed the "codes" used to identify the source of your report fields.

My: = a field from My Record (your personal information) | My:Company |

C: = a field from the Contacts screen | C:Phone |

G: = a field from the Group screen | G:City |

N: = a Note field | N:Contact |

A: = an Activity field | A:Create Date |

S:= a Sales Opportunity field | S:Amount |

System fields have no indicator.

Let's try adding sections to another report that has already been started for you.

Practice: Adding More Sections

Try It...

Step	What to do	How to do it/Comments
1.	Edit a different report template named **Activities by Contact**.	Choose **Reports**, **Edit Report Template...** from the menu, select **Activities by Contact**, click **Open**.
2.	Observe the report layout.	This is a simple report. It lists the Contact name, Company, and Phone.
3.	Add an **Activities** subsection to the **Contact** section of this report.	**Edit, Define Sections...**, select **Contact**, click **Add...**, choose **Activities**, click **OK**, and click **OK**.
4.	To the new section, add the **Date**, **Type** and **Regarding** fields from the **Activities** tab of the **Field List** dialog box. Do *not* add field labels.	On the Tool Palette, click the Field button and drag a box in the **Activities** section. 　field　 When the **Field List** dialog box is displayed (it's already on the **Activities** tab), remove the check from the **Add field label** check box. Select each field and click **Add**. Click **Close** when you're done and then click the Selection tool.
5.	Arrange the fields as they appear below, adjust the size of the section accordingly. Change the properties of the Regarding line to wrap if necessary.	Drag each field to its proper place, and then drag the **Activities** section label to close up the section.
6.	Print Preview your report. Save your work and leave the report displayed.	**File, Print Preview** **File, Save**

Activities by Contact

Date	My:Contact
	My:Phone

Contact	*Company*	*Phone*

Header			
Contact	C:Contact	C:Company	C:Phone
Activities	A:Date	A:Type	A:Regarding

New Fields

Footer	Page	Page

Report Filters

When you Print Preview, ACT! uses the current report filter settings (often the same thing as the current lookup). If you are working with a large database, previewing a report with no filter in place can take a very long time.

✔ You are most likely familiar with filtering reports, as you are asked to apply a filter every time you print any report. It is possible to define a *default* filter for your reports as well as change it when you use the report.

✔ Report filters define which records print in your report and, when applicable, what date ranges print for dated items like notes/histories and activities.

✔ Once you define a filter for your report, it always uses that filter unless you tell it otherwise.

✔ When a filter is defined for your custom report, Print Previewing the report uses the filter.

...define a default filter for a report

1. Display the report in Design view and choose **Edit, Define Filters...**.

The **Define Filters** dialog box displays (have you two already met?).

 Or right-click and select **Define Filters...**

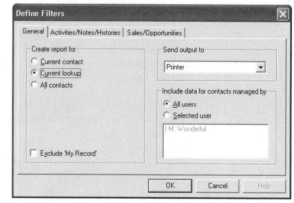

2. Specify the desired **Create report for** and **Send output to** options.

You can choose to print only the current lookup/group or all Contacts. You can default the report to Preview instead of sending it directly to the printer.

3. If you want to include date specific data or wish to eliminate certain types of activities from the report, display the appropriate tab of the dialog box.

Click the **Activities/Notes/ Histories** tab.

You can choose what to print as far as notes/histories and activities and specify date ranges to print as applicable.

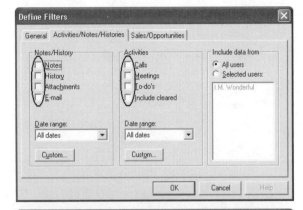

4. If you have included Sales/Opportunities data in your report, and wish to filter for specific types of data, display the **Sales/ Opportunities** tab and set the options to suit your needs.

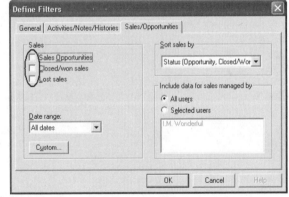

5. When you have set all of the desired filter options, click **OK**, and save your report.

You have just defined the default filter setting for this report.

You cannot generate a report filtered by a selected user unless that selected user is a logon user in your database. This seems obvious for a server database, but what if the Sales Manager is preparing reports from the laptop (with a sync version of the database)? Are the users enabled for login on the laptop. What about evil twins? Which evil twin maintains the activities, notes & histories?

Practice: *A Report Filter*

Step	What to do	How to do it/Comments
1.	Display the **Define Filters** dialog box for your **Activities by Contact** report.	Choose **Edit, Define Filters...** from the menu.
2.	Set the report to print the current lookup only. The report should assume you wish to Print Preview.	Select the **Current Contact lookup** and **Preview** options, click **OK**.
3.	Change the default Date Range to Current Quarter.	Anyone can select another time period if desired, however, Current Quarter will be the default.
4.	Save and close the report.	

Try It...

Scrunching Fields

As you place some types of fields on your reports, you may want to take out the space between those fields…you know…scrunch them together. For example, do you want the City Sate Zip fields to display like this…

Houston	, TX	713-661-
San Francisco	, CA	415-395-

Your text would display like this:

Houston, TX	713-661-
San Francisco, CA	415-395-

…removing extra space between fields

How To…

1. Display the report in Design view

   If you want to modify a label or envelope, click **File**, **Print**, change the **Printout type:**, select the template and click **Edit Template**.

2. Right-click on the first field in the series and select **Properties**

3. Click **Close up blank space**

   ☐ Don't print if duplicated
   ☑ Close up blank space
   ☐ Wrap text

4. Repeat steps 2 and 3 as necessary.

   Don't **Close up blank space** on the last field in the series (i.e. Zip.)

5. Click **OK**.

Practice: *Modifying an Address Label*

Try It...

Step	What to do	How to do it/Comments
1.	This time let's edit the Avery 5160 label to include the 2nd address line.	Click **File, Print**, change the **Printout type:**, select the template and click **Edit Template**.
2.	Shorten the Address 1 field to be about 2/3 the width of the label.	Click on the Address 1 field. Use the mouse to drag the selection box on the right to make the fields smaller.
3.	Change the properties of the field to remove extra space.	Right-click and select **Properties**. Click on **Close up blank space**, click **OK**.
4.	Now add the Address 2 field.	Click the Field icon. Drag the control to the right of Address 1. You can drag the control into the gray area. Select Address 2 and click **Add**. Click **Close**.
5.	Save and Print Preview.	Notice that the Suite numbers (from the Address 2 field on all the Contact records) now displays.
6.	Close the Label design view.	Click the Close button.　　　　☒

Using Custom Reports

Once your report is created and saved, you can use it to create reports for the current lookup.

...generate a custom report

How To...

1. Perform a lookup or display a group for the Contacts you wish to include in your report.

A report can print all Contact records or just the current lookup or group.

2. **Reports, Other Report...**

The **Open** dialog box is displayed with a list of report templates.

3. Choose the desired report template and click **Open**.

The **Run Report** dialog box is displayed (it should look familiar):

The **General** tab allows you to choose basic output options such as whether to use all contacts, current lookup or current contact only. You can also choose where the report will go (to the printer, preview, or to a file).

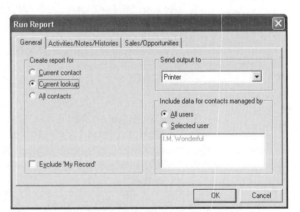

The **Activities/Notes/Histories** tab allows you to filter out histories, notes, etc. You can also choose date ranges for notes and activities.

Use the **Sales/Opportunities** tab to define filters for Sales data if it is included on the report.

When filtering dates, click **Custom...** and a calendar displays on which you can drag over a custom date range.

4. Choose the desired output options, and click **OK**.

☞ *The Report Designer only allows you to control the overall layout of the report, not individual Contact records. Basically you cannot edit the report after it is run. However, you can send the report to an editable file by choosing **File - Editable Text** from the **Run Report** dialog box. When you click **OK**, you are prompted for a file name and location (the file is saved in Rich Text Format (RTF)). You are then asked if you would like to open the file into your default word processor. You may open the file now, or open it later and edit your report ad nauseam.*

Practice: *Generating a Custom Report*

Step	What to do	How to do it/Comments
1.	If necessary, display the Contacts screen.	
2.	Display the **Clients** group.	Click the [<No Group>] Group button at the bottom of the window and select **Clients** from the list.
3.	Generate an **Activities By Contact** report using the current lookup. Observe the filter options (Current lookup and Preview) are already set for you.	**Reports, Other Report...**, choose the **Activities By Contact** report template, and click **Open**.
4.	Observe the preview.	It displays only the records in the current group.
5.	Close Print Preview.	**Close**

Try It...

Adding the Report to the Menu

If you use your custom reports constantly, you can add it to the menu quite easily.

...add a custom report to the menu

How To...

1. **R**eports, **M**odify Menu...

2. Click **A**dd Item....

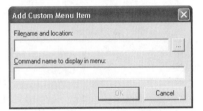

3. Click the Browse button to display an **Open** dialog box with a list of reports. Select the report you wish to add to your menu and click the **Open** button.

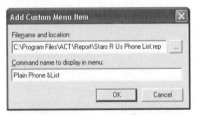

The selected file name and path are placed in the **Filename and location:** text box. The filename is displayed in the **Command name to display in menu:** box.

4. If you wish something other than the file name to appear on the menu, type a command in the **Command name to display in menu:** text box. You can underline a letter by placing an ampersand (&) in front of that letter.

When the command is displayed in the menu, the letter after the ampersand (&) is underlined.

5. Click **OK** to return to the **Modify Menu** dialog box. If you wish to add additional items, repeat steps 2 through 4. Otherwise, click **OK**.

The next time you display the **Reports** menu, the command you created is displayed at the bottom of the menu. Selecting the item runs your report.

	Practice: *Adding Your Report to the Menu*	
Step	**What to do**	**How to do it/Comments**
1.	Add the **Stars R Us Phone List** report to the menu. Make the menu read **Plain Phone List**.	**Reports, Modify Menu...**, click **Add Item...**, and click the Browse button. If necessary, display the folder where your report is stored, select the report, and click the **Open** button. (Use the **phonels6.rep** file if you did not create and save this file in a previous exercise.) In the **Command name** box, type **P&lain Phone List**, click **OK**, **OK**.
2.	Generate your report from the menu. Preview the report for all Contacts.	**Reports, Plain Phone List** Click **All contacts** and Send output to **Preview**, **OK**.
3.	Close Print Preview.	**Close**
4.	Remove your custom report from the menu.	**Reports, Modify Menu...**, select the **P&lain Phone List** report (if necessary), click **Delete Item**, **OK**.

Try It...

Review: *Running and Designing Reports*

Try It...

1. Lookup all records with **an ID/Status** of **Client**. Generate a **Contact Directory** report for the current lookup and preview it. Be sure there are 19 records in the report (or the same number of records as in the lookup). Close the report.

2. Modify the **Stars R Us Phone** List. Replace the Contact field which displays the name as:

> Fred Astaire

with the Last Name field, a comma (which would be a plain text field), and the First Name field to display as:

> Astaire, Fred

Set the filters for this report to Preview for the current lookup only.

3. Modify the Activities by Contact report.

Add a Sales/Opportunities section that contains the fields (without labels) for:
> **Status   Close Date   Sales Stage   Amount   Probability**

Create a Summary section for Activities (above) and a Summary section for Sales/Opportunities (above). In the Summary sections put Text Labels that say Activities and Sales/Opportunities respectively.

Close up any blank space.

Drag the Contact, Company and Phone fields down one line and move the Line from the Header section into the Contact section, above the Contact fields. Move the Contact field a little to the left and Bold it.

Feel really adventuresome? In the Sales/Opportunity section, include a **Summary field, Total** for **Amount**. (Don't forget to right-justify and line them up.)

Save and Print Preview.

Header	Contact		Company	
	C:Last Name	, C:First Name	C:Company	
Contact				
	Activities			
Summary of Activities				
Activities	A:Date	A:Type	A:Regarding	
	Sales/Opportunities			
Summary of Sales				
Sales	S:Status	S:Close Date	S:Sales Stage	

Advanced Groups

To be able to track information that relates to groups of records, you will:

- ☑ Create notes for different groups.

- ☑ Associate activities with groups.

- ☑ Customize group User fields.

Using Groups Creatively

You may be used to thinking about Groups as the feature that only collects contacts and displays them as a type of lookup. Well, Groups can collect things besides contacts. Groups can also collect activities, histories, notes, and sales opportunities, even if the Contact is not a member of the group.

Group Use Scenario

Let's say we have several projects that we need to keep track of...some big movie deals we are trying to put together. We need to keep track of who has agreed to participate in the project (group members). We also need to keep track of who we've talked to about which project and what they said...whether they have agreed to participate or not. So while the Contacts are not really group members (they haven't said yes to the project yet), you need a way to collect all of the activities, histories, notes, and opportunities that are associated with a specific deal (Group) where they can be easily viewed.

Confused yet? Let's see how it works.

Practice: *Creating 2 Movie Project Groups*		
Step	**What to do**	**How to do it/Comments**
1.	Open the Groups view.	Click the Groups button, if necessary.
2.	Create 2 new Groups called: **M1-Going Your Way** and **M2-Postman Never Knocks**	Choose **Group**, **New Group** from the menu or click the New Group icon. Type in the first Group name, then repeat for the second group.

Try It...

Group Activities

Even if you schedule an activity for someone who is not a member of a group, you can still associate that activity with a group. The group with which you associate an activity does not even need to have any members.

...associate an activity or history with a group

How To...

1. Create the activity or record a history.

Lookup the Contact and click the appropriate activity button.

Specify the details of the activity or the history as you usually would.

2. In the dialog box, click the drop-down arrow for **Associate with group:** and choose the group with which you wish to associate this task.

If you currently have a group displayed, the group name already appears in the box. You can change it if you wish.

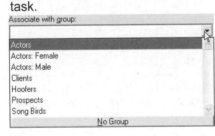

Associate with group:

| Actors |
| Actors: Female |
| Actors: Male |
| Clients |
| Hoofers |
| Prospects |
| Song Birds |
| No Group |

3. **OK**

The activity or history is set as usual, but also associated with the specified group.

If you display the Group window and click the **Notes/History** or **Activities** tab for the group, you will see any associated information listed there, and the names of the Contacts for whom the activities were created.

Try It...

Step	What to do	How to do it/Comments
1.	Let's record a cold call to Bing about the Going Your Way project to include details of: "He might be interested in the project. He wants us to call back next week." Schedule a follow up call for next week sometime. Don't forget to associate all of this with the **M1-Going Your Way** group.	Lookup Bing Crosby. Click the Record History icon. You'll have to change the type from Meeting to Call. Change the Regarding to Cold Call. In the **Associate with group:** area, select **M1-Going Your Way**. Enter some details of the call. Click **Follow Up Activity…** select some day next week, enter a regarding of Follow up. Don't forget to associate the activity with the **M1** group. **OK OK**
2.	View Bing's **Notes/History** tab. View his **Groups** tab. Is he a member of the **M1** group?	No he is not an **M1** group member.
3.	Display the Groups view and select the **M1** group. Click the **Notes/History** tab to see what you've been doing on the **M1** project.	Wow…there's Bing's phone call. Groups
4.	Display the **Activities** tab for the **M1** group to see what future plans you have to promote this movie deal.	At least one phone call scheduled.
5.	Display the **Contacts** tab to see who has signed up for the deal.	Guess we better get working. No one has signed up for the deal yet.
6.	OK, now go back to Bing and record another Cold Call regarding **M2**. Fill in the details as you like.	Return to Contacts view. Click the Record History icon. Change the type from Meeting to Call. Contacts Change the Regarding to Cold Call. In the **Associate with group:** area, select **M2-Postman Never Knocks**.

Filtering Group Notes

The **Notes/History**, **Activities**, and **Sales/Opportunities** tabs in the Group view have the ability to filter any combination of group activities. You control what is displayed here through the filter settings.

...filter any of the Group tabs

How To...

1. In the Group Window, display the **Notes/History** tab first. If the filter area is not displayed, click the **Filter** button at the top of the tab.

The **Filter** button hides or displays the filter area.

2. Select the desired **Show types** options.

These options control what will (or will not) be displayed in the list. Usually we leave them all checked.

3. Select **Show for** options.

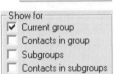

These options determine which Notes/History items will be displayed.

Current group displays only notes associated with the group. This is a good option.

☞ *Keeping a check in the **Contacts in group** option could hamper your database performance each time you open and move around in Groups, so uncheck it in the **Notes/History**, **Activities** and **Sales Opportunities** tabs.*

Contacts in group displays all notes/histories since the beginning of time for every Contact in the group...generally not what you want. Besides, read the note to the left.

4. As needed, choose **Dates to show:** options and **Select Users...** to further filter (or remove filters) from the Group Notes/History list.

The combinations are mind-boggling. (Well, they boggle our minds anyway.)

5. Display the Group **Activities** and the **Sales/Opportunities** tabs and review or change the filter options for them as well.

Practice: *Filtering the Group Display*

Try It...

Step	What to do	How to do it/Comments
1.	Hot dog! While Bing is not interested in **M2**, he signs up for the **M1** project. Add him to the **M1** group.	In Contacts view, click on Bing's **Groups** tab. Right-click, select **Group Membership...**, put a check beside the **M1** group.
2.	Return to Groups view. Now look at the **Notes/History** tab. Are there more histories there now, including the Cold Call about the **M2** project? We only want to see the Notes and Histories for *the M1* project	Click on the Filter button in the **Notes/History** tab. Notice how checking **Contacts in group** displays all histories for Bing, regardless of association. Uncheck it. Uncheck the same option in the **Activities** tab. Now only the activities you have planned to promote this movie are displayed.

Add Columns to View

Back in Contacts view, let's modify our layout tabs a bit to display more information. In the **Notes/History tab**, let's add a column that displays the Group association.

...add columns to list tabs

How To...

1. In the Contacts view, display the **Notes/History** tab first.

   Click on the **Notes/History** tab.

2. Right-click on the tab column headers and select **Add Columns to View...**

   Right Click

   garding

   Sort Ascending
   Sort Descending

   Add Columns to View...

3. Click on **Group** and click **Add**.

   As a note or history is associated with a group, you can see it.

4. Click **Close**.

 Repeat for the **A_ctivities** and the **S_ales/Opportunities** tabs

Practice: *Associate History with a Group*

Step	What to do	How to do it/Comments
1.	Add the Group column to the **Notes/History** tab in Contacts view.	Now you can see what Bing said about each of the movies we discussed with him.
2.	Add the Group column to the **Activities** tab in Contacts view.	

Try it...

Group Notes

By now you know the reasons for and the value of notes, activities, and histories as they pertain to your Contacts. These items track what you said, what they said, what you did, and what you need to do.

You can create a note for a group. That is, the note belongs to the group record and not for any one Contact in that group.

...create a group note

1.	Display the Groups window.	Click the View Groups button, if necessary. Groups
2.	Select the group.	Click the group (or subgroup) name in the list to the left of the Groups window.
3.	Display the **Notes/History** layout tab. This tab can display notes and history entries for members of the group and for the group as a whole.	Notes for individual members of the group may be displayed here. If a note belongs to a Contact record, a column identifies the Contact name.
4.	Click the **Insert Note** button at the top of the Notes/History list.	You can also click the Insert Note toolbar button.
5.	Type the note as you would for any record.	This note belongs to the group as a whole, not to an individual Contact.

How To...

Associating Notes with a Group

There are two ways to associate a Contact note with a group:

✔ Associate the note as you type it.

✔ Associate the note manually.

... associate a Contact note with a group

How To...

1. To associate a note with a group as you type, first select the group. If necessary, create a note for that Contact.

Click the Group button at the bottom of the Contact window and choose the desired Group from the list.

2. Create the note.

When a group is "active," any notes you create will be automatically associated with that group.

3. If the note already exists, locate the note in the **Notes/History** tab. If a Group column is not displayed in the list, add it.

To add a column to just about any list in ACT!, right-click anywhere inside the list itself and choose **Add Columns...** from the shortcut menu. A list of available columns is displayed. Drag the name of the column from the dialog box to the desired position in the list itself. If the column you want is not displayed, either it is not available for that list or it is already there (try scrolling to the right or left).

4. Click the Group column to display the drop-down list button, click the button, and select the desired group from the list.

Subgroups are listed with the name of their parent group, a colon, and the subgroup name.

Example: The Los Angeles subgroup you created earlier is listed as:

Actors:Los Angeles

Practice: *Groups of Notes (or is that Notes of Groups?)*

Step	What to do	How to do it/Comments
1.	Display the Groups screen.	Click the Groups button.
2.	Create a note for the **Hoofers** group. The note should read: **All Hoofers require additional insurance for feet.**	Click the **Hoofers** group, click the Insert Note button, and type these words of wisdom.
3.	Return to the Contacts screen. If necessary, display the **Hoofers** group. Does this note show up for any of the members of the group?	Click the Contacts button. Notes created for the group as a whole do not display for the individual members of the group.
4.	Display the Contact List and select the record for **Fred Astaire**. *Don't* do a lookup! It turns the group off.	Click the Contact List button, click somewhere on Fred's record.
5.	Create a note for Fred that reads: **Don't forget costume allowance for top hats.** Observe the **Group** column on the **Notes/History** tab for this note.	Click the Insert Note button to display the Contacts screen for the selected Contact and insert a note. Type the text of the note. **Note:** Because you are viewing a group, *not a lookup*, the note is automatically added to the Group notes tab.
6.	Display the **Groups** screen and observe the **Notes/History** tab for the **Hoofers** group. Display the **Filter** options if necessary and un-check the **Contacts in group** check box.	Click the Groups button. Notice that the group note does not indicate a Contact, while the note you *associated* with the group does.
7.	Return to the Contacts screen.	Click the Contacts button.

Try It...

Group User Fields

When you are in the Groups view, one of the tabs available to you is **Group Info**. You could customize these fields and use them for storing information about the group/project. What kind of information, you ask?

✔ You could enter the movie location.

✔ You could enter the start date of the movie.

✔ Movie budget, Director's name, length of time on location, etc.

We can modify and add Group fields the same way we added Contact fields.

...add columns to the Group tab

How To...

1. In the Groups view, click **Edit, Define Fields...**.

Groups

2. Verify that the **Record type:** displays as **Group** (instead of Contact.)

3. Modify or add fields as you did for Contact (starting on page 300).

4. Click **OK**.

Practice: *Modifying Group Fields*

Step	What to do	How to do it/Comments
1.	Display the Groups view. Change **User 1** to **Location**. Change **User 2** to **Start Date** and change the field type to Date.	Click the Groups button. Click **Edit, Define Fields...** click on **User 1** and change the field name. Groups. Click on **User 2** and change the field name to Start Date and change the **Type:** to Date. **Yes OK**
2.	The Location for M1 is Hong Kong. The Start Date is 2 months from now	Click on the **M1-Going Your Way** group. Click the **Group Info** tab and enter the Location and Start Date.

Try It...

Add Columns to the Groups Tab

The value of any Group field can be displayed in the Contacts view if the Contact is a member of the group.

How To...

...add columns to the Groups tab

1. In the Contacts view, display the **Groups** tab.

   Click on the **Contacts** icon if necessary. Click on the **Groups** tab at the bottom of the screen. Contacts

2. Right-click on the tab column headers and select **Add Columns to View...**

3. Any field created in the Group view can be displayed here.

4. Click **Close**.

Practice: *Modifying Groups Tab*

Try It...

Step	What to do	How to do it/Comments
1.	Lookup Bing Crosby. Add Location and Start Date to the Groups tab.	Click the Contacts button. Lookup Bing. Click on the **Groups** tab. Right-click on the tab column headers and select **Add Columns to View...** Click **Location** and click **Add**. Click **Start Date** and click **Add**. Click **Close**.
2.	Now we can check Bing's availability for other projects.	

Review: *Using Groups Creatively*

1.	George Cukor has agreed to direct the M1-Going Your Way. Add him to the Group.
2.	We completed a call to George on 12/14/2001 and forgot to associate it with the **M1** group. Make that change.
3.	Preview the Group Summary Report for **M1** group only.
4.	Schedule a Kick-off meeting for everyone in the **M1** group for next Friday.

Macros & Queries

To be able to make ACT! behave as you would like, you will:

☑   Record a macro.

☑   Run a macro.

☑   Assign macros to toolbars, menus, and shortcut keys.

☑   Customize ACT!'s behavior.

☑   Create and run Lookup By Example queries.

☑   Create and run Advanced Queries.

☑   Delete queries.

Macros

The more you use ACT!, the more likely you are to find yourself performing repetitive tasks. You know, those little annoying things that you do exactly the same way over, and over, and over, and over again?

Cheer up! ACT! has a macro recorder. Once you learn a few basic bits of information, you can automate many of those troublesome tasks.

Recording a Macro

Creating a macro involves performing a set of actions while a recorder is "watching." That part is simple, but there are a couple things of which you should be wary:

✔ You have the option to record mouse actions (clicks, drags, etc.). We recommend you *do not use this option.* Most mouse actions are recorded as coordinates on the screen instead of which menu or button you select. Since menus and buttons and other items can move (because of the resizing of a window or a change to a layout), a macro that runs fine the first time you use it may have a completely different effect the next time.

✔ There is no utility for editing existing macros. If you don't perform the task properly when recording your macro, you are doomed to record it again from the beginning (bummer, huh?).

...record a macro

1. Carefully think through and (if necessary) practice the task you wish to perform.

   We cannot stress this enough! You have to get it right the first time or record again.

2. **Tools, Record Macro...**

   The **Record Macro** dialog box displays:

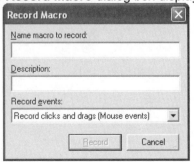

3. Type a name for the macro, type a description for the macro, and choose what to record.

The name will be used as the macro file name. The description is optional but can be useful. The **Record events:** option is very important, and it offers you three options:

Record clicks and drags (Mouse Events)
Everything
Record everything except mouse events.

☞ *Because of the difficulties inherent in accurately playing back mouse events, we recommend you choose the third option unless you have a specific reason to record mouse events.*

4. Perform the task you wish to record. Remember that if you want to manually select a menu option, press **[Alt]** to activate the menu line and then press the underlined letter of the desired menu option.

Perform the task carefully without using the mouse (unless you chose to record the mouse only).

5. Press **[Alt+F5]** to stop recording the macro.

You can also choose **Tools, Stop Recording Macro** from the menu.

Practice: *Recording a Macro*

Step	What to do	How to do it/Comments
1.	Let's assume you keep more than one ACT! database: perhaps one for business and one for personal use. You can record a macro that opens your personal database.	.
2.	Set up to record your macro. Name it **Open Personal** and ignore mouse actions. Start recording.	**Tools, Record Macro...**, type **Open Personal**, click the drop-down arrow for **Record events:** and choose **Record everything except mouse events**. Click **Record**.

Try It...

Step	What to do	How to do it/Comments
3.	Press [Ctrl+O] (shortcut for Open), type **personal**, and press [Enter].	Wait while the database opens.
4.	Stop recording your macro.	Press [Alt+F5], or choose **Tools, Stop Recording Macro** (use the mouse for this if you wish).
5.	Record another macro. Name it **Open Stars**. Record the opening of the file **Stars R Us**. Stop recording once the file is open. If you're prompted about rolling over activities, press [Enter] or [Esc] as part of the recording.	Repeat steps 2 and 3. Change the name of the macro and the path and file name (and the roll over prompt response, if necessary).

Running a Macro

Once the macro is recorded, it's ready to run whenever you need it. There are several ways to run your macros, the most direct is from the Tools menu.

...run a macro

1.	**Tools, Run Macro...**	The **Run Macro** dialog box appears.

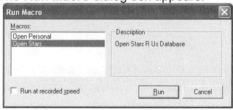

2.	Select the macro you wish to run.	If you typed a description for the macro, it is displayed in the box on the right of the dialog box.
3.	**Run**	You can also double-click the macro name to run it.

*Click the **Run at recorded speed** check box to run the macro at the speed which you performed the actions. If you paused for a 15 seconds before you typed the path and file name, for example, the playback pauses for the same length of time. This can be a useful way to observe what you did when a macro is not working properly. It can also show you just how slow a typist you really are (yikes!).*

Practice: *Run Your Macro*

Step	What to do	How to do it/Comments
1.	Run the **Open Personal** macro.	**T**ools, R**u**n Macro..., select the **Open Personal** macro, and click **R**un. The **Personal** file opens.
2.	Now run the **Open Stars** macro.	**T**ools, R**u**n Macro..., select the **Open Stars** macro, click **R**un. The **Stars R Us** file opens.

Try It...

Assigning Macros to Toolbars and Menus

You can probably see how running your macros using **T**ools, R**u**n Macro... could get old real fast; particularly if you run the macro frequently. There are three more efficient ways to run your macros:

✔ You can add it to a menu.

✔ You can create a toolbar button.

✔ You can create a keyboard shortcut.

All of the options have their advantages. However, to use one of these options, you must create a custom command for your macro.

How To...

...create a custom command from a macro

1. Create the macro (see page 404).   Don't you love it when we state the obvious?

2. **Tools, Customize Contacts Window...**

3. Click the **Custom Commands** tab and click **New** to create a new command.

   To create a custom command (in this case, one that will run a macro), all you need to do is fill out this form.

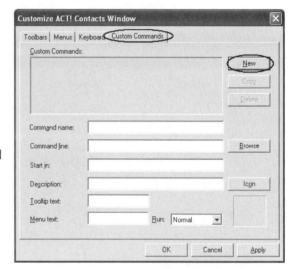

4. Type a **Command name:** in the appropriate text box.   Make the name meaningful so you will recognize it later.

5. Click the **Browse** button next to the **Command line:** text box. Locate and open the macro file.

   ☞ *If you know the path and name of the macro file, you can type it into the box instead of using **Browse**....*

   The macro file is probably stored in a folder named **Macro** under the folder named **Act**. Macro files have an **.MPR** file extension. Change the **Files of type** option (at the bottom of the open dialog box) to **Macros (*.mpr)** from the default executable files (***.exe**).

6. Type an optional **Description:** of the command, and/or type the optional **Button/tooltip text:**.   The description appears on the ACT! status bar when you point to a menu or toolbar button to which you have assigned the command. The **Button/tooltip text:** appears when the user points to a custom toolbar button.

7. Type the optional **Menu text:**. If you wish to have a letter underlined, precede it with an ampersand (**&**).

This text appears in the menu if you assign the command to a menu.

8. Once the desired items are set, click **Save**. You may then add additional commands if you wish. Click **Apply** when you are finished.

The custom command is added to the **Commands:** list. The dialog box remains displayed.

☞ *If you have access to icon libraries or custom icons, you can also assign a custom icon to your command. Click the **Icon** button, locate and select the file that contains the desired icon, and choose the icon. When you assign this command to a toolbar button, it displays the icon you selected.*

✔ You can create commands that run other ACT! reports, document templates, and even other programs. All that is necessary is to specify the path to the report template, document template, or the program's executable file, in the same way you specify the path to a macro. For example, if you frequently need to use the Windows calculator while you are working in ACT!, you can create a custom command that runs the program and adds it to the toolbar, the menu, or runs it with a keyboard shortcut.

✔ Later in this course, we will discuss the creation of Advanced Queries (page 423). These can also be used to create custom commands, and this can greatly facilitate the running of commonly used queries.

Practice: *Creating a Custom Command*

	Step	What to do	How to do it/Comments
Try It...	1.	Create a custom command for your **Open Personal** macro using the following settings: **Option** **Your Entry** Command name . **OpenPersonal** Command line ....**(Browse...** to locate file) Start in: ....(accept default) Description:. **Open Personal File** Tooltip text .... **Personal File** Menu text: .... **Pe&rsonal**	**Tools, Customize Contacts Window...** and click the **Custom Commands** tab. Click **New**. Enter the items shown at left. The file Command line is probably located on the C: drive in the: **\Program Files\Act\Macro** folder although it could be: **\Program Files\Symantec\Act\Macro** Click the drop-down arrow for **Files of type:** and choose **Macros (*.mpr)**. Click **Apply** when you're done. ☞ *If you did not successfully complete the creation of your two macros, you will find two macros named **Xpersonal** and **Xstars** in your class directory. Use browse to locate these macros.*
	2.	Create a custom command for the **Open Stars** macro using the following settings: **Option** **Your Entry** Command name ....**OpenStars** Command line ....**(Browse...** to locate file) Start in: ....(accept default) Description:....... **Open Stars File** Tooltip text ....**Stars File** Menu text: ....**S&tars R Us**	Click **New**, and follow the instructions for the previous command, substituting the new entries shown at left.
	3.	Save the new custom commands.	Click **Apply** leave the dialog box displayed.

Assign a Command to a Toolbar

Wow! That was a lot of work! And for what? Well, to be honest, nothing yet, but hang in there. The hard part is over and the best is yet to come. Now that you have created a custom command that runs your macro, you can assign the command to the toolbar, menu, or a shortcut key.

...assign a custom command to a toolbar

How To...

1. Define the custom command (see page 408).

   There we go again! You knew that, didn't you?

2. **Tools, Customize Contacts Window...** and click the **Toolbars** tab if necessary.

   The **Customize ACT!** dialog box appears.

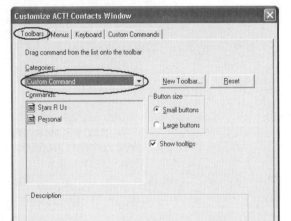

3. Click the **Categories:** drop-down arrow and choose the **Custom Command** from the list.

   Any custom commands you have created are displayed in the **Commands:** list.

4. Assuming you wish to add this command to the existing toolbar, drag the command from the window to the desired position on the ACT! toolbar.

 *You can also create a new toolbar by clicking **New Toolbar...** and giving it a name. Then drag the command to the new toolbar.*

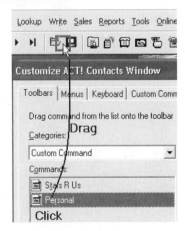

☞ *Once the button is on the toolbar, pointing to it displays the tooltip text you assigned when you created the command (if you assigned it). Clicking the button runs the macro. Pretty cool, huh? (We told you so.)*

Practice: *A Macro Toolbar Button*

Step	What to do	How to do it/Comments
1.	Assign the **Personal** command to the Contact Window toolbar. Position the new button to the right of the record Navigation buttons.	If necessary, choose **Tools, Customize Contacts Window...** and click the **Toolbars** tab. Locate and select **Custom Command** from the **Categories:** list. Drag the **Personal** command to the right of the record navigation buttons on the Toolbar.
2.	Add the **Stars R Us** command to the right of the Open Personal button if necessary.	Drag from the **Commands:** list to the toolbar.
3.	Close the dialog box.	Click **OK**.
4.	Observe your new buttons.	The buttons are identical in appearance.
5.	Point to each button and observe the tooltip. Click each button to open its respective file.	The tooltip identifies the database each button will open. You typed this tooltip when you defined the custom command (page 408).

Assign a Command to a Menu

Toolbar buttons are easy to access but not always easy to identify. Menu items, since they are text, tend to be a bit easier to identify with a glance.

...assign a custom command to a menu

How To...

1. Define the custom command (see page 408).

Are we becoming too predictable?

2. **Tools, Customize Contacts Window...,** and click the **Menus** tab.

The **Menu:** selections are displayed on the right.

3. From the **Categories:** drop-down list, select **Custom Command**.

Your custom commands are displayed in the **Commands** list.

4. Locate the main menu item in which you want your command to appear. And display its subordinate items.

Click the + to the left of the menu item to display a list of the items currently displayed in that menu.

☞ *Click a + to display the subordinate menu items. Click a - to hide them.*

5. Drag the custom command icon to the point in the menu list where you want the command to appear.

Your command is inserted into that menu's list.

6. Repeat with any other custom commands you wish to add. Click **OK** when you are done.

Practice: *Adding the Command to the Menu*

Try It...

Step	What to do	How to do it/Comments
1.	Add the **Personal** custom command to the **File** menu for the **Contact Window**. Position it above the **Close** command.	**Tools, Customize Contacts Window...**, and click the **Menus** tab. From the **Categories:** list, select **Custom Command**. Click the + to the left of **&File** in the **Menu:** column to display the File menu items. Drag the **Personal** command to the **&Open** command and release the mouse button (the item is added below the item to which you drag.)
2.	Add the **Stars R Us** custom command below the **Pe&rsonal** menu item you just added.	Follow the steps above for the **Stars R Us** command.
3.	Close the dialog box.	Click **OK**.
4.	Display the **File** menu and test your new commands.	**File, Personal** (Wait for the database to open.) **File, Stars R Us** You should have the two custom commands listed below the **Close** command. The menu text was determined when you defined the custom commands.

Assign Shortcut Keys to a Command

There are lots of neat and useful ways to activate your custom commands, aren't there? Well, there's one more.... For that command you execute one hundred times a day, you might want to assign a shortcut key.

✔ Shortcut keys allow the fastest access to your commands of all these methods.

✔ The only downside to shortcut keys is that you must *remember* the keystrokes in order to use them.

✔ Unless you have a photographic memory, we recommend you use this option only for those commands you use most frequently.

...assign a shortcut key to a command

1. Define the custom command (see page 408).

   We promise, this is the last time we mention it.

2. **Tools, Customize Contacts Window...**, and click the **Keyboard** tab.

   The **Customize ACT!** dialog box appears.

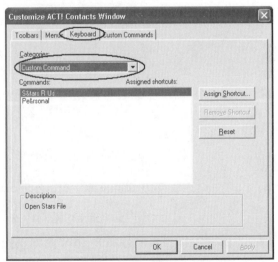

3. From the **Categories:** drop-down list choose **Custom Command**. A list of custom commands is displayed below.

   If any shortcut keys are currently assigned, they are displayed on the left side of the list.

4. Locate and select your custom command in the **Commands:** list.

   You can create or change shortcuts for any command in the list.

5. Click the **Assign Shortcut...** button.

The **Assign Shortcut** dialog is displayed:

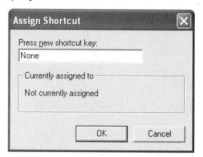

6. Press the key combination you wish to assign to the command. Check to see if they keys are already assigned.

When you press the keys, they appear as text in the **Press new shortcut key:** box. If the keys are already assigned, the **Currently assigned to** box displays that information.

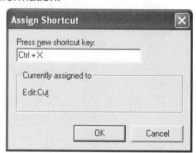

7. If the keys are already assigned, try another combination until you find one that is not currently assigned, and then click **OK**.

The new key combination displays to the right of the selected custom command.

8. Click **OK** to save your key assignments and close the dialog box.

Practice: *Shortcut Keys for Everyone!*

Step	What to do	How to do it/Comments
1.	Assign the shortcut key combination **[Ctrl+E]** to your **OpenPersonal** custom command.	**Tools, Customize Contacts Window...**, click the **Keyboard** tab, Choose **Custom Command** from the **Commands:** list (it should be at the bottom). Select **Pe&rsonal** from the list, click **Assign Shortcut...**, and press **[Ctrl+E]** (it should not be currently assigned). Click **OK**.
2.	Assign the shortcut key combination **[Ctrl+A]** to your **Stars R Us** custom command.	Follow the steps above for the **S&tars R Us** command.
3.	Close the dialog box.	Click **OK**.
4.	Test your new shortcut keys.	Make sure you are in the Contacts window, press **[Ctrl+E]** to open the **Personal** database. Press **[Ctrl+A]** to open the **Stars R Us** database.
5.	Use any of the methods you have created (button, menu, shortcut keys) to display the **Stars R Us** database.	

Try It...

Resetting Toolbars, Menus, and the Keyboard

Somewhere along the line, you may find yourself wanting to put a toolbar, menu, or shortcut key list back to its original configuration. You can go to each item and delete the commands you added, but what if you can't remember what you did exactly? Fear not! To return a menu, toolbar, etc. back to normal, all you have to do is reset it.

...reset toolbars, menus and shortcuts

1. **Tools, Customize Contacts Window...**

2. Click the tab that represents the item you wish to reset.

3. **Reset, Yes**

Pay attention! This option returns *all* menu, toolbar and keyboard shortcut options to their ACT! defaults. If you want to change only selected items, you need to do so manually.

Practice: *Clean Up Your Room (Part I)*

Step	What to do	How to do it/Comments
1.	First, make sure **Stars R Us** is the open database. If it is not, use your custom command to open it.	Use the toolbar, menu, or shortcut key to open the file.
2.	Reset your menu, toolbar and keyboard shortcuts.	**Tools, Customize Contacts Window...**, click the **Toolbars** tab, **Reset, Yes**. Click the **Menus** tab, **Reset, Yes**. Click the **Keyboard** tab, **Reset, Yes**.
3.	Delete the custom commands.	Click the **Custom Commands** tab, select **OpenPersonal** (if necessary), and click **Delete, Yes**. Repeat this process for **OpenStars**, and click **OK**.

Deleting a Macro

Some macros you keep forever, while others cease to become useful after a while. Don't clutter up your macros list with useless files.

...delete a macro

1. **Tools, Delete Macro...** The **Delete Macro** dialog box is displayed.

2. Select the macro you wish to delete, **Delete, Yes**. When you delete a macro you are given fair warning. Read it carefully.

Practice: *Clean Up Your Room (Part II)*

Step	What to do	How to do it/Comments
1.	Delete the **Open Personal** and the **Open Stars** macros.	**Tools, Delete Macro...**, select **Open Personal** (if necessary), click **Delete**, read the confirmation, and click **Yes**. Repeat for the **Open Stars** macro.

Queries

"What is a query?" he queried. "Why do you ask?" I queried back. A query is a question. When you "query" a database, you ask it a question. If you ask the question correctly, the database answers.

When you do a lookup in ACT!, you perform a query operation. The Lookup menu allows you to whittle your Contact List down to a manageable size. A lookup can be very specific or very general.

Example: You want to lookup only those records that have **Acme** in the company name **and** are located in **Cleveland Ohio**.

You could look up **Acme** in the **Company** field, then look up **Cleveland** in the **City** field, and **Ohio** in the **State** field. If you remember to select the **Narrow lookup** each time, you eventually get to the specified records. But, how many separate operations does it take? (Here's a hint: Less than 4 and more than 2.)

This technique, while effective, is a bit tedious. If you forget to click the **Narrow lookup** option, you lose your lookup so far and have to start all over again. There has to be a better way!

 *That "start all over" thing in the previous paragraph was just for dramatic effect. Actually if you forget to click Narrow lookup or add to lookup on one step of a multi-step lookup, you can choose **Lookup, Previous** to return to the previous step. We just wanted you to know.*

Lookup By Example

Lookup By Example allows you to specify all of your lookup criteria at once. You don't have to remember to add each criterion to your lookup; and you can view all of the criteria before you perform the lookup.

Lookup By Example allows you to use wildcards to specify unknown characters in your criteria. This allows you to find a string of characters in the middle or at the end of a field, or fields where the contents are similar. The wildcard character is an asterisk (*). Use the asterisk to represent letters that vary in your example.

Example: If you wish to find all records where the company name begins with the word **Acme**, you should provide an example like this:

Acme

If you don't specify a wildcard, ACT! assumes you want to look at the beginning of the field.

If you wish to find all occurrences of the word Acme in the company field you should provide an example like this:

Acme

The wildcard at the beginning **and** the end of the example tells ACT! you want any record that "contains" the word **Acme**. It is not much of a leap to see that ***Acme** would mean any name *ending* with Acme.

...use Lookup By Example

1. Display either the Groups or the Contact window.

    By Example is not available in some views.

2. **Lookup, By Example**

    An empty copy of the current Contact or Group layout is displayed. A special Query toolbar is displayed.

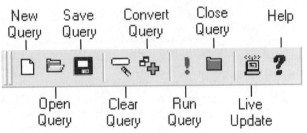

3. Type your criteria in the appropriate fields (use wildcards (*) when necessary).

    If you wish to use a different layout to do this, you may switch layouts while the Query By Example screen is displayed.

4. Click the Run button on the Query toolbar (it looks a little like a footprint, don't you think?)

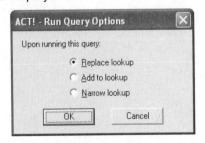

5. Click **Replace lookup, Add to lookup** or **Narrow lookup**

6. **OK**

    The lookup is performed for all of the specified criteria. You are returned to the Contact/Group screen with the new lookup in place.

☞ *If you specify criteria that do not fit any records in your database, ACT! lets you know. No lookup will be performed, and you must start from scratch (bummer, huh?).*

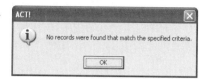

Practice: *Lookup By Example*

Step	What to do	How to do it/Comments
1.	Define a Lookup By Example that finds all records that start with **Acme**.	**Lookup, By Example** In the **Company** field, type **acme**.
2.	Run your query (replace the current lookup).	Click the Run button, **OK**.
3.	Observe the records the lookup found. Pay particular attention to **City**.	Some are in Los Angeles, while others are in Beverly Hills.
4.	Define a new Lookup By Example that locates all records with **Acme** anywhere in the company name, and are located in Beverly Hills.	**Lookup, By Example** In the **Company** field, type ***acme***, in the **City** field, type **beverly**, in the **State** field type **ca**.
5.	Run the query (replace the current lookup).	Click the Run button, **OK**.
6.	Observe the resulting records.	There should be 2 records in the lookup. You got all the "Acme's" in Beverly Hills, didn't you?

Creating Advanced Queries

If your query needs are more complex than Lookup By Example can handle, you may want to consider creating an advanced query. Don't let the name intimidate you. Advanced queries are not difficult to create and offer several advantages over Lookup By Example.

✔ You can easily convert a Lookup By Example into an advanced query.

✔ You can save an advanced query and use it again.

✔ You can more easily specify multiple conditions for one field with advanced queries.

...turn a Lookup By Example into an advanced query

1. Create your Lookup By Example.   See the procedure on page 421.

2. Click the Convert Query button on the Query toolbar.   The query is instantly converted to a set of advanced query statements.

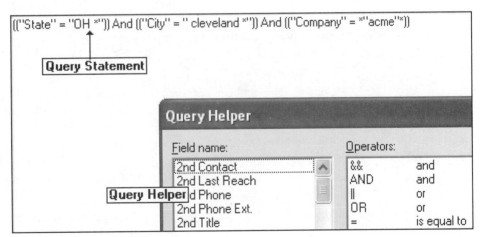

Practice: *A New Advanced Query*

Step	What to do	How to do it/Comments
1.	Create a Lookup By Example that locates all records containing the word **Film** in the **Company** field and **CA** in the **State** field. Do *not* run the query.	Choose **Lookup, By Example**. In the **Company** field, type ***film***, in the **State** field type **ca**.
2.	Convert to an advanced query.	Click the Convert Query button.
3.	Observe the query statements. Do not run the query yet.	The statements make sense, but would you remember where all those parenthesis and quotation marks go? Don't worry, you don't have to.
4.	Leave the query displayed.	((["State" = "CA"]*)) And ((["Company"]* = *"film"*))

...save an advanced query

1.	Create the query.	Convert a Lookup By Example or create a new advanced query.
2.	Choose **File, Save**, or click the Save button on the toolbar.	A **Save As** dialog box is displayed. The **Query** folder should already be displayed.
3.	Type a file name for the query.	ACT! places a **.QRY** extension at the end of the file name when you save.
4.	**Save**	The query is saved so you may use it again.

☞ *It's a good idea to save a query before you run it. This is particularly true if the query statement is complex and untested. If you run a query that contains a flaw (even a small one), it will return an incorrect answer (if it returns anything at all) and you have to start again from scratch. If you save the query first, you can open it, find out what is wrong, and fix it.*

Practice: *Saving the Query*

Step	What to do	How to do it/Comments
1.	Save the query, calling it **California Film**.	Click the Save toolbar button, type the file name in the appropriate text box, and click **S**ave. 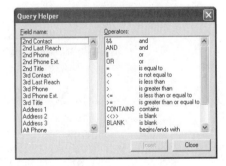
2.	Run your query (replace the current lookup).	Click the Run button, **OK**. How is this different? You can reuse this query.

The Query Helper

Converting a Lookup By Example into an advanced query is easy. Constructing an advanced query from scratch is hard (kind of like comedy). Fortunately, ACT! provides you with a helper...the Query Helper.

...display the Query Helper

1. Display either a Lookup By Example or an Advanced Query screen, and choose **Query, Show Query Helper...** from the menu.

   When you display an advanced query, the **Query Helper** usually displays automatically.

2. To hide the Query Helper, click the **Close** button in the **Query Helper** dialog box.

Try It...

Step	What to do	How to do it/Comments
1.	Create a new Lookup By Example, leave the fields blank, and convert it to an advanced query.	**Lookup, By Example** and click the Convert Query toolbar button. A blank query screen displays (scary, huh?).
2.	If the Query Helper is not displayed, display it now.	**Query, Show Query Helper...**
3.	Observe the two columns in the **Query Helper** dialog box.	On the left is a list of field names, and on the right is a list of operators that can be used to relate your criteria.
4.	Leave the screen displayed.	

☞ *You may notice more than one symbol for the same item (two symbols for **and**, two symbols for **or**, etc.). You may use either symbol in the advanced query window, but you should use the symbolic choice if you wish to use AND or OR in the same field when creating a Query By Example (use || instead of OR).*

Once the Query Helper is displayed, you use it to construct logical query statements. With it, you have a complete list of available fields and operators. The only thing you need to do is provide the examples.

...use the Query Helper

How To...

1.	Display the Query Helper, if necessary. Select the first field you wish to query from the **Field name:** list, and click the **Insert** button.	The field name is inserted into the Advanced Query screen.
2.	Choose a comparison operator and **click Insert**.	A variety of operators are listed to allow comparison of the field contents to your criteria in any number of ways.

3. Click at the end of the query statement and type the desired criteria.

Type your criteria as you would if you were defining a Lookup By Example.

4. If you wish to specify additional criteria, repeat steps 1 through 3 for each one.

There are a few rules of query making with which you should become familiar:

✔ Text criteria that consist of more than one word must be enclosed in quotes. This is not necessary if the criteria is a single word.
Example: City = Hollywood OR City = Los Angeles does not work.
City = Hollywood OR City = "Los Angeles" works.

✔ Each expression in your query must be complete.
Example: City = Hollywood OR "Los Angeles" does not work.
City = Hollywood OR City = "Los Angeles" works.

✔ Don't confuse the meanings of OR and AND.   What they mean to you and what they mean to a computer can be two different things.
Example: City = Hollywood AND City = "Los Angeles" - does not return an answer because it requires that both criteria be true *at the same time* for a record to match (a Contact address cannot be Hollywood *and* Los Angeles).

City = Hollywood OR State = CA returns any record where the city is Hollywood and every record where the state is CA. If you wanted to display only Hollywood, California, your statement should be constructed as follows:

City = Hollywood AND State = CA.

✔ Don't let the fact that there seem to be two symbols for the same operator bother you.
Example: Both **AND** and **&&** mean the same thing according to the Query Helper. Either operator works equally well in the Advanced Query window.

✔ If you use the > or < operators, you cannot use the * with the text criteria.

✔ If you want to specify criteria that looks for text anywhere in a field, use the CONTAINS operator from the Query Helper. Do not use the asterisk (*) wildcard at either end of the criteria like you would in Query by Example.

Example: If you create and run the advanced query **Company = *acme***, you get the expected results. But if you save this query, ACT! places quotation marks in the *strangest* places. **Company = "*"acme""***. The saved query does not work. If, instead, you specify **Company CONTAINS "acme"** the query works (and saves) properly.

✔ When you create your queries manually, mistakes happen (no, really, they do!). A simple

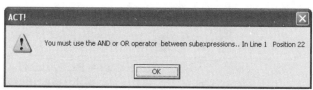

omission of an operator or a set of quotes can cause a query to malfunction or not to work at all. You can check your work by choosing **Query, Check Query Syntax** from the menu. If any errors exist, this utility finds them and tells you what they are.

✔ You can specify a sort order for your query result by choosing **Query, Specify Query Sort...** from the menu. A **Sort Contacts** dialog box displays where you specify up to three levels of sorting. This is saved with the query, so whenever you run it, the resulting records are sorted as you specified.

Practice: *Create and Save an Advanced Query*

Try It...

Step	What to do	How to do it/Comments
1.	Create a new advanced query, if necessary.	**Lookup, By Example** and click the Convert Query toolbar button.
2.	Display the Query Helper, if necessary.	If the Query Helper is not displayed, choose **Query, Show Query Helper**....
3.	Who haven't we talked to since 1996, but we have met with at some point? Create a query that displays only those records where the **Last Reach** field contains a date before 1/1/97 and the **Last Meeting** field is not blank.	Under **Field name:**, locate and select **Last Reach**, and **click Insert**. Select the **is less than** operator (**<**), **click Insert**, click at the end of the current statement, and type **1/1/1997**. Locate and select the **AND** operator and **click Insert**. Locate and select **Last Meeting**, **click Insert**, select the **NOT** or **!** operator, **click Insert**, select the **BLANK** or **<<>>** operator, and (finally!) **click insert**.

"Last Reach" < 1/1/1997 AND "Last Meeting" NOT BLANK

☞ *You must use a 4 digit year on your queries.*

4.	Save the query, naming it **Query 1**.	Click the Save toolbar button, type the file name, and click **Save**.
5.	Run the query (replace the current lookup). Click the **Status** tab and browse the three records to verify the Last Reach and Last Meeting dates.	Click the Run button, **OK**. One record has nothing in the **Last Reach** field. Obviously "less than" has a different meaning to ACT! than it does to us.
6.	Create a new advanced query.	**Lookup, By Example** and click the Convert Query toolbar button.

Step	What to do	How to do it/Comments
7.	Use the Query Helper to construct a query that will display records from **California** where the **Last Meeting** field is **BLANK** or records from **Texas** where the **Last Meeting** field is blank. Remember, each statement must be complete.	The correct syntax is displayed below:
	State = "CA" AND "Last Meeting" BLANK OR State = "TX" AND "Last Meeting" BLANK	
8.	Save the query, naming it **Query 2**. Run the query, replacing the current lookup, and observe the result.	Click the Save button, type the name, and click **Save**. Click the Run button, **OK.** There should be 30 records in the lookup.
9.	What do you think the result would be of the following query statement?	At first glance, it might seem to perform the same task as the statement you just created. *It won't!* The result of this query would be *all* records from **CA** or any record from **TX** where the **Last Meeting** field was **BLANK**.
	State = CA OR State = TX AND "Last Meeting" BLANK	

Once a query is created and saved, you can use it or modify it whenever you need it.

...use a saved Query

1. **Lookup, By Example**

2. **File, Open,**
    or
    click the Open toolbar button.
    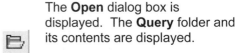
    The **Open** dialog box is displayed. The **Query** folder and its contents are displayed.

3. Select the query you wish to open and click **Open**.
    The query is displayed in the Advanced Query screen.

4. Click the Run button.
    Run the query as usual.

Practice: *Recycled Queries*

Try It...

Step	What to do	How to do it/Comments
1.	Open the query named **Query 1**.	**Lookup, By Example**, click the Open toolbar button, select the file, click **Open**.
2.	Do you remember the problem with this query?	The **Last Reach** statement displayed records that were before 1/1/97, but it also displayed records where the **Last Reach** field was blank.
3.	Add a statement that will require **Last Reach** to *not* be blank.	Use the Query Helper to add the following statement to the end of the current query: **AND "Last Reach" NOT BLANK**
4.	Save the query and run it. Replace the current lookup.	Click the Save toolbar button to update the query file, click the Run toolbar button, **OK**.
5.	Observe the resulting lookup. Did the change work?	Of course it did and we are crushed that you doubted us (sniff).

Adding a Custom Query to the Menu

You can now create complex and useful queries to isolate only those Contacts you need to deal with at the moment. But isn't the method of running those queries a bit clumsy? If you assumed there must be a better way, you were right.

✔ Take the most often used of your custom queries and add them to the Lookup menu. This is quick and easy.

✔ If you wish, you can define a custom command for the query, then create a toolbar button or shortcut key for it, or place it in any menu (including a new menu item of your creation). The procedure is the same as creating custom commands for macros (page 408 begins the section on creating custom commands).

ACT!

...add a custom query to the Lookup menu

1. **Lookup, Modify Menu...**

    If any commands have already been added to the menu, they are already listed here.

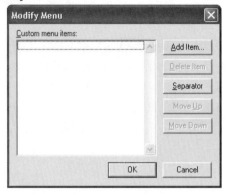

2. **Add Item...**

    The **Add Custom Menu Item** dialog box is displayed.

3. Click the Browse button to locate the query file. If you want the menu to display something other than the file name, type the text you wish to appear in the menu in the **Command name to display in menu:** text box. (If you wish, place an ampersand (&) in front of the letter you wish to be underlined.)

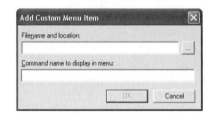

4. **OK**

    You are returned to the **Modify Menu** dialog box with your new command in place.

5. If you have more items to add to the menu, repeat steps 2 through 4. Click **OK** when you're finished.

    The new commands are now in your **Lookup** menu.

Practice: *Adding Queries To The Lookup Menu*

Step	What to do	How to do it/Comments
1.	Add The **Query 1** query to the **Lookup** menu. Leave the file name as the menu text, but underline the number **1**.	**Lookup, Modify Menu...**, **Add Item...**, click the Browse button (if necessary), locate the **Query** folder, select **Query 1**, **Open**, place an ampersand (&) in front of the number **1** in the **Command name to display in menu:** text box, **OK**.
2.	Add the **Query 2** to the **Lookup** menu. Underline the **2**.	Repeat the previous instructions, selecting the **Query 2** file. Click **OK** when you're done.
3.	Try your new menu items.	Display the **Lookup** menu and select each of the new commands in turn.
4.	Remove the two commands from the **Lookup** menu.	**Lookup, Modify Menu...**, select each of the commands you added in turn, and click **Delete Item, OK**.

Try It...

Deleting Query Files

There are several ways of deleting query files when you no longer need them. You can use a Browser window, the Windows Explorer, or you can delete them from within ACT!.

...delete a query file in ACT!

1. **Lookup, By Example**

2. **File**, **Open**,
   or
   click the Open toolbar button.

   A list of saved queries is displayed in the **Open** dialog box.

3. Select the file you wish to delete, press **[Delete]**, and confirm the deletion.

   You cannot mark multiple files using this method. If you have many files to deal with, we recommend that you use the Windows Explorer.

4. Click **Cancel** when you are done and click the Close button for the Example window.

You can also right-click a file in the Open dialog box and choose Delete from the shortcut menu.

Practice: *Deleting Your Queries*

Step	What to do	How to do it/Comments
1.	Delete the saved queries you created today. **California Film** **Query 1** **Query 2**	**Lookup, By Example** Choose **File**, **Open**, or click the Open toolbar button. Select each file in turn, press **[Delete]**, and confirm the deletion. Click **Cancel** when done. Click the Close button to close the Lookup By Example window and return to the database.

Review: Macros & Queries

	1.	Record a new macro that opens prints an envelope for the current contact. (Hint: In the Print dialog box, press E to change the Printout type. **[Tab]** to the next section and type the name/size of the envelope until it is displayed).
	2.	Test the macro.
	3.	Add the Envelope macro to the Write menu.
	4.	Put an icon for the Envelope macro on the toolbar.
	5.	Create a new advanced query named **Quarterly Review** that will display all records that have an edit date for the current quarter (Hint: >= to an beginning date and <= to an ending date)
	6.	Run the **Quarterly Review** query.
	7.	Delete the **Quarterly Review** query file. Delete the Envelope Macro as well if you don't plan to use it.

Synchronization

To be able to maintain up-to-date information with other ACT! users, you will:

☑ Discuss the concept of synchronization.

☑ Create remote databases for two of your employees.

☑ Practice setting up a shared folder and an e-mail synchronization.

Synchronizing Databases

If you are tied to your desk (and computer) all day, and/or if you are the only person in your company who needs access to your Contact data, you don't need to synchronize and you can close this book now.

Are they gone? Good... now we can talk.

Synchronization is the act of making the contents of more than one Contact database the same. Synchronization can be performed in a number of ways.

- ✔ You can synchronize directly - database to database.

- ✔ You can synchronize through a shared network folder.

- ✔ You can synchronize through e-mail.

Synchronization can be a two way process. You can both send and apply (receive) synchronization packets. This allows you to input different data into two separate databases and easily duplicate the Contacts in both directions. Both databases are "synchronized" with each other.

Synchronization can be selective. You can choose to send synchronization packets that contain only records that belong to specified groups.

The process of synchronization is a simple one once you get it set up. The process if setting up synchronization is not so simple, but not really that difficult. You may already be set up for synchronization. In this case, the only thing you have to do is perform the sync when necessary (or get ACT! to do it for you automatically).

 The following practice sessions assume you are reasonably familiar with Windows Explorer.

Let's take this process one step at a time.

1. Determine the Connection Method

If your computer is connected to a network, you will probably synchronize using a shared folder. If you are using a remote connection you may synchronize using e-mail.

✔ If you are synchronizing through a shared folder, you must know where the shared folder is located. Both the sender of the synchronization packet and the receiver must have this information.

✔ If you are synchronizing through e-mail, you need to know what e-mail program *your* system uses (Microsoft Outlook, Outlook Express, Internet Mail, Lotus Notes, etc.), and the e-mail address of the users with whom you wish to synchronize.

2. Set up Synchronization Folders or E-mail Addresses

In a real sync environment, you may use a combination of shared folder and e-mail syncing. There is really very little difference between the two methods as you follow the instructions.

Regardless of which method you select, you will need to make sure that these addresses are ready. If you plan to use shared folder, create the individual folders on the server for each sync user. If you plan to use e-mail, then you will need to have a valid e-mail address for all sync users as well as an e-mail address for the database administrator. You may want to consider getting a generic e-mail address like admin@stars-rus.com That way if the current user gets promoted or leaves the company, all remote setups do not have to be changed to reflect the e-mail address of the new database administrator.

3. Determine What Will Be Synchronized

Will you be synchronizing the entire database or only a part of it? ACT! allows you to sync portions of a database by selecting one or more Groups to send to a user.

For the next few practice sessions, you will synchronize from your **Stars R Us** database to a new empty database that we will create. To do this we will set up folders on the desktop. Let's pretend that these folders are actually on your computer and the local area network, and that we are going to maintain a master database on the network and a synchronized one on your computer. We are imagining that we have access to two computers. Your computer is one, the network computer is the other.

ACT!

Try It...

Practice: *Setting Up the Sync Folder*

Step	What to do	How to do it/Comments
1.	Open Windows Explorer.	Right-click on the **Start** button and click **Explore**
2.	Create a new folder under the default \Sync folder named \pal	Scroll down to Program Files, click on ACT and then on Sync. Select **File, New, Folder** and type the name "pal" and press **[Enter]**.
3.	Restore ACT!.	Click the **ACT!** button on the Windows task bar.

☞ *Normally, you would not set up synchronization folder on your PC, but on a server. We do this here to simplify the process of locating it and later deleting it when you are finished practicing.*

4. Define Users

Before you can setup synchronization with another user, you must create him or her. Each user must have a Contact record in your master database before you make them a user.

...define a new user

How To...

1. First, create a record in your database for the user you wish to create, then choose **File, Administration, Define Users**....

   The **Define Users** dialog box is displayed.

   The first page of this dialog box contains a list of current users for this database. From here, the administrator can define new users and delete existing users (power is intoxicating, isn't it?).

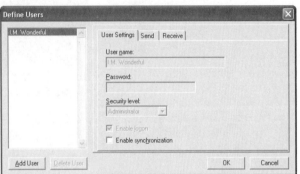

2. Click the **Add User** button . A new user (named **User1**) is created.

   Type the name of the user. Normally this should be the same as the name in their Contact record.

   Make sure the new user has a **Standard** security level (at least).

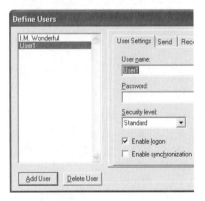

☞ *While matching the user name to the Contact name is not a necessity, it can make things easier later on.*

3. Click **OK**

4. Click **Assign Now...**.

    If you created several users in
    the previous steps, they will all
    be listed here. You assign one
    at a time.

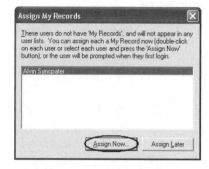

5. Click **Select...** to display a list of
    database Contacts.

    ☞ *If you forgot to create
    the Contact prior to
    creating the user, fill out
    the **Enter "My Record"
    Information** dialog box
    when it is displayed.*

6. Locate and select the Contact
    that belongs to the user name.

    Click **OK**.

7. If you defined more than one user, you will be returned to the **Assign My Record** dialog box. Repeat steps 5 through 7 until all users have been assigned to Contact records.

Once this user assignment process is complete, you are ready to create the remote database(s) and set up synchronization.

Practice: *Define a New User*

Step	What to do	How to do it/Comments
1.	Define a new user named **Alvin Syncpartner**. Alvin already has a record in the database.	Choose **File, Administration, Define Users...**, and click the **Add User** button. Type **Alvin Syncpartner**, make sure Alvin has a **Standard** security level, and that **Enable logon** is checked.
2.	Click **OK** and assign the new User to the **Alvin Syncpartner** Contact record. Click **OK** when you're done.	When you click **OK** the **Assign My Records** dialog box is displayed with Alvin's User name. Click **Assign Now...**, click **Select...** and select **Syncpartner, Alvin** from the list of Contact records.

Try It...

5. Create Database(s) With Which to Synchronize

Creating a new, empty database based on your master database is the easiest part of the set up process.

How To...

...create a new empty database

1. Open the master database.

   This is the database from which you will initially be sending sync packets.

2. **File, Save Copy As...**

   Select the **Create an empty copy** option.

   Enter the name for the new database in the **Filename:** area.

   ☞ *Use the browse button only if you need to save it to a non-standard drive or folder.*

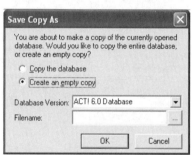

3. Click **OK**.

4. Click **Select...**

   This dialog box will probably display some information, which may or may not be what you want.

   In either case *do not* enter data into this form.

   Instead, click **Select...** to display a list of current Contacts.

   The **Enter "My Record" Information** dialog box appears.

5. Select the Contact to whom this new database will belong.

 It is very important for the synchronization user's Contact record in the master database and the remote database is exactly the same. By selecting the record from the master database and "sending" it to the new database as the "My Record", this is assured.

6. After a few moments, the new database is created (but not opened).

You remain in the original database. If you have other copies to create you may continue to do so.

Practice: *Creating & Setting Up a New Database*

Step	What to do	How to do it/Comments
1.	Create two new empty databases. Name the first one **Stars R Us-ASyncpartner** and save it to the default database folder. Be sure to select Alvin's name as the My Record. Create the second database as **Stars R Us-PFriday** and select Pal Friday for the My Record.	**File, Save Copy As...**, **Create an empty copy,** type **Start R Us-ASyncpartner**, and click **OK**. Click **Select...**, press **S** and/or scroll down and choose **Syncpartner, Alvin** from the list of Contacts, and click **OK**. Repeat the process for Pal.
2.	Open the new **Stars R Us-ASyncpartner** database. How many records does it contain?	**File, Open...** , select the file, **Open**. Only the My Record record appears in this database.
3.	Return to the **Stars R Us** database. Log in as I.M. Wonderful.	**File**, and choose **Stars R Us** from the list of recently open files at the bottom of the menu. When prompted to log in, delete Alvin's name and type **i.m. wonderful**. Click **OK**.

Try It...

Step	What to do	How to do it/Comments
4.	For the next exercise you will need to be sure that ACT! is set up to use Outlook as the e-mail package.	**Edit, Preferences**, click on the e-mail tab, change the **E-mail System Setup** if the default e-mail is not **MS Outlook**.
5.	You are ready to set up synchronization.	

6. Set up Synchronization

Now it's time to define how you will synchronize with the remote database. There are a lot of choices to make, but fortunately there is a wizard to help you with them.

...define a synchronization

1.	If necessary, open the master database (Stars R Us).	You will begin the process here.
2.	Choose **File, Synchronize Setup....**	The first **Synchronization Wizard** dialog box is displayed.

This dialog box is just an introduction. If you do a lot of this kind of stuff, click the **Don't show this screen in the future** check box and you will skip this step the next time you setup a sync.

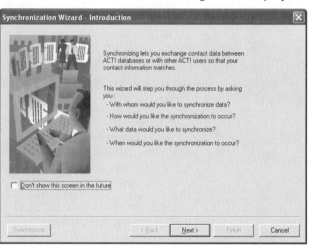

3.	Click **Next >**.	The second **Synchronization Wizard** dialog box is displayed.

This step is where you define the method of synching.

In this case **With other users**.

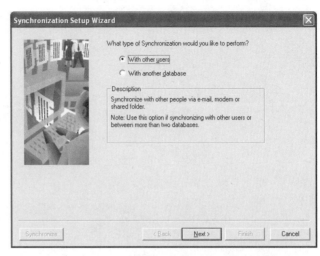

4. Click **Next >**.

The third **Synchronization Wizard** dialog box is displayed.

The **Send What** dialog asks you to choose whether to Send, Receive, or both and to verify what types of data you would like to synchronize. For example, you may want to synchronize Contact information but not Activities.

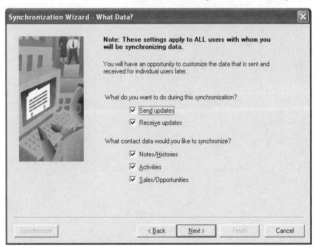

5. Make your choices and click **Next >**.

The fourth **Synchronization Wizard** dialog box is displayed.

The **With Whom?** dialog lists the available users to sync with (on the left) and which users have already been set up for syncing (on the right).

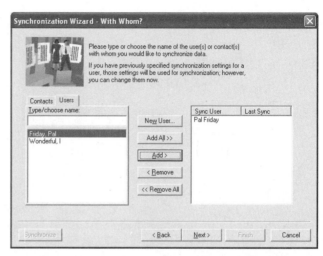

6. Select the first sync user in the left column and click **Add >** , repeat with any other sync users until they are listed in the right column. Click **Next>**.

The fifth **Synchronization Wizard** dialog box is displayed.

The **How?** dialog allows you to specify the method of sync packet delivery (E-Mail or Shared folder).

If you have more than one user defined, selecting each name displays a separate set of options.

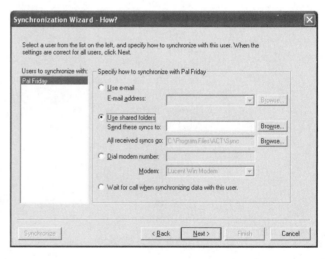

7. Select the first user name (if there is more than one). Select the **Use shared folders** option, then click the **Browse...** button to its right and locate the folder to which you will send the sync packet for this user.

Each remote user will have a different location. If you are using E-Mail, choose **Use e-mail** and enter their **E-mail address:** in the appropriate box.

8. When the sync method for all users has been set, click **Next >**.

The sixth **Synchronization Wizard** dialog box is displayed.

In the **Receive What Data?** dialog, you need to decide what information you will receive from each remote user. If you intend to use a collection group it will be set here as well.

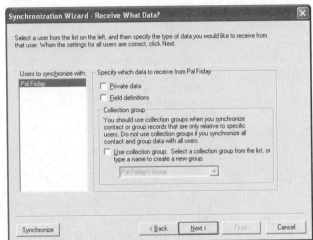

🖙 *If you are the administrator, you probably don't want to receive anything (let people like Alvin add fields…are you kidding me?) The only reason to use a collection group is if you intend to synchronize groups instead of all data in your database. If this is not the case, leave the option unchecked.*

9. Select each user and choose the desired receive options. When all users have been set, click **Next >**.

The seventh **Synchronization Wizard** dialog box is displayed.

In the **Send What Data?** dialog, specify what types of data you will *send* to each user. If you wish to send only certain groups, you can specify it here.

If you are the administrator, you probably want to check **Field definitions**.

10. For each user, specify the appropriate send options. When all users have been defined, click **Next>**.

The eighth **Synchronization Wizard** dialog box is displayed. (Will they never end?!)

This one is simple, If you choose **Yes** and click **Next>**, a dialog box displays in which you can specify an automatic sync schedule.

Leave the option set to **No** and it won't.

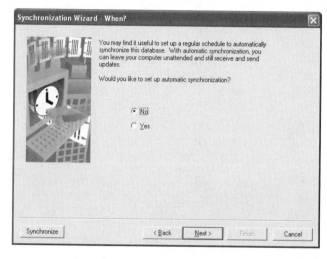

11. Choose the appropriate option and click **Next >** . If you chose **Yes** set the scheduled times and click **Next >** again.

The ninth **Synchronization Wizard** dialog box is displayed:

Yes, that's right, you're finished. Savor your victory and click **Finish**.

You will be deposited at the **Synchronize** dialog box because *You are ready to send!*

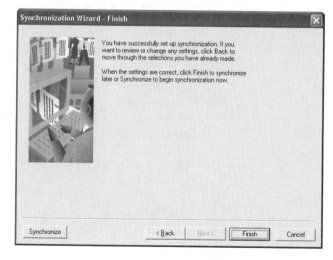

Send and Receive Options

Various options from the Synchronization Wizard might be worth discussing.

Send Options:

Send Private Data - This is used mainly when you are performing a synchronization with a database *you* will also use, such as desktop to laptop. Private data are those records and activities you designate as private when you create them. If you leave this option turned off, these records/activities are not included when you send a sync update. Private data is of little consequence if you are the only user of the database.

However, there is this to consider. If you are a laptop user and you never backup (let's be real now), and you are syncing to a database on your company's server, then syncing your private data is almost the same as backing up. No one on the master database can see the private records anyway unless they are logged on as you...not even the administrator.

Send database field definitions - When you change the definition of a database field, the change can have an impact on any data currently stored in that field. This is fine, as long as you are the only user of the database, but if you now wish to impose that change on other databases, make sure this option is on.

Send all records (next update only) - Check this option when you want your next update to send all of the records in your database. This is the default for the first synchronization. The option turns itself off automatically after the next update.

All Contacts and groups - Set this option if you want to do a complete synchronization. Those Contacts or groups that do not presently exist in the target database are created as part of the synchronization.

Selected groups - Set this option if you only want to send specific groups.

> **Example:** Your master database contains regional Contact information. Your representative in the Northeast has no need of Contact information in the Southwest and vice versa. Rather than clutter their databases with useless information, create regional groups for your Contacts and send only the appropriate groups to each person.
>
> When you click the **Selected groups** option, you may click the desired group names in the list below to choose which groups are to be sent to that user. A green checkmark indicates a selected group.

Receive Options:

Collection group - When you receive synchronization updates from other databases, you may wish to keep track of them and who sent them to you. To do this, you may specify a group into which all synchronized records from that user will be placed. Displaying the collection group allows you to see all new records added to the database by that user. If any of the received Contacts have been added to existing groups, they will still be members of those groups.

Receive private data - Once again, if you are applying a sync packet that contains your own records and activities, you will want to receive private as well as public data.

Accept database field definitions - Select this option if you want your database field definitions to keep pace with the database sending your synchronization packet. If they do not send their definitions, this option is meaningless.

Practice: *Set Up to Synchronize*

Step	What to do	How to do it/Comments
1.	Start the synchronization wizard..	Choose **File, Synchronize Setup...**. Click **Next >** at the introduction screen (if it is displayed).
2.	Synchronize with other users.	Make sure **With other users** is the selected option and choose **Next >**.
3.	For this sync you will send only; you will synchronize all data.	Uncheck **Receive updates**. Leave all other options checked, and click **Next >**.
4.	Add both **Alvin Syncpartner** and **Pal Friday** to the list of sync users.	Select Alvin in the list on the left, click **Add** to add him to the right column. Do the same for Pal and click **Next >**.
5.	Setup an e-mail sync for Alvin (alvin@stars-rus.com) and a shared folder sync for Pal (\sync\pal).	Click on Alvin's name and enter his e-mail address. Then click on Pal and click the **Use shared folders** option, click the **Browse...** button to the right of the **Send these syncs to:** text box, locate and select **\Sync\Pal**, click **Next >**.
6.	Do not receive private data or field definitions from Alvin or Pal. You will not use collection groups either.	Make sure none of these options are set and click **Next >**.
7.	Set the following options for both Alvin and Pal. Sync all Contacts and Groups, send field definitions, but not private data, and send all records, this time only.	Set the appropriate options for each syncer, click **Next >**.
8.	You do not wish to schedule automatic syncs at this point. Finish the wizard.	Make sure the automatic sync option is set to **No**, click **Next >**, click **Finish**.
9.	Observe the **Synchronize** dialog box and leave it displayed.	

Identity check - you are still the master database.

7. Perform the Synchronization

At this point you have defined the synchronization process as it relates to the master database. Now it is time to begin the process.

The first synchronization should be a complete circle. It involves three steps:

1. Send all records in the master database to the target database.

2. Apply the synchronization to the target database and send back to the master. This can be done in one step.

3. Receive the synchronization from the target to the master to complete the circle.

Once you have performed a complete initial synchronization, keeping the databases up to date with each other is as simple as telling ACT! to "synchronize now."

...send the first synchronization packet

1. If you will be setting up a sync with e-mail, be sure to disable your e-mail during this setup process.

In ACT!'s e-mail window, click on **File, Work Offline** This is only done for the *first* sync that you perform for this new user.

2. **File, Synchronize....**

You have already defined the synchronization so you are ready to rock (did we really say that?).

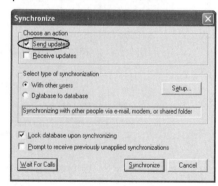

3. Since this is the first time you have sent a sync from the master, choose **Send updates** only.

 There is nothing to receive now anyway.

3. Click **Synchronize**.

The first packet is sent to each of your sync users. A progress bar is displayed as the process proceeds.

4. Now it's time to receive the sync at the remote database.

☞ *Anytime you want to make changes to the synchronization process, whether it is for a single user or for the entire process, you can revisit the synchronization wizard by choosing **File, Synchronize Setup...** from the menu. Walk through the process making any necessary changes and the next time you sync, the new settings will be used.*

Practice: *Begin the First Sync*

Step	What to do	How to do it/Comments
1.	Disable your e-mail.	In ACT!'s e-mail window, click on **File, Work Offline** This is only done for the *first* sync that you perform for this new user.
2.	Send the initial synchronization to the remote databases.	The dialog box should still be displayed, The **Send updates** check box should be the only one checked in the **Choose an action** box. click **Synchronize...** (tough wasn't it?).

One of the packets was sent to the shared sync folder and the other packet was attached to an e-mail and is now currently in your Outlook Outbox. |
| 3. | Open Pal's database first to apply the shared folder sync. | Open **Stars R Us-PFriday**. |

Try It...

Identity check - you are now the remote database, pretending to be Pal.

Applying a synchronization requires no prior setup other than making sure ACT! knows where to look for your received packets. When you instruct ACT! to receive synchronization, it will look everywhere a sync packet could be, and if it finds one, it will apply it by running the Synchronization Wizard. Essentially, you receive the sync and define how your data is to be returned at the same time. Let's see how it works....

8. Tell ACT! Where Sync Packets Will Be Located

This is a critical step. When you wish to apply a synchronization to your database, the ACT! program must know where to look for the synchronization data (called a **synchronization packet**). When you tell ACT! to apply a synchronization, it looks in this location.

This information must be specified for each computer using ACT!

✔   You can specify a folder of your own creation (which most likely will be on a shared network drive).

✔   You can use the default folder already defined (usually **c:\program files\act\sync**).

In either case, you must be aware of which folder is specified for each computer.

...specify the synchronization folder

1.	**E**dit, P**r**eferences...	The **Preferences** dialog box is displayed.
2.	Click the **Synchronization** tab.	

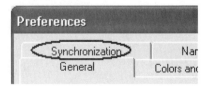

3. The current path for synchronization files is displayed in the **Location for received synchronizations** area. If you wish to change it, click the **Browse...** button and specify the new folder location.

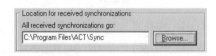

4. **OK**

The new location is saved. From now on, when you apply a synchronization packet, this computer looks in that folder.

9. Synchronize

The time has come to take the final step. This time we are combining the How to... and the Practice: sessions into one.

Practice: Receiving the First Sync

Step	What to do	How to do it/Comments
1.	Remember you are pretending to be Pal and are currently in Pal's database. So you need to change your default sync folder location to look for Pal's sync packet.	**Edit, Preferences...** and click the **Synchronization** tab. Change the **All received synchronizations go** text box, to Pal's sync folder (click **Browse...**, select the folder, and click **OK**). C:\Program Files\ACT\Sync\pal This is where the synchronization packet was sent from the master database. Click **OK**.
2.	Begin a Receive-only synchronization for this database. Your e-mail window will open first so that ACT! can determine if there are any sync packets there to apply..	Choose **File, Synchronize**.... Check the **Receive updates** check box, and un-check the **Send updates** check box. Click **Synchronize**. At this point, ACT! will go looking for synchronization packets. When it finds them, it notifies you.

Try It...

Step	What to do	How to do it/Comments
3.	Since I.M. Wonderful does not exist in this database yet, choose **Create a new user named:** and accept the proffered name (this is the name of the person who sent the packet).	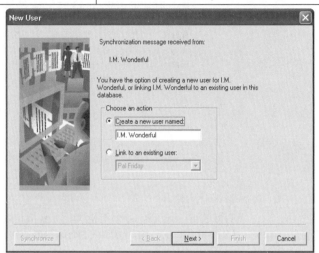

You will almost always select the option that ACT! presents for you here.

Click **Next>**.

Step	What to do	How to do it/Comments
4.	You recognize this one don't you? Here you specify how you synchronize **back** to the user who sent you this packet. Specify to send to the **C:\Program Files\Act \Sync** folder	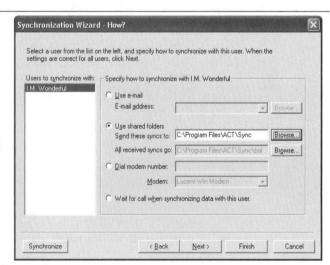

Step	What to do	How to do it/Comments
5.	Proceed through the **Synchronization Wizard** dialog boxes. In the Receive What dialog box, remember to Receive field definitions that were sent from the master. No other options in the sync wizard are usually changed.	When you reach the last Wizard dialog box and click **Finish**, the synchronization packet is applied to your database. When the process is complete, you have the same records in your new database as you had in **Stars R Us**.

E-mail Synchronization

You already know how to synchronize using e-mail, because you know how to do a shared folder sync. The differences are:

✔ You must have ACT! (yours and theirs) set up to use e-mail.

✔ You specify an e-mail address instead of a folder path when you set up the users sync.

✔ The receiver must apply the first sync packet manually.

The first time a user receives a synchronization message, it may be necessary for them to apply the attached packet manually. Synchronization messages have a subject of **ACT! Sync**. The synchronization packet is an attachment to the message.

...apply the first e-mail sync packet

1. Open the **E-mail** window in ACT!.

E-mail

You should use ACT!'s e-mail window to apply the first packet..

2. Double-click your e-mail's Inbox to display the messages.

3. Locate the message with **ACT! Sync** as the subject. Double-click it to open it.

4. Double-click the attachment icon. The synchronization setup wizard will run.

   The attachment is in the upper-right corner of the e-mail.

5. Follow the steps in the wizard to setup synchronization with the sender (review starting on page 457).

   Do this just as you would with a shared folders sync, but specify an e-mail address instead of a folder to which to send packets back.

The next time you receive a sync packet, you can apply it manually (the setup wizard will not run) or you just tell ACT! to synchronize and it will look in your Inbox for sync packets and apply them for you.

Shared folder and e-mail synchronization are compatible. That is, you can set up a synchronization that uses either method for different users.

Practice: *Alvin's Turn*		
Step	**What to do**	**How to do it/Comments**
1.	Open Alvin's database. ☞ *Remember you are now pretending to be Alvin and are currently in his database.*	
2.	Apply the first e-mail sync (it will still be in the Outbox).	Open the **E-mail** window in ACT!. Double-click the Outbox. Double-click the message intended for Alvin to open it. Double-click the attachment icon <ACT! Sync>. The synchronization setup wizard will run.

Try It...

Try It...

Step	What to do	How to do it/Comments
3.	Since I.M. Wonderful does not exist in Alvin's database yet, accept the option of **Create a new user named:** and click **Next>**.	
4.	Enter I.M.'s e-mail address: im@stars-rus.com and click **Next>**.	In real life, you would be careful to enter the correct e-mail address.
5.	Proceed through the **Synchronization Wizard** dialog boxes. In the Receive What dialog box, remember to Receive field definitions that were sent from the master. No other options in the sync wizard are usually changed.	When you reach the last Wizard dialog box and click **Finish**, the synchronization packet is applied to your database. When the process is complete, you have the same records in your new database as you had in **Stars R Us**. You will be returned to the e-mail window.
6.	When you manually apply the first sync, you will have to send out the sync, so… Synchronize the database.	**File, Synchronize**, verify that both Send and Receive Updates are checked. Click **Synchronize**.
7.	In the ACT! E-mail window drag the e-mail intended for I.M. into the Inbox.	We are still in a test setup environment.
8.	Both Alvin's and Pal's database are now ready for distribution. Time to move back into the master database. Open **Stars R Us**.	**File, Open**, click on **Stars R Us** and click **Open**.

Step	What to do	How to do it/Comments
9.	Verify that your sync folder is set properly (you are now back in the master database) Then apply the syncs.	**Edit, Preferences...** and click the **Synchronization** tab. Click the **Browse...** button to change the **All received synchronizations go** location to your default: c:\program files\act\sync **OK**
10.	You can now re-enable your E-mail. If this were a real database, it would be time to move it to the server to move it back into production.	**File, Work Offline** (to remove the check).

What changes are made when a packet is applied?

✔ Deleted records from the other database are not deleted, but a lookup is created that displays all records deleted from the source database. You can use this lookup to delete these records or leave them alone. To display the "deleted" lookup, choose **Lookup, Synchronized Records, To Be Deleted**. To delete all of these records, display the **To Be Deleted** lookup, press **[Ctrl+Delete]**, and click the **Lookup** button and confirm the deletions (be sure this is what you want to do before you confirm).

✔ A lookup is also created that displays all synchronized Contacts. You can use this lookup to display the last records added or changed by a synchronization. To display this lookup, choose **Lookup, Synchronized Records, Last Synchronized**.

✔ Records that have had changes made are changed in the target file.

✔ Records added to the master file are added to the target file. (This assumes they are part of the groups being synchronized if that option was set.)

Automatic Synchronization

As you have seen, setting up a synchronization can take some time, but once ACT! knows what it's doing, keeping your databases synchronized is a "piece of cake." If you regularly perform the synchronization task, you might consider letting ACT! synchronize automatically. You may have set this option when you set up the synchronization, but if you didn't then, you can either run the setup wizard again, or you can use the **Preferences** dialog.

...enable automatic synchronization

How To...

1. **Edit Preferences...**, click the **Synchronization** tab, and click the **Schedule** button.

The **Synchronization** dialog page is displayed.

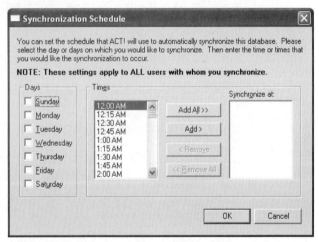

2. Set the options to suit your needs.

    ☞ *You must select at least one day of the week or automatic synchronization will not take place.*

These options are easy to set and understand.

3. **OK**

Automatic synchronization will now take place according to the schedule.

☞ *In order for automatic synchronization to work, your computer must be running and ACT! must be open. The synchronization addresses/locations must be accessible (this may require being logged on to your network). If this is not possible, you must perform your synchronization manually. If this is the case, set a synchronization reminder to help you keep your synchronization up to date.*

Review: *The Final Exercise*

Try It...	1.	List the necessary steps to set up synchronization. 1. 2. 3. 4. 5. 6. 7. 8. 9.
	2.	In the **Stars R Us** database (logged in as I.M. Wonderful), schedule a meeting with Rin Tin Tin for tomorrow at 10:00 a.m. You're going to discuss his contract.
	3.	Send a synchronization update.
	4.	Open Pal's database and apply the update from her sync folder.
	5.	Check to see if the meeting with Rin Tin Tin appears.
	6.	Reopen the **Stars R Us** database and login as I.M. Wonderful.
	7.	Minimize ACT! to display the Windows desktop. Locate the **pal** sync folder you created earlier. Delete the folder.
	8.	Return to ACT!. Reset the default sync folder to its original setting. **C:\PROGRAM FILES\ACT\SYNC**
	9.	You may now exit ACT!.
	10.	Pat yourself on the back.

Appendix

Using ACT! with your PDA

If your life is full of appointments or you find yourself wishing you had the phone number of your favorite client at times when you can't get to your PC right away, you may want to invest in a PDA (Personal Digital Assistant) such as a Palm OS powered handheld (also known as Palm Pilot, Visor, etc.) or a Pocket PC. It is easy to share your ACT! contacts' name address and phone number data as well as your scheduling information with most PDAs on the market.

Synching ACT! with a Palm

Palm OS devices are easy to find in almost any office supply stores. They became popular because of their quick, simple, and easy to use interface.

ACT! has developed two different software packages that link the ACT! database with the Palm

The **ACT! Link 2.0** is a free link from ACT! that synchronizes basic 'Rolodex' style information to the Palm Address Book, Date Book, and To-Do list features that are built in to the Palm, so that you can get to your contact data and calendar information while away from your PC.

In addition to the basic phone and address information that the ACT! Link 2.0 syncs between your desktop and the Palm, custom options also allow you to select four additional user fields and a maximum of the 10 most recent Notes and Histories.

Let's say that one of the fields that you customized in your ACT! database is named "Directions." In the field you could enter the basic directions to the client office (which exit to take...turn left here...etc.) If you select to synchronize that field with the Palm, you could review that information in the morning as you leave for your first appointment. How cool would that be!

☞ VERY IMPORTANT...Backup your database first in case anything goes wrong.

...setup your Palm

How To...

1.	Install the Palm Desktop software that came with your PDA.	When the Palm Desktop software has been installed, the red and blue circling arrows will display in the lower-right corner of the Taskbar.

2.	Start the install of **ACT! Link 2.0**.	It may be on your original installation disks from ACT!, but you can also download the most recent **ACT! Link 2.0** at no charge from the ACT! web site (www.act.com). It's always a good idea to check for newer versions of this link.
3.	Click **OK**.	To close the Hot Sync Manager Application (if prompted.)
4.	**N**ext>	At the Welcome Screen.
5.	**Y**es	To accept the Software License Agreement.
6.	**N**ext>	To accept the default Program Folder location.
7.	Click **Change Database...** to identify your ACT! database.	

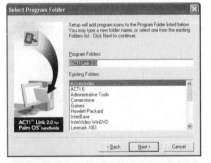

8.	Select your database from the list and click **Open**.	

9.	**N**ext>	To accept the ACT! database.

10. Select one of the **Overwrite** options and click **Next>**.

     *One of the **Overwrite** options is recommended. Synchronize (as a first time setup option) has the potential for doubling the contacts in your ACT! database.*

11. **Yes**

To verify that you understand the implications of the option you selected. (Read the warning and be sure that you do understand that using one of the Overwrite options will overwrite ALL of your data on one of the platforms.

12. Verify that the **Launch ACT! Link 2.0** option is checked and click **Finish**

13. Close the ACTLinkreadme.txt, if necessary.

The Global Settings dialog should be displayed.

14. Click on the ACT! Contacts icon at the left. Then click on the **Options...** button.

     The Options dialog will offer powerful options to customize your ACT! Palm link.

15. Select to synchronize all contacts or only the groups you want to synchronize with your Palm.

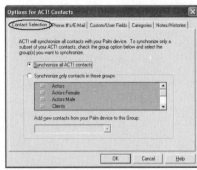

16. Click on the **Phone #'s/E-Mail** tab and change which phone numbers are synched to your Palm, if desired.

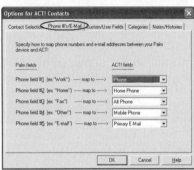

17. Click on the **Custom/User Fields** tab and select the fields you want to synchronize to the Palm.

   All fields in your ACT! database are available.

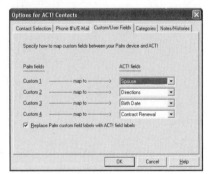

 Good place for the "Directions" field if you created it.

   Place a check in the **Replace Palm custom field labels with ACT! field labels** to replace the Palm label of "Custom 1" with the associated ACT! label (i.e. "Directions").

18. Generally no changes are made on the **Categories** tab.

   Categories are usually mapped to the ID/Status field.

19. Click on the **Notes/Histories** tab to change the number or type of notes and histories that will synchronize with your Palm.

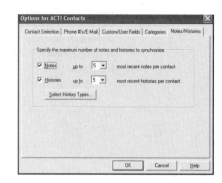

 *Click on the **Select History Types…** to view the different types of history that can be synced with your Palm*

20. **OK**

21. Click on the **ACT! Activities** icon to change the starting date of Activities (Meetings and Calls) that will sync.

22. Click on the **ACT! To-Do's** icon to change the starting date of To-Do's that will sync. You probably don't need to create any special mapping for priorities.

23. **OK**

24. Press the sync button on your handheld to start the process.

 If you selected one of the Overwrite options, by default the next time you synchronize your ACT! and Palm, the data will…..synchronize.

…modify your ACT! Palm Sync setup

How To…

1. Click on the **Palm HotSync Setup** icon on the ACT! toolbar.

  You can also click Start, Programs, ACT! Link 2.0 Configuration

 *ACT! has developed two different software packages that link the ACT! database with the Palm. The **ACT! Link 2.0,** that we just discussed, is a free link from ACT! that synchronizes basic 'Rolodex' style information along with Notes and Histories to the Palm.*

***ACT! for Palm OS** is its own application which maps all 60 of ACT!'s pre-defined fields (including the 15 User fields) to the Palm. Group and Sales Opportunity information is also synchronized to the Palm. In essence, it is like a mini-version of ACT! on your Palm. You can get more information about this more full-featured product from the ACT! website at www.act.com. While you are there, you should also check out **The Official ACT! for Palm OS QuickStudy Guide** (an e-book sold on ACT!'s web site). It really is the best book available for learning how to use the ACT! for Palm OS on your PDA…well…we might be biased about that.*

Syncing ACT! with a Pocket PC

While Pocket PCs (PPC) have Palm-like functionality, these devices use a slimmed-down version of Windows and have much greater processing power, memory, and graphics capability than Palm OS devices. A PPC is usually a bit larger than a Palm device, but still uses the stylus and on-screen keyboard for input.

Your ACT! contacts and calendar can also be synchronized with a Pocket PC. You can sync your entire database or only selected groups.

☞ *VERY IMPORTANT…Backup your database first in case anything goes wrong.*

...setup your Pocket PC

How To...

1. Install the PocketPC software (ActiveSync) that came with your PocketPC.

2. Start the install of the **ACT! Link for Pocket PC** software.

   If the software is not on your ACT! installation CD, you can download or order it from the ACT! website (www.act.com).

3. **Next>**

   At the Welcome Screen.

4. Place a checkmark in one of the options discussing potential product conflicts and click **Next>**

   Be sure that you have uninstalled any conflicting products prior to installing the ACT! Link for Pocket PC to avoid problems with data duplication.

5. **Yes**

   To accept the Software License Agreement.

6. Enter the **Serial:** number that was delivered with your software and click **Next>**.

7. **N**ext>

To accept the default Program Folder location. The program will then display a Setup Status screen.

8. Click **Settings** to change your default ACT! database and to customize your sync options.

    Click **Browse...** if necessary to change the database (the last database that you opened has been selected).

9. Click **Group Settings** to select which groups you wish to synchronize with the PDA.

    OK

10. Click **Note and History Settings** to select the number and type of Histories that will by synced.

    OK

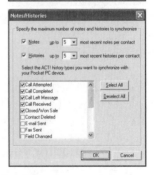

11. For the first sync, it is recommended that you select **ACT! contacts overwrite Pocket PC contacts.**

12. Click the **Activity** tab to verify the settings. For the first sync, it is recommended that you select **ACT! timed activities overwrite Pocket PC contacts.**

13. Repeat with the **To-do** tab.

14. **OK**

15. **Yes** to keep the settings that specify that the data on your Pocket PC will be replaced.

16. Back in the ACT! Configuration window, click **Next>** and then **Finish.**

You can then click **Exit** to leave the main Installation screen.

17. Place your Pocket PC in its cradle to begin the sync process.

 If you selected one of the Overwrite options, by default the next time you synchronize your ACT! and PocketPC, the data will.....synchronize.

...modify your ACT! Link for Pocket PC setup

1. Click on the **ACT! Link for Pocket PC Settings** icon on the ACT! toolbar.

  You can also click Start, Programs, ACT! Link for Pocket PC, ACT! Link for Pocket PC Settings.

Index

[Ctrl+Q] = SideACT!
[Ctrl+Z] = Undo Action
[Spacebar]=Tag Record
[Ctrl+N] = New Database

[Ctrl+X] = Cut
[Ctrl+C] = Copy
[Ctrl+V] = Paste
[Ctrl+O] = Open Database

[Ctrl+S] = Save
[Ctrl+Del] = Delete Contact
[Ins] = New Contact
[Ctrl+Shift+S]=Send to Outlk

[Ctrl+L] = Schedule Call
[Ctrl+M] = Schedule Meeting
[Ctrl+T] = Schedule To Do
[Ctrl+Shift+D] = Reschedule

[Ctrl+D] = Clear activity
[Ctrl+Shift+E]=Clear mult actv
[Ctrl+I] = Attach file
[Ctrl+H] = Record history

ACT!

	F1	F2	F3	F4	F5	F6	F7	F8	F9	F10	F11	F12
Ctrl				Close Database	Lookup Blank	Cycle Window			Groups Tab	Control Menu	New Sls Opp	
Alt				Exit ACT!	Macro Rec/Stp	Timer Toggle	Spell Check		Activities Tab			Import
Shift	What Is?			Start Timer	Day Calendar	Cycle Tabs		Tag/Edit Mode	Note/His Tab	Right-click	Tag All	
	Help	Popup	Week Calendar	Mini-Calendar	Month Calendar	Prev Layout	Task List	Contact List	Insert Note	Groups Wndw	Contact Wndw	Save As